George E. Goodrich

The Centennial History of the Town of Dryden. 1797-1897

George E. Goodrich

The Centennial History of the Town of Dryden. 1797-1897

ISBN/EAN: 9783337426118

Printed in Europe, USA, Canada, Australia, Japan

Cover: Foto ©ninafisch / pixelio.de

More available books at **www.hansebooks.com**

THE

CENTENNIAL HISTORY

OF THE

TOWN OF DRYDEN,

1797--1897.

COMPILED AND EDITED BY

GEO. E. GOODRICH,

WITH THE AID OF THE CENTENNIAL EXECUTIVE COMMITTEE
AND MANY OTHERS.

J. GILES FORD, PRINTER:
THE DRYDEN HERALD STEAM PRINTING HOUSE.
DRYDEN, NEW YORK.
1898.

PREFACE.

which appear have been provided upon the request of the Committee by the persons represented, or their friends, and the portrait of no living resident of the township will be here found. Little attention has been given in this work to the present, while the great effort has been to resurrect and preserve the past, representing so far as possible old land-marks and dwelling upon old habits and conditions as they formerly existed. The table of contents and list of illustrations immediately following will serve the purpose of a more complete index which it had been intended to supply at the end of the volume. Such a one had been partly prepared, but when the types were all up it was discovered that we had already occupied more than the space provided, and this feature was therefore reluctantly given up.

While it would be inadvisable here to attempt to mention all who have lent a helping hand to the preparation of this work, the writer wishes to acknowledge his special obligations to Chas. F. Mulks, of Ithaca, a descendant of the Ellis family, of Dryden, for his exhaustive and painstaking researches, of which this book has the benefit, and without which it would suffer, especially in the matter of statistics and genealogy, as well as in general accuracy. We are also under great obligations to Ex-Governor William Marvin, of Skaneateles, formerly a Dryden boy, now ninety years of age, who, with his own trembling hand, has, by letters and manuscripts, answered many inquiries and supplied much information not otherwise obtainable.

To the members of the Committee, one and all, whose names are given upon the reverse of the title page, the public will be indebted for whatever shall be found worthy to be preserved in the future from this first attempt to accurately record and perpetuate at length the annals of the town of Dryden. G. E. G.

ERRATA.—Page 91, for "Chapter XXIV," read "XXV." Page 115, line 8, after "and," read "pay of." Page 122, for "Israel Hoy," read "Hoyt." Pages 221, 223, for "Aaron Albright," in headline, read "Andrew." Page 254, after "Assumes the god," near the bottom of the page, read "Affects to nod."

TABLE OF CONTENTS.

	CHAPTER.	PAGE.
Prehistoric Conditions,	1	1
Indian Occupation,	2	4
The Approach of Civilization,	3	6
The First Settlement,	4	10
The First Resident Freeholder,	5	13
Other Settlements of 1798 and 1799,	6	17
Settlements from 1800 to 1803 Inclusive,	7	20
The Political Organization of the Town,	8	23
Events from 1803 to 1812,	9	28
The War of 1812,	10	30
Events from 1812 to 1822,	11	33
Review of the Pioneer Period,	12	35
The Period of Development—Transportation,	13	40
Immigration and Emigration,	14	43
Occupation of the Inhabitants,	15	45
Review of the Development Period,	16	47
The Civil War Period,	17	50
The War of the Rebellion,	18	52
Personal Record of Dryden Soldiers,	19	55
Internal Improvements,	20	68
The Period of Maturity,	21	70
Dryden Village in the Pioneer Period,	22	73
Pioneer Families of Dryden Village,	23	78
Dryden Village in the Development Period,	24	89
Dryden Village in the War Period,	25	94
Dryden Village in the Maturity Period,	26	98
Anecdotes of Dryden Village,	27	105
Schools, Churches and Cemeteries of Dryden Village,	28	107
The Southworth Library,	29	113
Willow Glen,	30	116
West Dryden,	31	121
Varna and Fall Creek,	32	131
Etna,	33	137
Isaiah Giles and Gilesville,	34	144
McLean and Malloryville,	35	149
Freeville,	36	152
The Octagonal School-House,	37	159
Further History of the South-west Section,	38	162

CONTENTS.

	CHAPTER.	PAGE.
Further History of the North-west Section,	39	167
Further History of the North-east Section,	40	175
Further History of the South-east Section,	41	180
The Dryden Agricultural Society,	42	184
The Ellis Family in Dryden,	43	191
The Snyder Family in Dryden,	44	194
The McGraw Family in Dryden,	45	199
The Benjamin Wood Family in Dryden,	46	202
John Southworth,	47	208
Milo Goodrich,	48	212
Jeremiah Wilbur Dwight,	49	215
John C. Lacy,	50	218
Andrew Albright,	51	220
Other Dryden Men of Note,	52	224
The Dryden Centennial Celebration,	53	244

LIST OF ILLUSTRATIONS.

	PAGE.
Township Map,	Pocket inside front cover
John Ellis, "King of Dryden,"	Frontispiece
Dryden Lake,	3
The New Log-Cabin,	12
Dryden Center House,	41
The Old Brick Store,	91
Dryden Woolen Mill,	95
Park and M. E. Church,	100
Main Street, Dryden,	104
Map of Dryden Village, (facing)	104
The Presbyterian Church,	109
Jennie McGraw-Fiske,	113
The Southworth Library,	115
West Dryden M. E. Church,	123
Mrs. Alletta George,	127
Map of Varna,	130
Varna, from R. R. Station,	132
Main Street, Varna,	134
Map of Etna,	136
Etna, West Side,	139
Etna, East Side,	143
Samuel Mallory,	150
Freeville Grist-Mill,	152
Shaver's Hotel,	153
Freeville Junction,	155
Map of Freeville, (facing)	156
The Octagonal School-House,	160
Church at Snyder Hill,	167
Ellis Hollow Church,	168
Main Building, Dryden Fair,	185
Scene at Dryden Fair,	189
Major Peleg Ellis,	192
John McGraw,	200
John Southworth,	209
Milo Goodrich, (facing)	212
Jeremiah Wilbur Dwight, (facing)	215
John C. Lacy, (facing)	218
Andrew Albright, (facing)	220
Smith Robertson,	225
William Marvin,	227
Richard Marvin,	229
Thomas J. McElheny,	230
Orrin S. Wood,	232
Otis E. Wood,	234
John Miller,	236
Samuel D. Halliday,	238
George B. Davis,	239
John D. Benton,	240
Dr. Francis J. Cheney,	242
Warren W. Tyler,	243
Inside the Log-Cabin,	251
Joseph E. Eggleston,	261
"Everything Goes,"	263
The George Junior Republic,	157

THE CENTENNIAL HISTORY

OF THE

TOWN OF DRYDEN.

CHAPTER I.

PREHISTORIC CONDITIONS.

The complete history of every atom of matter extends back to its creation; so the early history of the territory now known as the town of Dryden, is coeval with the formation of the present surface of the earth itself. While the scope of our work will be mainly confined to the century period immediately following the first settlement of the township by its present race of inhabitants, a brief reference to its earlier conditions will here be permitted, bringing it down to the time when our History properly begins.

Our knowledge of the earth's early history must be principally derived from the science of geology, which teaches that this portion of the state of New York was once the bottom of an ancient ocean, of which the sea shells and fossil fishes, found in the stratified layers of our native rocks, and the extensive beds of salt which are now known to underlie the surface of certain sections, if not all of our county, seem to afford abundant proof. Scientific scholars tell us that the northern part of our state first emerged from this prehistoric sea, which, gradually receding toward the south, left bare the native stratified rock formation of our locality in what the geologists term the Chemung period of the Devonian age. They teach us that subsequently powerful forces, by means perhaps of icebergs and glacial action, brought here and scattered about boulders and gravel beds from older and more northern geological formations, at the same time plowing up and pulverizing into soil the native strata, and scooping out our valleys, in some places so deep as to form the beds of the numerous lakes which are a marked physical feature of Western New York. These lakes and valleys, with their intermediate ridges of hills and uplands, usually extend in a general north and south direction, the hills of our township varying from 1500 to 1800 feet above the present sea level, while the beds of some of the neighboring lakes, Seneca for example, lie below the surface of the ocean itself. Just how these results were brought about must still be a matter for scientific study, but certain it is that this process of creation or development, whatever it may have been, resulted in leaving a rolling surface and a deep and fertile soil covering the beautiful hills and dales of our county of Tompkins.

When first discovered by civilized man our town was a dense forest, mostly of hemlock and hard wood timber, liberally sprinkled with large trees of white pine, which in some places grew to be so thrifty and thick as to monopolize the soil and overshadow and crowd out the inferior growth. How many generations of these undisturbed forest trees grew and decayed before being seen by the first settler, must be a matter of pure speculation; how this primeval forest appeared to the hardy pioneers who cleared it from the sites of our present homes, must be to us a subject for interesting reflections.

The physical features of the country which have suffered the least change in their appearance during the century period of our history, are the larger streams, which "while man may come and man may go" still "flow on forever" from their fountains to the sea. When first discovered, Virgil, Fall and Cascadilla creeks, although unconscious of their present names, with more obstructed channels but with larger volumes of water, drained the same valleys through which they still flow. They were then in their wild, untrained and unbroken state, unsaddled by bridges and unbridled by mill dams, but they took the same general courses which they now pursue, and were the first landmarks in the boundless forest. The hills, too, although hidden from view by the foliage of the unbroken shade, must have presented the same general form as now. Our Dryden lake, since enlarged by artificial means, still had an existence as a small body of water, when nature turned it over for the use of man. For unknown ages its tiny waves broke on the lonely shore, or, in more placid mood, its calm surface, all unseen, reflected the shadows of the virgin forest of pine with which it was completely surrounded.

DRYDEN LAKE.

Photo by Silcox.

CHAPTER II.

INDIAN OCCUPATION.

Although there is no record that the town of Dryden was ever the site of any permanent Indian settlement, there is abundant evidence that the Indians occupied it as a hunting ground. The little flint arrowheads which are still found, especially along the banks of the streams and upon the shores of the Lake, are unmistakable proof of the presence of the Indians, and the chips of flint, the waste product of the rude manufacture of these arrowheads, and other implements of stone found frequently about the shores of the Lake, indicate that at some time they had there at least a temporary encampment. The nearest Indian villages of which we have any authentic account were the habitations of the Cayugas, near the present site of the city of Ithaca, and extending on both sides of Cayuga Lake to its outlet. Central New York, when first known to civilization, was the home of the "Iroquois," a term applied first to five and afterwards to six confederated Indian tribes, which included the Cayugas, and is said to have constituted the most powerful force of Indians on the American Continent. We may perhaps claim some significance in the fact that the territory which now constitutes the central and western part of the Empire State was once the home and hunting ground of the victorious Iroquois, the conquerors of all the neighboring tribes. It was said that such experiences had the New England tribes of Indians suffered from the Mohawks—the eastern branch of the Iroquois—that the very mention of the name of "a Mohawk" caused them to flee with terror. The Iroquois had recently conquered the Adirondacks on the north and the Eries and Hurons on the west, and after becoming known to white men, in one of their southern excursions, they rescued from their enemies the whole tribe of Tuscaroras of North Carolina, whom they brought home with them and adopted as the sixth branch of their nation.

The conditions and habits of these aborigines form an interesting study to those who have investigated the subject. The first white men to go among them, except occasional fur traders, were the missionaries of the French Jesuits, who for a century prior to the English occupation of their territory, had lived and labored among them in the vain effort to effect their conversion to their form of Christianity. These, like other American Indians, from the first seemed to take much more naturally to the vices than to the virtues of their white brothers and the sacrifices of those zealous men, who left their pleasant homes in France to live and work among the Indians of North America for their education and development in the Christian faith, were worthy of better success than resulted. But the reports which these French Catholic priests sent back to their native country of their experiences among them are now found carefully preserved in French monasteries, and constitute one of the most interesting and trustworthy sources of our knowledge of the actual condition in which the Indians were then found. The "relations" (as they are called) of one Father Carheil, who spent over twenty years of his life among the Cayugas, and who in the year 1672 describes Lake Tiohero (now Cayuga) and the beautiful country surrounding it, with its abundance of fish and game, have thus recently been resurrected and translated into English, throwing much light upon this subject so interesting to the antiquarian.

In the French and Indian wars, which preceded the Revolution, the Iroquois, in spite of the French priests, took sides with the English, and rendered efficient assistance in the conquest of Canada from the French. When the War of the Revolution followed between the English colonies and their mother country, the Iroquois at first decided to remain neutral, but the most of them were afterwards persuaded to join their old allies, the English. This exposed the outposts of the colonies to a merciless enemy in the rear, and the frightful massacres of Cherry Valley and Wyoming were among the results. Fortunate it was for the early settlers of our locality that these bloody times passed before they ventured into the Western Wilderness.

To avenge these outrages and to punish the hostile Indians and drive them from the neighborhood of the advance settlements, an invasion of the Iroquois country was executed in the year 1779, known as "Sullivan's campaign," which, after a battle with the combined forces of Indians and Tories near Newtown (now Elmira), resulted in their complete defeat, followed by the subsequent overrunning of the Indian country and the destruction of their villages, including those along Cayuga and Seneca lakes. This campaign, forming a part of the Revolutionary war, planned by Washington and executed by Generals Sullivan and Clinton with a force of about five thousand men, detachments of which marched within a few miles of the town of Dryden, and perhaps within its borders, resulted in the complete humiliation of the fierce Iroquois, and opened the way for the subsequent purchase and settlement of this section of Western New York, over which up to that time they had held absolute sway. With the exception of the Oneidas, who had remained friendly to the colonies, and a part of the Onondagas, whose descendants still remain on their reservation near Syracuse, the Iroquois were driven from this part of the state never to return in large numbers. Some took refuge in Canada and along the Niagara frontier, others, including a number from the Cayuga and Seneca tribes, were colonized in the extreme western part of this state, while most of the Cayugas were induced to make their homes in the Indian Territory, where their descendants now reside in considerable numbers. Thus it happened that the early pioneers of our town escaped all annoyance from hostile Indians, who had been effectually driven out of the country before any settlement was attempted.

Those readers who desire to follow more minutely the details of "Sullivan's Campaign" will find the journals of the officers of that expedition, with full explanatory notes and maps, given in a large volume recently published by the State, a copy of which can be found in the Dryden village school library.

CHAPTER III.

THE APPROACH OF CIVILIZATION.

The War of the Revolution was practically ended in 1781, two years after Sullivan's Campaign was carried out against the Indians of Western New York. Within the next ten years the remnants of the Iroquois confederacy ceded their lands, by various treaties, to the State. Conditions favorable to the settlement of this locality were thus rapidly developed. Other sections of the country, both north and south of us, more readily reached by means of navigable lakes and rivers, were already occupied by the pioneer settlers, while the ridge separating the head waters of the St. Lawrence from those of the Susquehanna, of which our town forms a part, was still uninhabited. In February, 1789, the N. Y. State Legislature passed a law for surveying and setting apart for the use of its soldiers of the Revolution who then survived, a large section of land between Seneca and Oneida lakes afterwards known as the "Military Tract," comprising nearly two million acres, and including the town of Dryden, which was designated in the survey as Township No. 23. This tract was surveyed in the years 1789 and 1790, and divided into twenty-six townships, to which two more were afterwards added, making twenty-eight in all, each being about ten miles square and containing one hundred lots of about one mile square each. Dryden is one of the few to retain nearly its original dimensions. The little notch which formerly existed in the southeast corner of the town before the seven lots were set off to Caroline, was caused by the overlapping of the territory known as the Massachusetts Ten Townships upon the Military Tract, the West Owego Creek, which rises in Dryden near the southwest corner, being the west boundary of the former. The lots of Dryden were surveyed in the year 1790, by John Konkle, of Scholarie. In the southeast corner of each lot was set apart one hundred acres, known and frequently referred to in old descriptions, which are brought down into deeds of even this date, as the "State's Hundred Acres," which the owner had the option of exchanging for an equal number of acres of the U. S. lands in Ohio; and out of each lot was reserved a piece of fifty acres, known as the "Survey Fifty Acres," which was retained by the surveyor for his services, unless redeemed by the owner at eight dollars. So poor were the early inhabitants in those days, and so scarce was money, that many of them were unable to raise the eight dollars necessary to save the Survey Fifty Acres of their lots even on these terms.

Out of each township one lot was reserved for gospel and school purposes and another for promoting literature, the gospel and school lot in Dryden being No. 29 and the literature lot No. 63. The other lots were drawn by ballot in the year 1791 by the New York soldiers of the Revolution, each private and non-commissioned officer being entitled to draw one lot. A copy of the "Balloting Book" containing the names of the soldiers of the Revolution by whom the lots of the town of Dryden were originally drawn, can now be found in the Tompkins county clerk's office. This method of distribution of the land of the township by ballot, accounts for the fact that the early settlers of the town did not come in large colonies from any particular part of the older settlements, but came singly or in small groups from localities widely separated.

Prior to this time all of the western part of the state was embraced in the old county of Montgomery, but in the year 1791 Herkimer and Tioga counties, the latter including Dryden, were set off from Montgomery and in 1794 Onondaga county, then made to include all of the Military Tract, was formed and set off from Tioga and Herkimer. Thus our Township No. 23 was, from 1791 to 1794, a part of Tioga county, becoming in 1794 a part of Onondaga county, and so remained until it was appropriated to form a part of the new county of Cayuga in 1799, and was afterwards set off to form a part of the present county of Tompkins upon its organization in the year 1817.

It is thus seen how it happens that all of the records of land titles of the town of Dryden, prior to 1817 and subsequent to 1799, are found in the clerk's office of the county of Cayuga, the records of our own county commencing with its formation in the year 1817. Township No. 23, while in Montgomery county, was included in the political subdivision of Whitestown; upon its incorporation into Tioga county in 1791 it became a part of the old town of Owego; but when it was absorbed by Onondaga county it was at first included, in its political existence, with the present townships of Enfield and Ithaca in the original town of Ulysses, the organization of which dates back to the formation of Onondaga county in 1794. On Feb. 22, 1803, Township No. 23 was set off by itself, having been previously named Dryden by the commissioners of the land office, in honor of John Dryden, the English poet. The townships of Ithaca and Enfield remained a part of Ulysses, in their political organization, until four years later.

But few of the soldiers of the Revolution came and settled upon the lots which fell to them. The old veterans of those days, like some of later times, cared more for their present comfort than for an opportunity of finding new homes in the wilderness of the Military Tract. Nor can the old Revolutionary soldiers, after having passed through the hardships involved in the seven years' war with England, be blamed for shrinking from the privation and suffering incident to pioneer life in a new country. Many of them disposed of their titles for a mere trifle. For instance it is said that the original owner of the lot of 640 acres upon which the Dryden Center House now stands, sold it for a coat, hat, one drink of rum, and one dollar in money, and that the soldier who drew Lot No. 9 sold it for one "great coat." "Land sharks" existed even in those days and many of the soldiers' claims to the territory of Dryden were bought up for a trifling consideration by speculators in the East, who held them for advanced prices, at which they were sold to those who became actual settlers.

So great a length of time elapsed between the drawing of the lots and the actual occupation of them, and so many loose and fraudulent transfers were made of them in the meantime, that the uncertainty of titles resulting was one of the troubles which vexed and disappointed the early settlers, much more than we of the present day can realize. Some, however, of the original owners retained their lots and occupied the lands which the government had given them as a bounty for their services. As an example, Elias Larabee, who drew Lot No. 49, including the southeast quarter of Dryden village, came and lived for a long time upon his lot, and one of his descendants, Daniel Law-

THE APPROACH OF CIVILIZATION.

son, a pensioner of the War of the Rebellion, still owns and occupies a small part of it.

The town having been surveyed in 1790 and the lots being drawn in 1791, the next question was how were these possessions in the wilderness of the Military Tract to be reached. The first settlers had already arrived at Owego and Elmira by way of the Susquehanna and Chemung rivers, while others had come to Syracuse and Auburn by way of the Mohawk and Seneca rivers and the lakes, and settlements had been commenced in and about Ithaca and Lansing, on the banks of Cayuga Lake, by parties who had taken these routes, but there was no direct practicable way to reach from the east the elevated watershed lying between the two, until a road was cut through the woods from Oxford on the Chenango River to Ithaca at the head of Cayuga Lake, which was done in the years 1793, 1794 and 1795, by Joseph Chaplin under a contract from the State. Mr. Chaplin was the first settler in the town of Virgil and we quote from Bouton's History of that town, pages 9 and 10, concerning him and his work as follows :

"To facilitate the settlement of this section of the country, a road was projected connecting Oxford with the Cayuga Lake, to pass through this town [Virgil.] Joseph Chaplin, the first inhabitant, was intrusted with this work. The instrument by which he was authorized to engage in it was authenticated on the fifth of May, 1792. He spent that season in exploring and surveying the route, the length of which is about sixty miles. He came to Lot No. 50 [of Virgil], which he owned and afterwards settled, erected a house and prosecuted his work, having a woman to keep the house and cook for workmen. The work of cutting and clearing the road was done in 1793-4; so that he moved his family from Oxford over it in the winter of 1794-5, employing six or seven sleighs freighted with family, furniture, provisions, etc."

But it seems that when he had completed the road as far as Virgil he was persuaded by some settlers from Kidder's Ferry (near Ludlowville) to continue the road from Virgil through to that point, as it then contained more inhabitants than Ithaca. Having done so he presented his bill to the Legislature, which rejected it on the ground that he had not complied with the terms of his contract, which required the road to be built to Ithaca. He then returned and in the year 1795 cut the road through from Virgil to Ithaca known as the "Bridle Road," and thus became entitled to his pay, the first road opened by him being now known as the old State Road, extending between the towns of Dryden and Groton and through Lansing to the Lake.

The foregoing is the version of this matter which has appeared in the local histories previously published, but it is now claimed, with better reason as it seems to us and more consistently with the conditions which are known to have then existed, that the Bridle Road was the trial route first partly opened by Chaplin, and which the state government refused to accept because it did not terminate as required by the contract at a point on Cayuga Lake, the early Ithaca settlement being at least a mile from its nearest shore; and that he then fulfilled the letter of his contract by afterwards opening the old State Road to Kidder's Ferry, leaving the first route only a bridle path which Capt. Robertson, as we shall see hereafter, was obliged to widen in order to reach with ox teams by way of Ithaca his site on Lot 53 of Dryden.

We are told that in this work of cutting these new roads through the wilderness, Mr. Chaplin was assisted by his step-son, then a young man, Gideon Messenger by name, who is the ancestor of the present Messenger family of Dryden and the uncle of H. J. Messenger, of Cortland. From Bouton's History we learn that this same Gideon Messenger was the first town clerk of Virgil in 1795, afterwards its supervisor, and that he passed over the State Road from State Bridge, in the eastern part of Virgil, to Cayuga Lake, before there was a single habitation in the whole distance. (Bouton's Supplement, page 39.)

CHAPTER IV.

THE FIRST SETTLEMENT.

It seems to be conceded that the first actual settler in the town of Dryden was Amos Sweet. Our information upon this subject is derived almost entirely from the "Old Man in the Clouds," the fictitious name of the author of a series of articles published in "Rumsey's Companion," the first newspaper published at Dryden, in the years 1856 and 1857, and which were, in fact, compiled by the editor from the information afforded by old men, then living, but since dead, and in that way preserved. We quote from the first number as follows:

"It was in the spring of 1797, that a man by the name of Amos Sweet c me from the East somewhere, and, after ascertaining the location of his lot, put up a log house about ten feet square, just back of where now resides Freeman Stebbins [now John Munsey] in this village, where himself, his wife, two children, his mother and brother all lived.

THE FIRST SETTLEMENT. 11

This would seem to be a very small and rude habitation to the people of our present gay and beautiful village. It was built of logs about a foot thick; these were halved together at the ends and the cracks chinked in with split sticks and mud. The house was eight logs high, covered with bark from the elm and basswood. Through one corner an opening was left for the smoke to pass through, there being no chimney or chamber floor. The fire-place was composed of three hardhead stones turned up against the logs for the back, and three or four others of the same stamp formed the hearth, these being laid upon the split logs which formed the floor. Inasmuch as there was no sash or glass in those days in this vicinity, their only window consisted of an opening about eighteen inches square cut through the logs, and this, to keep out the inclement weather, was covered with brown paper, greased over to admit the light. The door was also in keeping with the rest of the house, being composed of slabs split from the pine and hewn off as smooth as might be with the common axe. The hinges were of wood and fastened across the door with pins of the same material, serving the double purpose of cleet and hinge. In this house, thus built without nails and with benches fastened to the sides of the house for chairs, eating from wooden trenchers and slab tables much after the fashion of the door, did this little family of pioneers live."

But the title to the lot upon which Mr. Sweet built seems to have been defective and one Nathaniel Shelden appears to have had the real ownership, for in 1801, he compelled Mr. Sweet and his family to leave it. Elsewhere Mr. Sweet is spoken of as a "squatter," or one having no title, and Mr. Shelden is represented as using "fraudulent means" to dispossess him, but charity for both of these early pioneers compels us to believe that the difficulty grew out of the great uncertainty and confusion which then existed as to the titles derived from the old soldiers of the Revolution, some of whom had undertaken to sell the same lands several times over to different parties. At any rate Sweet was compelled to leave his pioneer home in 1801, and soon after, as the account says, "he sickened and died, and his remains, together with those of his mother and two children," were buried directly across the road from the Dryden Springs Sanitarium. The house remained for some time after, for we are told that it was used as the first school house for the children of the early settlers in the year 1804.

The new log cabin constructed during the summer of 1897 on the grounds of the Dryden Agricultural Society was built of green chestnut logs and modeled after this first pioneer house in Dryden. It is intended to be preserved and it is hoped it will long remain as a relic of that kind of architecture, once so prevalent here, where now only the decaying remains of two or three log houses can be found in the whole township.

The fact that we now find no signs of the graves where Mr. Sweet and his family are said to have been buried, strikes us at first as singular, but a little reflection and an examination of the customs of the early settlers in that regard, supplies us with the explanation. The pioneers had too much to do to spend much time or effort in the burial of their dead and were too poor to go to much expense in such matters. Mr. Bouton, in his History of Virgil, says that the first gravestone in that town was erected in 1823, although deaths had occurred there from its earliest settlement. He also explains their method of selecting places for the burial of their dead, which seems to us strange. We quote from pages 13 and 14 of the Supplement, where he speaks of a stranger who lost his way and perished in the woods, and mentions that he was buried near where he was found.

"Only a few families at this time (1798) resided in the town, which extended over ten miles of territory. There was no public burying ground and it was not possible to know where it would be located. * * * Families buried their dead on their own premises, and others, strangers and transient persons, were permitted to be laid in these family grounds. Ultimately it came to pass that one or more of these grounds came to be considered *public*, in a subordinate sense. There were a large number of them which continued in use after the public ground was opened."

Grave-stones as seen in old cemeteries, where any existed at all, were then of the simplest character, many being made of native flag-stones, and the coffin of the pioneer was a coarse wooden box manufactured by the local undertaker, fifteen dollars paying for the very best.

When we come to think of it, a cemetery would not be much of an institution in an early settlement in the woods, especially where the living inhabitants had all they could do to keep soul and body together. Far different is it in a community of a century's growth, where now our cemetery tombstones, many of them imported from Italy and Scotland, represent the expenditure of very many thousands of dollars, and the earth beneath them already envelops the forms of the ever-increasing, yet silent, majority.

CHAPTER V.

THE FIRST RESIDENT FREEHOLDER.

While Amos Sweet was the first man to take up his residence in Dryden, he seems never to have held permanent title to any of its real estate, and, so far as we can learn, he left no relatives or descendants from whom any of the present inhabitants can trace their ancestry. We know not whence he came, except from the "Old Man in the Clouds," who says that he came from "the East somewhere," and our short story of his appearance and residence here is an unsatisfactory and a tragic one. We have already given all the facts which we can learn of him except the statement derived from an old obituary notice of Seth Stevens, a relative of the early Rummer family in Dryden, which relates that Stevens, while probably residing in Virgil, helped to build the first log house in Dryden, presumably the Amos Sweet house. We have accidentally come across his signature as a witness to an old Dryden deed, which shows that he could write, an accomplishment at that time none too common.

The next settlement in the township was made by a man whose life had a permanent influence upon the town, and who well-earned the title which was afterward given him of being the "Father of the Town," having been its first resident freeholder and afterward its first supervisor.

In the year 1797 there lived near Schuylerville, Saratoga county, N. Y., George Robertson, a young carpenter and millwright, who by patient industry had acquired a home and a little property, but whose ambition prompted him to become a pioneer in the undeveloped wilderness of the Military Tract. His father, Robert Robertson, who had recently died, had in 1769 emigrated with his family, consisting of his wife, Josephine, and two small children, young George and his older sister, Nancy (McCutcheon), from near Glasgow, Scotland, to Saratoga county, where, upon the breaking out of the Revolution, the father enlisted and gallantly served throughout the struggle for independence. The old flint-lock musket which he carried in the army of Washington under the command of General Philip Schuyler, by and after whom one of his sons was named, is still kept as a treasure in the family and was on exhibition at Dryden's Centennial Celebration.

Young George Robertson, in 1797, had an opportunity of purchasing Lot No. 53, of Dryden, from a neighbor, Benoni Ballard, the soldier to whom it was allotted, and in the autumn of that year he made a prospecting tour on foot from Saratoga county to Dryden, reaching Lot 53 by way of the Mohawk Valley, Auburn, Cayuga Lake and Ithaca, returning by way of the Bridle Road through the present site of Dryden village, to Oxford, and thence by way of Utica to his home. Upon this preliminary visit the only habitation which he found in Dryden was that of Amos Sweet, described in the last chapter, where, as he related, there was a clearing of about half an acre which he called a "turnip patch."

Being pleased with the new country and possessed of a courage which, we fear, would be lacking in these days of luxury and refinement, Robertson sold his home and with the proceeds completed the purchase of Lot No. 53 for eight hundred and fifty dollars. He left his wife and two children for the time being and set out in February, 1798, with a sleigh loaded with such implements and provisions as could be carried, drawn by two yoke of oxen, for the long journey. He was accompanied by at least two young men, including his younger brother, Philip S. Robertson, and Jared Benjamin.

Of Philip S. Robertson we shall have occasion to say more here-

THE FIRST RESIDENT FREEHOLDER.

after as being one of the pioneers of the northwest section of the town, but of Jared Benjamin we shall say here, lest it be omitted hereafter, that he was then a lad sixteen years of age who had been apprenticed to George Robertson to learn the carpenter's trade and who was induced to accompany him into the wilderness by the promise of eighty acres of land, and who, during the journey and for the first year of the settlement, served as the housekeeper and cook of the party. He afterwards served as a soldier from Tompkins county in the War of 1812, after which he journeyed and settled further west, but his son, Charles Benjamin, returned to Dryden and at one time occupied and enlarged the Dryden village tannery and afterwards built a tannery at Harford, one of the old buildings still standing there unoccupied near the railroad station; and his son is Chas. M. Benjamin, now one of the proprietors of the Ithaca Journal. Another of the descendants of this pioneer lad, Jared Benjamin, is Mrs. D. B. Card, of Dryden.

To return to our narrative, it is claimed by some that Walter Yeomans, and by others that Moses Snyder also accompanied George Robertson on this pioneer journey, but neither are mentioned in the first account, published forty years ago when the facts were more attainable, and either may have come a year or two later, although it is certain that both were early pioneers of Dryden from Saratoga county.

The pioneer party were three weeks on the journey, coming by way of the Mohawk Valley, Utica, Hardenburg's Corners (now Auburn), reaching Ithaca (then called "Markle's Flats,") where there were then three log houses, March 1, 1798. It took the whole of the next day to widen the Bridle Road through from Ithaca to Lot 53, upon which Mott J. Robertson, the youngest son of Captain George Robertson, now resides, so as to admit of the progress of the team and baggage. They arrived towards evening on March 2nd and made hasty preparations to spend their first night on the site of their new home. In later years Captain Robertson pointed out to his sons the very spot, now located between the highway and railroad track near the west line of Lot 53, where, on that March evening, on split basswood logs, they ate their first meal and stretched themselves out to spend the night, having provided the oxen with the tops of the basswood trees for a supper of browse. A fall of two inches of snow during the night caused Philip S. to get up and stretch over them a blanket on stakes, to protect them from the storm. The next morning the men set to work to build a log house and make a clearing so as to secure a crop of grain that season. The trees were chopped down, girdled and burned, the seed was dragged in with the aid of a tree top as a harrow, and the rich, mellow, new ground yielded abundant harvests in that and the succeeding years. Thus the energy and prudence of young George Robertson enabled him to harvest the first considerable crops in the town, and when the subsequent settlers came to him to obtain seed grain, it is said that he supplied those who had no present means of paying for it, but refused those who had money which would enable them to get it elsewhere, lest he should not have enough to supply all of his poorer neighbors. Whether such a policy of supplying only those who had no money could be successfully carried out in these times, may be seriously questioned, but it served to exhibit the unselfish character of Capt. Robertson and entitled him to the gratitude of his fellow pioneers, as well as to that of their posterity. His wife and children came on, the next season (1799), in care of her brother, Wm. Smith, of Saratoga, who, after viewing the uninviting prospect of the single log house, surrounded for a short distance with the clearing full of charred stumps and then by the dense wilderness, advised his sister to return with him to his home in Saratoga, but she bravely resolved with her husband to share the hardships and reap the rewards afforded to pioneers in a new country. Their son, Robert R., whose birthday was April 7, 1800, was for a long time supposed to have been the first white child born in the town of Dryden, but we now learn upon reliable authority that Melinda, the daughter of David Foote and the mother of Mrs. Darius Givens, now residing in Dryden village, was born at Willow Glen, on February 21, 1800, and was therefore the first native-born child, while Robert R. was the first native-born male citizen of the town.

The heroic and unselfish conduct of Captain Robertson, and his industrious and prudent life, together with abilities of no common order, gave him prominence in our early history and when the town came to be organized as a separate political township in 1803, he was made its first supervisor. Although not the first settler, he was the first resident freeholder of the town, raised the first crop of any account, and, his house being a hospitable refuge for the early settlers perhaps less provident than he had been, he is credited with being the first innkeeper of the town in 1801. These facts well entitled him to be regarded, as he was by the early settlers, the "Father of the Town of Dryden." He was afterward a captain of the State militia and the field opposite the present residence of his son, Mott J. Robertson, upon which this log house was built in 1798, was the training ground for the early yeomanry of Dryden, who were here required to be annually drilled in military tactics. Captain Robertson died April

4, 1844, having raised a family of thirteen children, many of whom have held positions of honor and trust in this and other states, at least two of his sons having served as sheriffs of the county of Tompkins. His oldest child, Nancy, married Thomas Bishop and she and her oldest brother, Thomas, lived and died in the town of Lansing. Robert died in Chautauqua county, N. Y. Phœbe became the wife of Peter V. Snyder, and Corilla the wife of Wm. Brown, who, with her brothers, John, Theodore, Cyrus and Hiram D., made their home in Albion, Mich. Pauline became the wife of Benjamin F. King, at Parma, Mich., and Philip died in Crawford county, Pa. Smith, of whom we shall say more hereafter, resides at Eau Claire, Wis., and Mott J., the only son now residing here, is one of the present Centennial Committee of the town of Dryden.

CHAPTER VI.

OTHER SETTLEMENTS OF 1798 AND 1799.

In the fall of 1798, three families settled at Willow Glen. They consisted of Ezekiel Sanford, his wife and one son, David Foote, his wife and four daughters, and Ebenezer Clauson, his wife, one son and two daughters, making in all a party of fourteen persons, who came to Dryden over the new State Road, from the Chenango river, with a single team of oxen drawing a heavy ox sled of the olden times, which was made with wooden shoes and a heavy split pole. This conveyance carried all of the household furniture of the three families, which we infer from that fact could not then have been very rich in housekeeping materials. Sanford located opposite the residence of the late Elias W. Cady, Clauson on the premises now owned and occupied by Moses Rowland, while Foote built his log hut between the two. They are said to have passed a very "comfortable winter," subsisting largely upon the abundant game found in the new country, the oxen being supplied with plenty of browse from the trees. That they were able to live through the winter at all in this way is a mystery to us of the present age, who are supplied with so many of the comforts and luxuries of life. It seemed to the writer at first impossible that cattle could be wintered on "browse" without hay or grain, but he is assured by old men that such is not the case, and that it was not uncommon in old times when fodder was scarce to fell trees in the woods, especially maple and basswood, so that cattle could have access to the tops for their subsistence. We are also reminded that wild deer wintered in the woods in this locality, when the snow was deep, without this assistance of the woodman. These new settlers did survive and seem to have prospered in their new homes, and as proof of these facts we know that our present popular highway commissioner, Sanford E. Smiley, is one of a large number of direct descendants of that same pioneer, Ezekiel Sanford, one of the party who wintered their oxen on browse and themselves on the "abundant game found in the new country" in the winter of the year 1798-9. Like Amos Sweet, who had preceded them one year, they seem to have had, when they came, no permanent title to the land upon which they located, but came empty handed to grow up with the new country as they did, having become the ancestors of many of its now prosperous inhabitants.

The writer was at first unable to learn whether any of these three pioneers except Sanford left descendants now residing in the township, and was surprised to learn that both Mrs. Darius Givens and Mrs. Robert Sager are grandchildren of that same David Foote. Clauson, with all his family, is believed to have moved further west, one of his daughters having married a brother of Wyatt Allen, formerly of Dryden.

Others who settled in 1798, coming here from Lansing, where they had sojourned a short time, were Daniel White and his brother-in-law, Samuel Knapp, a soldier of the Revolution, who was engaged in the battles of Trenton, Princeton, Stony Point, Brandywine and Monmouth. Knapp took up his location on Lot No. 14, where he raised a large family and died July 1, 1847, aged 91 years. His remains are buried in the Peruville cemetery. Mr. White gave his attention to the construction of the first grist-mill of the town, which stood about forty rods west of the present grist-mill in Freeville, just north-west of where the highway now crosses Fall Creek. He procured a stone which he found on the Thompson (now Skillings) farm, split it and himself dressed out and took to the mill the first millstones, which answered the purpose and were in constant use until the mill was reconstructed in 1818. His mill was completed in 1802, prior to which time the pioneer was obliged to take his grist to Ludlow's Mill (now Ludlowville) to be ground, or pound it into meal in the hollow of a large stump, as was sometimes done by hand. During the past summer parts of this boulder out of which Mr. White worked these first millstones, were brought to the grounds of the Dryden Agricultural Society by Samuel Skillings, a descendant of Samuel Knapp, and left near the new log cabin, where they will remain as a relic and reminder of the use which Mr. White made in 1802 of a part of this rock. Besides being a practical miller, Mr. White was an ordained deacon of the M. E. church and preached on the Cayuga circuit in 1802, and for several years afterwards. He came to Lansing from Pennsylvania, but was originally from Roxbury, Mass., and died at the age of seventy-eight, leaving a family of fourteen children, of whom the only present survivors are Daniel M. White, of Dryden, secretary of the present Centennial Committee, Mrs. Anna Montfort, of Peruville, and Mrs. George F. A. Baker, of West Dryden. Many of his grandchildren and great-grandchildren are now living.

Aaron Lacy, father of the late John R. Lacy, came from New Jersey and settled at Willow Glen early in the year 1799, on the corner since occupied by the Stickles family.

Zephaniah Brown came from Saratoga and settled on Lot 71, adjoining the town of Ithaca, in the year 1799, cutting the first road from that portion of the town to Ithaca, which was extended two years later by Peleg Ellis to the Ellis Hollow neighborhood. Brown seems to have been the first pioneer in that part of the town and resided for a number of years on the farm since occupied by Chauncey L. Scott. But in about 1830 he and his family moved to Michigan, leaving, so far as we can learn, no descendants in the town.

Tradition has handed down to us an incident worthy of being here preserved of the first visit between the two pioneer families of Peleg Ellis and Zephaniah Brown, after a path had been made connecting their respective clearings in the forest. Mrs. Ellis came to make her call upon her new neighbor on horseback, one of her little girls sitting in front of her and the other behind. As they emerged from the woods into the clearing Mrs. Brown saw them and anxiously called out to her husband in a voice loud enough to be heard by Mrs. Ellis: "Zephaniah! Zephaniah! Mrs. Ellis is coming. What shall we have for tea?" To which her husband replied in a voice still heard by the visitor: "Make a shortcake! Make a shortcake and put the cream in thick; put it in thick, I say."

Society did not then require of Dryden neighbors the formalities, and shall we say hypocrisy, now in vogue; but who can say that there did not then exist among these pioneers dressed in homespun clothing and living in their log houses in the clearings, more genuine, heartfelt hospitality than exists to-day among their more polished descendants in their expensive mansions, furnished with all that modern luxury and elegance can suggest?

CHAPTER VII.

SETTLEMENTS FROM 1800 TO 1803 INCLUSIVE.

In the year 1800 Lyman Hurd came in from Vermont and settled with his wife and children at Willow Glen, on the corner opposite the blacksmith shop, now vacant. His house which he built there was then the best in town because it had a chimney, the others having merely a hole in the roof for the smoke to pass out. This chimney was not made of bricks and mortar, but of sticks and mud, built up from the beam over the fire-place in cob-house fashion, such as was known in those days as a "stick chimney," the best that could be made with the material at hand. Mr. Hurd brought with him a pair of horses, the first seen in the new settlement, but unfortunately one of them died during the first winter, not being able perhaps to subsist upon "browse," which, as we have seen, was about all the food for domestic animals which the town then afforded. In this dilemma Mr. Hurd and his hired man went off through the woods to Tully and there procured an ox, which they brought home and harnessed in with the surviving horse by means of what was called a half yoke, and the "Old Man in the Clouds" certifies to us that for all purposes, "such as plowing, logging, going to mill and to meeting, this team worked together admirably."

Other settlers of the same year were Nathaniel Sheldon, the first physician to reside in the town, and Ruloff Whitney, who built the first sawmill of the town, which was located on Virgil creek, on the road leading north from Willow Glen, which was opened at this time by the authorities of the town (still Ulysses) to connect at this point the "Bridle" road with the old "State" road. This mill was located upon what has since been known as the Joseph McGraw farm, and furnished the first lumber for the new settlement. Ruloff Whitney was also the first bridegroom of the town, having wooed and won one of Virgil's fair daughters, Miss Susan Glenny, whom he married in this, the first year of the nineteenth century, or perhaps more accurately speaking the last of the eighteenth. From this time on settlers were numerous and will be noticed further on when we come to treat of the separate localities of the town with which they are associated, mentioning here in detail only those who, to some extent, are prominently connected with the history of the town, as a whole.

Among these were the two brothers John and Peleg Ellis, who came originally from West Greenwich, Rhode Island, and first settled in

Herkimer county of this state, from which John came to Virgil in 1798, having purchased of the Samuel Cook estate Lot No. 23 of that town, upon which he remained about three years. In the meantime his brother Peleg, having exchanged with this same Cook family his home in Herkimer county for Lot No. 84 of Dryden, in the locality since known as Ellis Hollow, first came out to view his new possessions in the fall of 1799. He had difficulty at first to locate his newly acquired property in the universal forest, until meeting with Captain Robertson, he received such directions as enabled him to find it, by means of a map and the marked trees which, when properly understood, indicated the boundaries of the recently surveyed lots. Having found his property he immediately commenced chopping for a clearing, and he is said to have passed eleven days alone at work without once seeing a human being. On the eleventh day Zephaniah Brown, who, as we have seen, had already settled on Lot 71, hearing the sound of the axe came up with his gun in hand to make his first call upon his new neighbor.

Returning home to spend the winter, Mr. Ellis came on, the next summer, with his family, then consisting of his wife and two daughters, and built on the headwaters of Cascadilla Creek, which flowed through his lot, his first home of logs, in which he lived for eight years. Here, on January 30, 1801, was born Delilah (Mulks), the oldest of the family of Major Ellis to be born in Dryden, the two eldest daughters having come here with their parents. We shall have occasion to refer to Major Ellis hereafter as the captain of the first company of Dryden men to engage in the War of 1812, having afterward been commissioned as major of the militia of the olden time. He lived on the farm which he had thus commenced clearing in 1799 for nearly sixty years and died there on his eighty-fourth birthday, May 9th, 1859. Four of his family of twelve children are still living, one of them, Mrs. John M. Smith, still occupying the homestead. Major Ellis is said to have been a man universally esteemed for honesty and the qualities which make a good citizen and a faithful friend.

His brother John, whom we left in Virgil, sold his property there and came to Dryden in 1801, first settling here on the farm near Malloryville, since owned by A. B. Lamont, where he remained about three years. Afterwards he also resided in Ellis Hollow near his brother; but a few years before his death, which occurred April 10, 1846, he took up his final place of residence in the town on the place now owned by J. Wesley Hiles, one-half mile north of Dryden village.

nearly opposite to the farm where his grandson, Geo. A. Ellis, now resides. From the date of his residence here to his death, John Ellis seems to have been the most prominent citizen of the town. Before the county of Tompkins was organized he held the position of Judge of the Court of Common Pleas of Cayuga county, and afterwards he held the same office in Tompkins county. He was chosen supervisor of the town for twenty-seven years, was a member of the State Legislature in 1831 and 1832, besides holding many minor offices. Subsequent politicians must despair of equalling his record as an office holder, and we must all concede that he was entitled to the designation which was given him at the time, of being "King of Dryden." Among his many descendants are Thomas J. McElheny, of Ithaca, John E. McElheny, of Dryden, and the late Jennie McGraw-Fiske, to whom we are indebted for the Southworth Library. Judge Ellis is said to have been a man of commanding presence, keen and quick in the use of his intellectual powers. A portrait of him, painted in Albany during his attendance at the State Legislature, is still owned by his grandson, John E. McElheny, and was on exhibition at Dryden's Centennial Celebration, a copy of which is the frontispiece of this volume. For further particulars concerning John and Peleg Ellis see the subsequent chapter of this History which treats of the Ellis Family in Dryden.

In the year 1801 the first merchant of the town, Joel Hull, from Massachusetts, settled at Willow Glen, taking up his abode on the corner now occupied by Moses Rowland. He was also the first resident surveyor in the town, but it is said that he was neither a hunter nor a shingle maker, two qualifications which all other early settlers were supposed to possess. He was, however, a man of much intelligence, the first town clerk, in 1803, and a man whose advice was sought in legal matters, being an expert in drawing deeds and contracts. His store was opened in an addition to his house in 1802. His stock of goods was purchased at Aurora and consisted of a chest of old Bohea tea, which he sold at one dollar per pound, a quantity of Cavendish tobacco, at three shillings per pound, and two or three rolls of pig-tail tobacco, at three cents per yard, cash. As money was scarce, barter was in order, and one bushel of ashes would buy one yard of pig-tail. His stock also included a keg of whiskey, two or three pieces of calico and some narrow sheetings. He ventured more extensively in trade afterwards and failed in business, thus setting a bad example which succeeding merchants have too often followed. He and his family afterwards removed to Pennsylvania. An incident of him is vouched for by the "Old Man in the Clouds" which ought to be preserved, as illustrating the condition of the country at that time, and is as follows: In the spring of 1803 he received, from some distant friends in the East, a pig, which was allowed to run at large about the house and in the woods and grew to be a fine shoat of sixty to eighty pounds. One day as Mr. Hull was chopping wood at his door he heard the pig squealing in the edge of the clearing, some fifteen rods distant, as if something unusual was the matter. A windfall of large pines lay between the house and the standing timber, which concealed the location from which the sound was heard, but taking his axe in hand and followed by his oldest son and Thomas Lewis, Mr. Hull rushed to the rescue. Arriving upon the scene he discovered a large bear, with the pig closely embraced in its fore paws, marching off towards the swamp. The bear shortly arrived at a log over which he was struggling to carry his prize, when Mr. Hull dashed up from behind and drove his axe into the head of the robber, killing him instantly and exclaiming at the same time, "Damn you, Bruin, I'll teach you the result of stealing my only pig in broad daylight." The pig, though badly injured, recovered and reached full grown proportions.

In the year 1801, there arrived from New Jersey the Lacy brothers, Richard, Thomas, Daniel, Benjamin and James, who located, the first, where Jackson Jameson now lives, the next three in Dryden village, and the youngest, James, near Dryden Lake. All afterwards removed farther west, except Benjamin, the father of the late John C. Lacy, of whom we shall have more to say hereafter in connection with Dryden village. In the same year two brothers, Peter and Christopher Snyder, came from Oxford, N. J., and commenced a clearing on Lot 43, to which they emigrated in the following season, as will be seen at length in a succeeding chapter upon the "Snyder Family in Dryden."

William Sweezy lived one-half mile north of Varna and a man by the name of Cooper settled one-half mile south of Etna as early as 1801.

Andrew Sherwood, a soldier of the Revolution, who was the ancestor of another family which has multiplied and flourished in Dryden, came with his son Thomas and settled on Lot No. 9 in the year 1802.

CHAPTER VIII.

THE POLITICAL ORGANIZATION OF THE TOWN.

From 1794 until 1803, as we have seen, Township No. 22 (including all the present towns of Enfield, Ulysses, and Ithaca, town and city) was merged in its political organization with Township No. 23 (Dryden) under the name of Ulysses. In the year 1794, the assessed valuation of the whole town, as thus constituted, was £100, and the tax levied £12 and 10 shillings, as they then counted money, being a tax of more than twelve per cent on the valuation. In 1797, the population of the whole town of Ulysses was returned at 52 and the valuation at $4,777, our decimal system of currency having been substituted for the old English form of money. In 1798 the population had increased to 60 and the valuation to $5,000. In the year 1800, the census shows a population of 927, a rapid increase, which continued for some years, but not more than one third of it belonged to what is now Dryden. On the jury list of Ulysses for 1801, are found the names of three men who resided in Township No. 23, viz: Peleg Ellis, Ichabod Palmerton, and Jehiel Bouton. At the town meeting of Ulysses, held at the home of Nathaniel Davenport (the location of which is now in Ithaca) in March, 1802, it was voted "that the township of Dryden be set off from Ulysses." From this we infer that the name Dryden was commonly applied to Township No. 23 before it had a separate political existance, which was effected by an Act of the Legislature passed Feb. 22, 1803. At the first town meeting, held at the home of Captain George Robertson, March 1, 1803, the following officers were chosen:

Supervisor—George Robertson.
Town Clerk—Joel Hull.
Assessors—John Ellis, Joel Hull, Peleg Ellis.
Constable and Collector—Daniel Lacy.
Poormasters—William Garrison, Philip S. Robertson.
Commissioners of Highways—Lewis Fortner, Ezekiel Sanford, William Harned.
Fence Viewers and Overseers of Highways—Amnah Peet, Ebenezer Clauson, David Foote, Joseph Schofield.
Pound Master—John Montayney.

It must have been a veritable paradise for office seekers in those days, for every one could hold an office and still have offices to spare.

We give in this place the full list of Supervisors, Town Clerks, and Justices of the Peace of the town to the present time, thus calling to mind many prominent citizens of by-gone days:

SUPERVISORS.

George Robertson,	- 1803	William Miller,	- - 1805
John Ellis, - -	1804	John Ellis,	- - 1806-12

POLITICAL ORGANIZATION.

Jesse Stout,	- -	1813	Smith Robertson,	- 1851 3
John Ellis,	- -	1814	Hiram Snyder, -	1854 6
Parley Whitmore,	-	1815	Jeremiah W. Dwight,	- 1857 8
John Ellis,	- -	1816	Lemi Grover, -	1859-61
Parley Whitmore,	-	1817	Caleb Bartholomew,	- 1862
John Ellis,	- -	1818-34	Luther Griswold,	- 1863-5
Joshua Phillips,	-	1835 37	John M. Smith, -	1866 71
John Ellis,	- -	1838	James H. George,	- 1872 3
Joshua Phillips,	-	1839	Edwin R. Wade, -	- 1874
Elias W. Cady,	-	1840 1	Harrison Marvin,	1875 9
Henry B. Weaver,		1842 3	James H. George,	- 1880 1
Jeremiah Snyder,	-	1844	George M. Rockwell, -	1882 4
Wessels S. Middaugh,	- 1845 7		James H. George, -	- 1884 5
Albert J. Twogood,	-	1848	George M. Rockwell, -	1886 7
Hiram Snyder,	-	1849	John H. Kennedy,	1888-95
Charles Givens,	-	1850	Theron Johnson,	- 1896 7

TOWN CLERKS.

Joel Hull,	- -	1803	Walker Marsh, -	- 1844 5
William Miller,	-	1804	Nelson Givens,	1846 7
Joel Hull,	- -	1805 7	Walker Marsh, -	- 1848 9
Derick Sutfin,	-	1808	Nelson Givens,	1850
John Wickham,	-	1809	Oliver Stewart, -	- 1851 3
Thomas Southworth,		1810-11	Richard M. Beaman,	1854 6
Isaiah Giles, -	-	1812	George H. Houtz, -	1857 74
Parley Whitmore,		1813 14	George S. Barber, -	1875 7
Josiah Newell,		1815 16	John S. Barber, -	- 1878
Henry B Weaver,		1817 19	DeWitt T. Wheeler, -	1879
Benj. Aldridge,	-	1820 31	Geo. H. Houtz, -	- 1880 7
Abram Bouton,	-	1832	C. B. Snyder, -	1888 9
Hiram Bouton,		1833	Henry C. Warriner,	- 1890
Henry B. Weaver,		- 1834 9	Fred E. Darling,	1891 3
Rice Weed,	-	1840	John M. Ellis, -	- 1894 5
Bryan Finch,	-	1841	Fred E. Darling,	1896 7
C. S. C. Dowe,	-	1842 3		

JUSTICES OF THE PEACE.

Derick Sutfin, -		1803	Samuel Hemmingway,	1803
Ruloff Whitney,	-	1803	Isaiah Giles, -	- 1810

HISTORY OF DRYDEN.

Ruloff Whitney,	-	1810	Abraham Tanner, -	1857
Jacob Primrose, -		1811–12	Alviras Snyder, -	1858
Ithamar Whipple,	-	1811-12	James H. George, -	1859
James Weaver,	-	1818	Thomas Hunt, -	1860
Jesse Stout, -	-	1818	Edmund H. Sweet, -	1861
Parley Whitmore,	-	1818	Alviras Snyder, -	1862
Rice Weed, -	-	1825	James H. George, -	1863
Thomas Hance, Jr.,	-	1825	Isaac Cremer, -	1864
Jesse Stout, -		1825	Abraham Tanner, -	1865
Wessels S. Middaugh,	-	1829	Hananiah Wilcox, -	1866
James McElheny,	-	1830	James H. George, -	1867
Schuyler Goddard,	-	1831 2	Thomas Hunt, -	1868
Rice Weed, -	-	1833	Hiram Bouton, -	1868
William H. Miller,	-	1833 4	Hananiah Wilcox, -	1869
Ephraim Sharp,	-	1835	Wm. W. Snyder, -	1870
Moses C. Brown, -	-	1836	Almanzo W. George, -	1871
Henry B. Weaver,	-	1837	Geo. E. Goodrich, -	1872
Moses C. Brown, -	-	1837	John W. Webster, -	1873
Parley Whitmore,	-	1838	Warren C. Ellis, -	1873
Rice Weed,	-	1838	John Snyder, -	1874
Wm. H. Miller,	-	1838	Almanzo W. George, -	1875
Elijah Fox,	-	1839	Wm. H. Goodwin, Jr.,	1876
Parley Whitmore,	-	1840	Wm. J. Smith, -	1876
Rice Weed,	-	1841	John W. Webster, -	1877
Nicholas Brown,	-	1842	John T. Morris, -	1878
Thomas Hunt,	-	1842	Geo. R. Burchell, -	1878
S. S. Barger, -		1843	Wm. E. Brown, -	1879
Abraham Tanner, -		1844	Geo. E. Monroe, -	1880
Walker Marsh,		1845	Geo. E. Hanford, -	1881
S. S. Barger,	-	1846	Geo. Snyder, -	1882
Thomas Hunt,		1847	Wm. J. Shaver, -	1882
Abraham Tanner, -		1848	Wm. E. Brown, -	1883
Walker Marsh,		1848	Geo. E. Underwood, -	1883
Andrew P. Grover,	-	1849	Geo. E. Monroe, -	1884
Thomas Hunt,		1850	Alviras Snyder, -	1885
Abraham Tanner, -	-	1851	Artemas L. Smiley, -	1886
Andrew P. Grover,	-	1852	Geo. E. Underwood, -	1886
Walker Marsh,	-	1853	Wm. E. Brown,	1887
Abraham Tanner,	-	1854	Artemas L. Smiley, -	1887
Eleazer Case,	-	1855	Geo. E. Monroe, -	1888
William Scott,	-	1856	Everel F. Weaver, -	1889

Geo. E. Underwood,	-	1890	Geo. E. Hanford,	-	1893
Samuel S. Hoff,	-	1891	Geo. E. Underwood,	-	1894
Wm. E. Brown,	-	1891	Erastus M. Sager,	-	1895
J. Dolph Ross,	-	1892	J. Dolph Ross,	-	1896
Geo. E. Hanford,	-	1892	Bert D. Conklin,	-	1897

We thus have before us the names of the men who for nearly a century have had the care and management of the political organism known as the "Town of Dryden." The only material change in the territorial extent of the township was made in 1887, when the easterly seven lots of the southern tier were set off and annexed to Caroline, for the reason that they were located much more conveniently to Slaterville as a business center than to any similar place within the town of Dryden. The town meetings were early held at different hotels in the town, subsequently more often at the Dryden Center House, until within a few years past, during which they have been held in election districts. The town was formerly divided into four, but now consists of six election districts. In the old times one of the duties of people at town meeting was to apportion the income derived from the gospel and school lot between the support of the churches and schools, the statute requiring that it should be annually distributed by the voice of the people at town meeting so that each should have some share. In accordance with this requirement it used to be a standing custom at every town meeting to pass a resolution that of the gospel and school funds "six cents be appropriated for the support of the gospel and that the balance be devoted to school purposes." This was done not from disregard for the welfare of the gospel, but was in accordance with the general spirit of the country, which, while liberally providing for public education in the common schools, declined to impose any compulsory tax upon the people directly or indirectly, for the support of sectarian or religious institutions. The gospel and school lot was for a long time rented and the rents applied annually as above stated, but subsequently the lot was sold and the proceeds, about eleven thousand dollars, now forms the town school fund, which is loaned by the supervisor on bonds and mortgages and the interest applied annually for the benefit of the common schools of the township.

CHAPTER IX.

EVENTS FROM 1803 TO 1812.

One of the memorable occurrences of this time in the town of Dryden was the "Great Eclipse" which was witnessed June 16, 1806, when total darkness came on suddenly at mid-day, and the fowls went to their roosts as though it were night. This was the only total eclipse of the sun to be visible in this section of the country during the nineteenth century, and, as we may well imagine, it made a deep impression upon the minds of the early inhabitants, who, as we may safely say, were more superstitious and less informed upon those subjects than are we of the present age. It furnished a means of fixing dates, and old people in later years were accustomed to speak of things as having taken place before or after the "Great Eclipse," as the case might be. The immigration to the town was very rapid during this time, so much so that when the government census came to be taken in 1810, it was found that the town of Dryden alone contained 1,893 inhabitants, considerably more than one-third of the number of the present population of the town.

We shall speak more particularly hereafter in connection with Dryden village, of the arrival of the Griswolds from Connecticut and the Wheelers from New Hampshire in 1802, and of Jacob Primrose and others who settled at West Dryden, when we treat of that particular locality. Thomas Southworth, a tanner and currier, originally from Massachusetts, and his son John, then ten years of age, located first at Willow Glen in 1806, and we shall have occasion to refer to them often hereafter in connection with Willow Glen, and Dryden village to which they afterward came. Rev. Daniel McArthur, from Scotland, settled in 1811, on the farm which was after his death owned and occupied by the late Ebenezer McArthur, who in his will (having no surviving children) devised it, subject to the life estate of his wife, to the town of Dryden as an addition to the school fund of the town.

At about this time a small company of emigrants from the north of Ireland, who had temporaraily made a home in Orange county of this state, located in the South Hill neighborhood at a place which, from this fact, has since been known as the Irish Settlement. This colony included Hugh Thompson, who became a rigid and prominent member of the Presbyterian church in Dryden village, William Nelson, the father of Robert Nelson still residing in town, and Joseph McGraw, Sr., who in after years was known to the writer as an active, talkative,

EVENTS FROM 1803 TO 1812.

but quick-witted old man, displaying in his ready speech a rich Irish brogue. His son John, born in this "Irish Settlement" in 1815, became one of the most accomplished and successful business men which this or any other town ever produced, and his family will merit from us later a special biography. We here give the list of those, some of whom have not already been mentioned, who are known to have become inhabitants of the town before 1808, many of them being the ancestors of their now numerous descendants and of many of whom we shall again have occasion to speak when we come to mention the particular families or localities with which they are associated. The list is as follows:

Bartholomew, Jesse,
Barnes, Ichabod,
Brown, Zephaniah
Brown, Reuben,
Blew, Michael,
Brown, Israel
Brown, Obadiah,
Brown, Obadiah, Jr.,
Bailey, Morris,
Bush, Peter,
Carr, Job
Carr, Peleg,
Carr, Caleb,
Conklin, John,
Clark, Samuel,
Callon, William,
Cornelius, John,
Carpenter, Abner,
Cass, Aaron,
Dimmick, Elijah,
Fortner, Lewis
Fulkerson, Benjamin,
Genung, Benjamin,

Girvin, Samuel,
Gray, George,
Giles, Isaiah,
George, Joel,
Griswold, Edward,
Griswold, Abram,
Grover, Andrew,
Hile, Nicholas,
Horner, John,
Hart, Joseph,
Hollenshead, Robert,
Hoagland, Abraham,
Hemmingway, Samuel,
Jennings, Benjamin,
Jay, Joshua,
Jameson, Thomas,
Lewis, Amos,
Lewis, David,
Legg, Matthew,
Luther, Nathaniel,
Luce, Jonathan,
Mineah, John,
McKee, James,

McKee, Robert,
Ogden, Daniel
Owens, Timothy,
Pixley, Enoch,
Palmerton, Ichabod,
Rhodes, Jacob,
Southwick, Israel,
Skellinger, Samuel,
Snyder, Jacob,
Smith, William,
Teeter, Henry,
Van Marter, John,
Wheeler, Seth,
Wheeler, Seth, Jr.,
Wheeler, Enos,
Woodcock, Abraham,
Wickham, John,
White, Richard,
Waldron, John,
Weeks, Luther,
Whipple, Ithamar,
Yeomans, Jason,
Yeomans, Stephen,

We may here properly refer to the fact that the population of the town of Dryden, as well as of our county in general, was early made up of individuals from different, though nearly related nationalities and from localities widely separated. Ethnological scholars tell us that the superiority of the Anglo-Saxon race is accounted for from the fact that it is made up of a union of different races having at no remote period the same common origin. The Saxon, Norman, Dane and ancient Briton were none of them especially distinguished as a nationality by themselves, but when united for a number of generations the result was the formation of the Anglo-Saxon race, whose power and influence among the nations of the earth now surpasses all others, and whose language, it is now conceded, will in time become the universal language of the world. May we not in like manner expect great results from the development of a population whose progenitors included the McGraws, McElhenys, Nelsons, McKees and Lormors, emigrating from Ireland; the Lamonts, McArthurs, Robertsons and Stewarts direct from Scotland; the Snyders and Albrights, of Dutch, as well as the Dupee and DeCoudres families, of French ancestry, while the great majority of the early settlers, the groundwork, so to speak, of the new society, were of the genuine New England Yankee stock of recent English derivation, many of them coming here from the very confines of the "Nutmeg State."

CHAPTER X.

THE WAR OF 1812.

In the minds of the great mass of people of the present age, the importance of our war with Great Britain, known as the War of 1812, is overshadowed and lost sight of in view of the War of the Revolution which preceded it by about thirty-five years. It is not so regarded by the careful student of history. The earlier war made our country free, but it required the latter to make us really independent and respected as a nation. The latter war also did much to strengthen the bond of union between the colonies and to make of us a nation rather than a mere confederation of states.

Our ancestors were poorly prepared for either conflict with the mother country, supplied as she was with powerful armaments and standing armies, and it was only the necessities of the occasion which seemed to suddenly call forth and develop in them the courage and heroism which enabled them to succeed. History affords but few instances where an inferior number of untrained men, called suddenly and unexpectedly to arms, have overwhelmingly defeated trained soldiers as did Jackson with his hasty recruits at New Orleans; and we are not required to look so far away from home for instances of the same character. On the Niagara frontier in 1814 ("on the lines," as it was termed in those days.) General (then Colonel) Winfield Scott and his brave followers, usually opposed to superior numbers of the enemy, performed feats of military strategy and heroism, in the battles of Lundy's Lane and Chippewa, which forced from the unwilling British officers exclamations of wonder and admiration, and cannot be read by us to-day without arousing pride within us, that we are among the descendants of such heroes. As we read of these instances we can hardly realize that they are not the events of some far-off country, belonging to some remote period of time, while they actually did occur within the present century and within five hours ride by rail from where we now live. With the exception of some skirmishes with the Indians, and some events of the same character near Oswego, this is the nearest that war ever came, and we trust it is the nearest it ever will come, to our doors. How many of us realize that the company of Dryden militia which went out to "the lines" under Captain (afterwards Major) Peleg Ellis, in July, 1812, were taken prisoners together with Colonel Winfield Scott at the battle of Queenston, which proved to be the Bunker Hill or Bull Run of that war, but was followed by hard earned victories which in the end placed the balance largely in our favor and secured a triumphant result?

It is to be regretted that we—and especially our young people—in choosing our reading matter, select descriptions of incidents far removed from us in time and space, or more often amuse ourselves by reading the alluring inventions of fiction ; and then, when we chance to visit Niagara Falls and see on the opposite shore the imposing and magnificent Brock monument, 194 feet high, constructed of Niagara limestone and erected on Queenston Heights, the most prominent landmark as seen from Lewiston on the American side, we are compelled to remain silent or expose our ignorance by asking what that imposing column was designed to commemorate. If my readers will obtain from the Southworth Library, or elsewhere, "Lossing's Field Book of the War of 1812," a large and interesting volume, devoted to the description and illustrating the leading events of this war, they will find that the perusal of it will well repay their effort and enable them to repel to some extent at least the charge so often made with a degree of truth, that Americans are wofully ignorant of their own history. They will find in it a reference to Colonel (afterwards General) Bloom, of our adjoining town of Lansing, and afterwards sheriff of Tompkins county, and to the regiment (which included the first Dryden company) which he led at Queenston, where he was wounded. We are indebted to the researches of Charles F. Mulks, of

Ithaca, for the information that Aaron Cass, one of the Dryden company from near Ellis Hollow, was struck on the head by a British cannon ball and instantly killed while the regiment was crossing the Niagara river in boats to take part in the battle of Queenston. Cass had been a distinguished soldier of the Revolution from Connecticut, was a brother-in-law of Aaron Bull, and settled in Ellis Hollow in 1804. Other soldiers of the Dryden company were Aaron Genung, from near Varna; Arthur and Stephen B. June, Marcus Palmerton, Jonathan Lace, George McCutcheon and Peter Snyder. With the exception of the statement that Judge John Ellis afterwards went out to "the lines" with the second Dryden company of militia, leaving but fourteen able-bodied men in the township, these are all of the recorded facts which we are able to give concerning Dryden's participation in the War of 1812. It is regretted that the accounts of Dryden's volunteers of that date are so meager, and it reminds us of the necessity of committing to a written record the achievements of the Dryden soldiers in the War of the Rebellion, before all of them shall have passed away, or they, too, will be lost to local history.

We are fortunately able to give from the relation of Thomas J. McElheny, whose mother was a niece of Major Ellis, an incident of the battle of Queenston which he has often heard his great-uncle relate, and which is as follows: As the Dryden company were crossing the Niagara river to the Canada side, Stephen B. June, impressed with the importance of the occasion and boiling over with the true martial spirit, arose in his boat and swinging his hat defiantly called out as the watchwords of the expedition: "Death, Hell or Canada." This was early in the morning of the day when everything was hopeful and but few of the enemy were in sight. The battle of the morning was successful. A landing on the Canada shore was effected, the Queenston Heights were gallantly scaled and captured and the Commanding General Brock of the enemy was mortally wounded in the conflict. But in the afternoon the reinforcements of the enemy arrived in overwhelming numbers, while the help expected from the American side failed to appear, and after a brave but hopeless effort at resistance, the whole American force, including Colonel Scott and Captain Ellis with their followers, were taken prisoners. Not seeing his townsman, Stephen B. June, among the prisoners, Captain Ellis went back on the battle field to look him up, and after searching found him very severely wounded by a ball which had entered his mouth and passed out of the back of his neck, just below the base of the skull, fortunately missing the spinal cord. Finding that June was alive and still conscious, although fearfully wounded, Captain Ellis asked him which it was now, "Death, Hell or Canada," to which the wounded soldier feebly but firmly replied: "I can't tell quite yet, Captain, which it is, but when the British bullet struck me I thought I had them all three at once." June lived to return home and, if we are not mistaken, some of his family descendants are still inhabitants of the town.

Since writing the above we learn that Geo. R. Burchell, Esq., of Dryden, is a great-nephew of that same Stephen B. June, although the most of that family have removed to Alleghany county and further west. The original commission of Major Ellis as captain, issued to him February 11, 1811, by Daniel D. Tompkins, then governor of the state, is one of the relics which were on exhibition at Dryden's Centennial Celebration.

CHAPTER XI.

EVENTS FROM 1812 TO 1822.

In the year 1813 there was published at Albany the first edition of "Spafford's N. Y. State Gazetteer," which contains the earliest description of the town of Dryden which we have found, and probably the first ever printed, which we therefore reproduce here in full as follows:

"DRYDEN—A post-township in the southeastern extremity of Cayuga county, 35 miles S. of Auburn, 170 west of Albany; bounded N. by Locke, E. by Virgil in Cortlandt county, S. by Tioga county, W. by Seneca county [which then included Ithaca] and the town of Geneva [Genoa (?) the part now Lansing.]

"It is 10 miles square, being one of the military townships, and has a considerable diversity of surface, soil and timber.

"Fall Creek of Cayuga Lake with several branches spreads over the northern and central parts, and Six Mile creek, a fine mill stream, rises in the S. E. corner, runs into Tioga county and returns across the S. W. towards the head of Cayuga Lake. There is also another small stream, and there is an abundance of mill seats, with considerable tracts of alluvion; though the general character is hilly with pretty lofty ridges. The soil of the alluvion is warm, rich and productive; that of the uplands rather wet and cold, but excellent for pasture and meadow. There are two grain mills and carding machines. There are some congregations of Baptists and Presbyterians who have houses of worship, but I am not informed of their number; and 4 or 5 school houses. The settlements were commenced about 1800, and in 1810 the population amounted to 1890, when there were 310 families and 213 senatorial electors. The whole taxable property, as assessed in 1810, $84,099. There are 3 turnpike roads that cross this town, besides common roads in various directions. The inhabitants are principally farmers whose farms and looms supply much of their common clothing.—*N. T. R. P.*"

In the year 1814 at a special town meeting a board of town school superintendents was first elected, consisting of Joshua Phillips, Peleg Ellis and John Ellis. Afterwards in the same year they met and divided the town into fourteen school districts, which have since been increased to twenty-seven. The amount of public school money disbursed by this board to all the districts in 1814 was $192.47, not one quarter of the amount now annually received by the Dryden village district alone. In no department of public affairs has there been such a marked and continual improvement as in the matter of education in the common schools. Our young people should realize that in school opportunities they have a great advantage over the school children of even twenty-five years ago, while their privileges in this respect are not to be compared with the very meager opportunities which were offered for school education in the Pioneer Period of Dryden's history.

The year 1816 was known as the "cold season," in which nearly all of the crops were destroyed by summer frosts, and great scarcity, almost a famine, resulted. It should be borne in mind that there were no such means of transportation then as now to relieve a section where the crops had failed, and no great supply of produce was carried over from year to year.

In this year, 1816, Elias W. Cady moved in from Columbia county and located on the farm near Willow Glen which he owned and occupied for more than sixty years, becoming one of the most prosperous farmers of the town. He was a member of the State Legislature in 1850 and 1857, and his grandson, John E. Cady, has in recent years twice held the same position. Elias W. Cady in his later years used to delight to tell how, when he first came to Dryden, Parley Whitmore, who kept a store in Dryden village near where the M. E. church now stands, refused to trust him for a few pounds of nails, and he was obliged to take a load of produce to Albany to get them.

In the next year, 1817, the new county of Tompkins was formed, and Dryden became a part of it, instead of being the southeast cor-

THE PIONEER PERIOD.

ner of Cayuga county. Cortlandt county (so spelled in those days) had been formed in 1808, and an unsuccessful effort was made in the Legislature in the same year, supported by petitions from some of Dryden's citizens, to make this town a part of it.

A state census made in 1808 shows that the number of electors at that time in the town of Dryden whose farms exceeded in value £100 (about $500) each, was seventy-four; two others had farms exceeding in value £20 (about $100), while the number of electors who rented tenements of the yearly value of forty shillings was returned at 174. The census of 1810 having shown a population in the town of 1890, that of 1814 shows an increase to 2545, while that of 1820 returns a population of 3995, showing a very rapid increase and reaching, near the end of the first quarter of the Century Period, a number slightly exceeding that of the present population, the highest number ever reached being 5851 returned in 1835, while the latest returns, according to the census of 1892 after the loss of seven lots in 1888, show a present population of 3912. The causes which have influenced this sudden increase and afterwards the gradual decrease of our population will be treated of in a separate chapter hereafter.

CHAPTER XII.

1235123

REVIEW OF THE PIONEER PERIOD.

We have now hastily passed over the first twenty-five years of the history of the town of Dryden, as a whole, commencing from the first settlement in 1797 and extending to the year 1822. We shall refer to it hereafter as the Pioneer Period, being the first quarter of the century of Dryden's inhabitation by her present race of population. To obtain a correct and reliable view of this period, we have been obliged to look back beyond the reach of human memory and to rely upon such information as tradition and the fragmentary records of those early times afford. Reliable memoranda of those times, when obtainable, have been quoted minutely as furnishing the most trustworthy means of obtaining a correct idea of the condition and habits of our ancestors in that distant period.

We can readily understand that the wilderness was not transformed into fine cultivated fields, such as we now have, during that time. The best of the farms must have been thickly beset with stumps and cradle knolls when the year 1822 dawned upon the new country. Farming tools and implements of husbandry were then few and of the rudest character. Mr. Bouton says that the first cast iron plow seen in the town of Virgil was introduced there in the year 1817, and we may assume that Dryden was not much in advance of her older sister town in that respect. Hitherto plowing had been done with a home-made wooden implement, held with a single handle, the original "mould board" being of wood instead of iron. Fortunate was the farmer in those days who possessed a sickle with which to cut by hand his grain standing in the fallow, a handful at a time, and when it had been threshed with the flail, the willow fan and riddle afforded the best means of cleaning it for use or market. Such roads as then existed through the woods would now be considered almost impassable and all means of transportation were so difficult and expensive that people lived as far as possible upon their own productions. Log houses were the rule and frame buildings the exception, even at the end of this period. We have queried as to whether any old houses, first constructed in those times, still exist, without becoming much the wiser for the speculation; but we mistrust that the little red house, now used as a storage building on the Burlingame farm, near the reservoir of the Dryden Village Water Works, is among the oldest survivors of former dwellings. It was the home of Edward Griswold, Sr., when he was the owner of a large part, at least, of the lot (No. 39), a mile square, near the center of which it still stands. John C. Lacy, in his Reminiscences, states that within his recollection (he was born in Dryden in 1808) the Dr. Briggs house, originally built by Dr. Phillips, on South street, but now moved off and occupied by John McKeon, on Lake street, was the finest house in Dryden village.

All of the dwellings of this period were lighted as well as heated from the fire in the open fire-place, tallow candles even at this time being a luxury only to be used on special occasions. Many a time has the thrifty, industrious housewife of our ancestors, with the aid of the numerous small children "who played around her door," gathered in at twilight a supply of pine knots so that she might have them to throw on the fire as needed to enable her to spin by their light in the long fall and winter evenings. We regret that we are unable to do justice to the pioneer Mother of that period, for the reason that no record was ever made and kept of her hardships and privations, there having been no "strong-minded women" in those days to record them; and our only remedy is to give to her a full half of all the credit which belongs to the pioneer families for all of that which was accomplished.

Sheep husbandry prospered in the new country as soon as the

sheep could be protected from the wild animals of the surrounding forests, and the cultivation of flax was early introduced. So abundant was the flax seed left after the fiber was worked up into cloth, that an oil mill to express the linseed oil was early in operation on what is now South street in Dryden village, the heavy frame of which mill still serves to support a dilapidated barn, the covering of which was put on new since its use as an oil mill was discontinued. The plain clothing of the family was made from homespun linen and woolen cloth, coarse and heavy but at the same time strong and durable.

Joseph McGraw, Sr., already referred to as the father of the millionaire, John McGraw, came into the settlement in this period as a professional weaver, going from house to house to work on the hand looms of those days and to instruct others in the art; and his fellow townsman, Benjamin Wood, the grandfather of our ex-governor, A. B. Cornell, at the same time was known and employed as a "reed maker," manufacturing by hand from reeds the delicate parts of the looms by which the warp was manipulated in the process of weaving. Mr. Wood early resided near Willow Glen in the little old wood-colored house recently taken down on the farm formerly owned by Charles Cady; but afterwards he became the proprietor of the premises near Etna, known as Woodlawn. A subsequent chapter will be devoted to Mr. Wood and his family.

We have intentionally omitted from our narrative some hunting and fishing stories which have come down to us, suspecting that even the good and true old men of those times, like their descendants, might be given to exaggeration upon those subjects, and preferring to leave them out altogether rather than to furnish exaggerated fiction under the guise of reliable history. We should, however, say something concerning the wild animals which were native here when disturbed in their haunts by the pioneers.

Of the larger animals the deer were very abundant and did not wholly disappear from the forests of the town until about 1835. It seems to be stated upon good authority that Peleg Ellis, during the first autumn of his settlement in Dryden, killed eighteen deer so near his log house that he drew them all up to his door upon his ox sled. The woods were full of small game and the squirrels and chipmunks were so abundant that when the raising of grain was first attempted in the small clearings entirely surrounded by the forest, it was almost impossible to save it from destruction by these pests. It was only by persistent trapping and hunting and sometimes by the use of poisoned bait that the crop was secured. The bears and wolves were somewhat troublesome, but they soon avoided the neighborhood of the settlements. The only animal which seriously endangered human life, and that not often except when hunted and at bay, was the cougar, or puma, or American lion as it was sometimes called, and often referred to by old people as the painter or panther, but improperly so, the true panther being a denizen of Africa. This cougar or puma was a cat-like carniverous animal about five feet long, of a reddish brown color above and nearly white underneath, being closely related to the leopard family of animals. It was King of Beasts on the American continent, nearly all of which it originally inhabited, and woe to the unsuspecting deer or other animal which passed under the tree from which it was watching to spring upon its prey. It had a peculiar cry which was sometimes mistaken for that of a human being in distress, and many were the thrilling stories told of it by the early settlers, although it was too cowardly to often attack mankind.

The American eagle, too, in early times made his home in Dryden, as appears from the following account published in the Ithaca Daily Journal of April 20, 1880, as copied from the Dubuque (Iowa) Times of an earlier date:

"In the years of 1828-9 a man discovered an eagle's nest in the top of a pine tree on the bank of Fall Creek in the town of Dryden, Tompkins county, N. Y., east of the town of Ithaca. The tree was cut and three young bald-headed eagles just ready to fly left the nest before the tree reached the ground. They were caught. One of them was presented to Roswell Randall, a wealthy and prominent merchant residing in Courtland Villa, Courtland county, N. Y. He caged, fed and cared for the bird two or three years. It grew fast and became a very large, noble bird of attraction. Mr. Randall placed the caged prisoner by the side of the front walk leading to his beautiful mansion, in the foregrounds, that visitors and passers-by could easily enjoy the sight. Finally the bird caused so much trouble that Mr. Randall gave it to William Bassett, a near neighbor, who was an engraver and silversmith; in politics an old line Whig. In 1831 a Fourth of July celebration was had in the village. Mr. Bassett being a public spirited man, added largely to the enjoyment of the day by preparing a silver clasp with these words engraved upon it, viz: 'To Henry Clay, of Louisville, Ky., from Wm. Bassett, of Courtland Villa, Courtland county, N. Y.,' and riveting it loosely, around one of the legs of the eagle carried the bird and placed it on top of the cupola of the Eagle Hotel in the village, its head in a southwest direction. The military corps and citizens being drawn up in front of the hotel, the eagle was set at liberty. It stood erect upon the cupola, made three flaps with its wings, then set off southwest. The military were ordered to fire, the citizens, swinging their hats, gave three cheers for Henry Clay. The eagle continued its course till out of sight."

This was on the Fourth of July, 1831. The sequel subsequently appeared in the Western papers giving an account of a "large bald-headed eagle being shot by an Indian on a high, towering bluff on the west bank of the Mississippi, about three miles north of Dubuque, on the eleventh day of July, 1831, measuring seven feet three inches from tip to tip of outstretched wings, having an engraved silver clasp riveted around one of his legs reading as follows, viz: 'To Henry Clay, of Louisville, Ky., from Wm. Bassett, of Courtland Villa, N. Y.' In seven days from the time this noble bird graced the dome of the Eagle Hotel and set sail in the direction of Henry Clay's residence he was shot as above stated."

This incident was first furnished to the press by G. R. West, who was present at the celebration at Cortland in 1831 and saw the eagle take its flight from the old Eagle Hotel, which stood where the Messenger House is now located in Cortland village, and the promontory on the Iowa bank of the Mississippi river, where the eagle was shot as above stated, has since been known as "Eagle Point," and is a land-mark for all steamboat men on the upper Mississippi.

But the most interesting of the native animals which inhabited Dryden was the beaver. These industrious creatures were about the size of a small dog, and lived on the bark of trees, taking up their habitations in colonies of fifty or more each, in the streams, across which they built dams with wonderful instinctive sagacity. They formed houses of sticks plastered with mud so regular and perfect that they seemed almost to be the work of human hands. It was some time before the writer could ascertain to a certainty that the beaver inhabited Dryden. The name "Beaver Creek," applied to a sluggish, muddy stream in the northeast corner of the township, first suggested the thought and was followed up by inquiry which develops the fact that the remains of a beaver dam could be distinctly seen in the woods on this creek as late as twenty-five years ago. These interesting animals carried so much value in the fur upon their backs that they could not long survive the efforts of the pioneer hunters to capture them, and hence they early disappeared from this section of the country, so that their former presence here had been almost forgotten.

CHAPTER XIII.

THE PERIOD OF DEVELOPMENT—TRANSPORTATION.

We now enter upon the second quarter-century of Dryden's inhabitation, extending from 1823 to 1847 inclusive, which, for the want of a more appropriate name, we shall refer to as the "Period of Development." The term development might properly be applied to the entire period of Dryden's history, but we feel justified in applying it especially here from the fact that during this particular time the town supported, and was developed by the aid of, its largest number of inhabitants, and the change of its territory from a "howling wilderness" to a productive, civilized country township was more rapid at this time than at any other. We shall not attempt to review the events of this period so much in their chronological order as was done in treating the "Pioneer Period," but we shall view the development of our subject from several different standpoints, first giving attention to the matter of transportation.

As we have already seen, the earliest pioneer settlers came bringing their scanty supplies on ox-sleds with wooden shoes, the primitive "Bridle Road" presumably not being adapted to transportation by wheeled vehicles, even in the summer time. At the end of the first twenty-five years the principal thoroughfares had become passable by wagons and stages, the stumps having been removed, the low places being filled with corduroy crossing and the principal streams being spanned with pole bridges. Our highways are none too good at the present time, but we can realize that very much has been done, and much time and labor has been required, to bring them to even their present state of development. Those of us who have occasion to use "woods roads" of the present day are not surprised to read the accounts of the frequency with which the early teamsters became "mired" in using the only means of transportation which was then afforded. In view of these circumstances we are not surprised to learn that the first mail was carried by a man on foot between Oxford and Ithaca from 1811 to 1817, and that the first stage commenced running between Homer and Ithaca through Dryden in 1824. Other localities seem to have been more early favored than ours in this respect and the Bath and Jericho Turnpike, chartered by the State in 1804, and later forming a part of the old Ithaca and Catskill stage route and still known as the "turnpike" from Slaterville to Ithaca, passing through the southwest corner of our town, was one of the

DEVELOPMENT—TRANSPORTATION.

early thoroughfares connecting the East with the West. But during the period of which we are now speaking transportation on the principal highways, in the absence of all other means, was very much employed, and upon the Bridle Road between Dryden and Ithaca nearly, if not quite, a dozen local hotels or "Taverns," as they were then called, ministered to the wants of travelers and teamsters, and in so doing conducted a thriving business. One of them was the Dryden Center House originally built and operated early in this period by Benjamin Aldrich, already mentioned among the early town officers.

DRYDEN CENTER HOUSE.

Unlike most of these country inns the Center House has not been permitted to run down, but under the management of its present proprietor, Gardner W. S. Gibson, has been repaired and improved so that it now presents a modern appearance, fully in keeping with its prominence in the early history of the town. Here for a long time town meetings were held and the official business of the town transacted and it is still patronized as the proper place for holding town caucuses. It was not uncommon in those days for such farmers as Edward Griswold and Elias W. Cady to take a wagon load of produce to market at Albany, returning with a load of store goods, and at certain seasons of the year the roads to Syracuse were lined with teamsters returning with wagon loads of salt, lime and plaster, after having taken loads of farm produce to market. Towanda, then the head of navigation on the Susquehanna river, was also a favorite shipping point at which Dryden farmers marketed their produce.

The Erie Canal ("Clinton's Ditch" as it was derisively called in those times) was opened to navigation in 1825, and in the absence of railroads it soon became a great aid in the means of transportation. Some of the later settlers of this period, James Tripp, for example, who came in from Columbia county in 1836, shipped their goods by way of the canal and drove across the country with their horses and wagons. The Ithaca & Owego Railroad, the second to be chartered in the State, passed over a small corner of Dryden and was opened in 1834, but it was operated wholly by horse power in those days, and gave but little indication of the efficiency, as a means of transportation, afforded by railroads of the present time. Still until the financial panic of 1836, which was a temporary set back, this was a time of rapid growth and prosperity. Permanent buildings were constructed and manufacturing enterprises were instituted. The only brick dwelling ever constructed in Dryden village was built by John Southworth in 1836. The Mallory brothers, from Homer, in 1826 located on Fall Creek at a point since called from them, Malloryville, and there operated a saw-mill, chair factory, carding and cloth dressing machinery and a dye house, employing from thirty to forty hands, and prospering until their mills were destroyed by fire in 1836, when they removed farther west. One of these Mallory brothers (Samuel) recently died at Elkhorn, Wisconsin, in his ninety-ninth year.

One of the distressing occurrences of this time, but one which we do not feel at liberty to omit from our History, which professes to speak of all the prominent events, resulted from the connection of the murderer, Edward H. Ruloff, with the town of Dryden. In the year 1842 he served as a school teacher in Dryden village and numbers of his pupils are still residents here. He came originally from the province of New Brunswick. On December 31, 1843, he married Miss Harriet Schutt, a lovely Dryden girl seventeen years of age, who had been one of his pupils. They moved to the town of Lansing. In 1845 a daughter was born to them, but shortly afterwards the wife and daughter disappeared, the only visible means of their disappearance being a large strong wooden box with which Ruloff was seen to drive away in a wagon towards Cayuga Lake.

He was soon after arrested in the West and brought back to this county; the bottom of the lake was dredged for the box in vain, and, there being no direct evidence of murder, Ruloff was finally sentenced to ten years in State's Prison for abducting his wife. Having served his term he was released and disappeared from public view until the year 1871, when he was convicted of participating in a robbery and murder at Binghamton, for which he was executed. He was a singular character, being a profound and diligent student, and his career was an interesting, though terrible one, afterwards being made the subject of magazine articles upon moral insanity, of which it seemed to furnish a striking example.

CHAPTER XIV.

IMMIGRATION AND EMIGRATION.

If we examine a small inland body of water, such as our Dryden Lake—known to the early inhabitants as "Little Lake"—we shall find that it is connected with a small stream known as the inlet and a larger one called the outlet. During the spring floods the inflow is greater than the outflow, the result being that the water rises in the lake until it reaches what is called "high water mark." Then during the dry summer and autumn, as the inflow is rapidly decreased while the outflow continues unabated, the supply of water is reduced until "low water mark" is reached. Now, if we will picture to ourselves our town of Dryden as the dry bed of a lake, to which the tide of immigration commenced to flow in 1797, and continued to flow rapidly until 1835, when the increasing outflow of emigration exceeded the diminishing inflow of immigration, and has so continued ever since, we shall have in mind before us the comparison sought for, to correctly illustrate this subject. Many of the early inhabitants or their children continued their migrations to points farther west. For example we have seen that a number of the children of Captain Robertson, the first freeholder of the town, early sought new homes in the West, where they have made reputations for themselves. Of the five Lacy brothers all of whom settled here in 1801, four in later years moved on further west, while only one, the father of the late John C. Lacy, remained. Until we come to consider it carefully, but few of us can realize the great and continuous drain which has been made upon the older settlements of the East to build up and populate the Great West during the past seventy-five years.

The writer was strikingly reminded of the reality of this fact upon his first visit to the West some twenty-five years ago. At the end of his journey he found himself in an inland town of the state of Michigan, imagining himself to be a stranger in a strange land. Having occasion to call upon a justice of the peace he stopped at the first office which displayed a sign of that character, hesitating to introduce himself as from Dryden, N. Y., doubting whether the inmate of the office had ever heard of such a place. Mustering up his courage, however, he ventured to state to the officer where he was from, and you may imagine his surprise upon the magistrate's extending his hand saying: "Why, I used to live in Dryden," and he immediately commenced inquiring about some of the old citizens of Dryden, whom he had known here thirty years before. A gentleman who happened to be in the office reading a newspaper, here interrupted by saying: " I never lived in Dryden, but my wife used to be a resident of that town." The surprise and revelation was complete, and further experience in states farther west has confirmed the fact, that the great western part of our country is thickly sprinkled over with inhabitants who have either themselves been at some time residents of Dryden or whose ancestors came from our town. Hardly a city of any size or a county in any of the Western States can be found to-day which has not some inhabitants who in this way derive their origin from the town of Dryden. They are found among all the classes and conditions of the Western population, from the farmer and common laborer to the Legislators and Judges, the town of Dryden having recently furnished to one of the newly formed Western states its first elected governor.

If all of the western population who can trace their origin directly or indirectly to the town of Dryden, could have been brought together at our Centennial Celebration, the whole township would have been taxed to its utmost to furnish accommodation for the vast concourse of people, and the grounds of the Agricultural Society would have been inadequate to furnish them standing room.

In view of these facts it is no disparagement to the town that its population has decreased for the past sixty years. The Great West has continually been offering superior advantages to our young men, the more ambitions and adventursome of whom have been and still are taking advantage of these opportunities, leaving behind the more conservative (and shall we say less enterprising?) to till the same farms and pursue in a quiet way the same avocations as was done by our fathers before us. And yet, in spite of this drain upon the best life blood of the population, we shall submit to those former residents who shall from time to time revisit us, that we have not permitted the town to run down in its enterprise and productiveness, but that with the aid of improved machinery and better buildings and methods, the farms, as a whole, have been improved and rendered more productive, while the general business interests of the people, with better means of manufacture and transportation, and superior educational advantages, have not suffered in comparison with the earlier times. There is coming a limit to this outflow of population, the Great West is filling up, and the time is sure to come when the tide of migration will ebb back to our shores, and then the town of Dryden will support a greater and we trust a more prosperous population than ever before.

CHAPTER XV.

OCCUPATION OF THE INHABITANTS.

During this "development" period Dryden was emphatically a lumbering town. Agricultural operations had been developed sufficiently to support the population, but the surplus product of the township at this time in this era of building was mainly pine lumber of a superior quality. This did not need to seek a distant market but was in ready demand at the low price which then prevailed of from four to five dollars per thousand feet by the country immediately north and east of us, which was not well supplied with pine timber. The following statistics concerning Dryden are gathered from the second edition of "Spafford's N. Y. Gazetteer," published in 1824, and furnish valuable data bearing upon this subject of the occupation of the people:

Number of grist-mills in town, 4; saw-mills, 26; fulling-mills, 2; carding-machines, 4; distilleries, 5; asheries, 4; population, 3,950; taxable property, $208,866; electors, 733; farmers, 2,005; mechanics, 132; shop-keepers or traders, 4; number of families, 634; acres of improved land, 14,323; number of neat cattle, 3,670; number of horses, 674; number of sheep, 6,679; number of yards of cloth manufactured in families in 1821, 37,300!! Number of school districts, 20; public school money in 1821, $576.05.

We observe from this record the small number of horses kept compared with cattle; the small number of store-keepers compared with the number of farmers and mechanics, and the small amount of taxable property, not being one-fifth of what the farm buildings of the town are to-day insured for in the Dryden and Groton company.

In the year 1835 the number of saw-mills in operation was fifty-three, all employed in working up the great quantity of timber, mostly pine, which produced the ready money for the people, the predominance of which industry greatly retarded other farming interests. The picturesque fences of pine stumps, now disappearing, but which have served their purpose in this form for half a century, often attract the attention of strangers and are reminders of the former abundance of pine. Any person who has occasion to pass through the woodland remaining on the Dryden hills to-day may observe the large weather-beaten but almost imperishable pine stumps still standing in the woods, from which the wealth of pine timber was taken in this period of our history. Every merchant of those times kept in connection with his store a lumber yard, where he received from his customers lumber in exchange for goods. John McGraw, then a clerk in a Dryden village store, obtained his first lessons in the lumber business in handling the local pine timber of the town, from the profits of which he obtained his start in the financial world, and afterwards applying his experience thus obtained to larger operations elsewhere, he amassed the fortune which netted over two million dollars to his estate after his decease. Dryden must then have presented the appearance of a vast lumber camp, the fifty-three saw-mills, all run by water power, giving employment to a great many men in cutting logs, drawing them to mill, and manufacturing and marketing the lumber, operations all requiring much more labor to produce the same results then than now. Like all lumbering communities Dryden did not present a very advanced or refined state of development in that period, and John Southworth, who was a keen and careful observer of men and things in those times in which he participated, used to say in after years that the Dryden farmer, who occasionally took out of his clearing in those days to the county seat of this or an adjoining county with his ox team a load of lumber, or perhaps a cargo of charcoal, or sometimes a few barrels of potash salts leached from the ashes gathered after the burning of his fallow, when he was interrogated by the tradesmen to whom he sold his products as to where his home was, would admit with no little hesitation and embarrassment, that he lived "just in the edge of Dryden."

A great change has taken place since that time. The pine timber lands, so valuable to the lumbermen, but after the removal of the timber, so beset with obstacles in the shape of the pine roots and stumps, so troublesome to the agriculturist, have at length been subdued and reduced to cultivation, and prove to be possessed of rich and enduring qualities of fertility. The disposition of the Dryden farmers to devote

THE DEVELOPMENT PERIOD.

their efforts to dairying instead of grain-raising has tended to improve rather than diminish the natural resources of the soil. In place of the original pine timber, excellent farm buildings have been supplied, and the Dryden farmer is no longer ashamed to acknowledge the location of his home. In fact his tendencies now seem to be in the other extreme, and subject him to the charge that he believes that his town was created a little better than the rest of the world in general. The interest which was manifested in the celebration of Dryden's Centennial, is proof of the pride which her inhabitants now take in acknowledging and honoring their native town.

CHAPTER XVI.

REVIEW OF THE DEVELOPMENT PERIOD.

We have failed to mention the war with Mexico, which occurred during this period from 1846 to 1848, resulting in the addition to our country of a vast amount of western territory, including California. This war did not excite great interest in the state of New York, and so far as we can learn no organized effort was made in Dryden to promote it, and no volunteers, except perhaps a few scattering adventurers, went from Dryden to engage in it. It was a Southern measure, not over popular at that time in the North, although in its results it proved to be important and highly beneficial to the country at large.

This was an era of prosperity in which the value of real estate and other property maintained a healthy improvement. As the water power used by the saw-mills ceased to be required for that purpose on account of the rapidly decreasing supply of saw logs, attention was given to other kinds of manufacturing to which these water powers were adapted; and hence many of the mills and factories of the town date back to this period.

During this time stoves to a great extent took the place of the old-fashioned fireplaces, and tallow candles furnished the means of house lighting in the evening, supplemented toward the end of this period by sperm oil lamps and an explosive burning fluid compounded of camphine and alcohol.

The anti-slavery movement developed largely during this time. The census of 1820 shows that there were then held in the county of Tompkins fifty slaves, of whom thirty-two were held in the town of Caroline, nine in the town of Hector, six in the town of Danby and three in Ulysses (then including Ithaca), but none were then held in the towns of Dryden, Groton or Lansing. In the preliminary draft of this chapter we said that we found no evidence that negro slavery ever existed in the town of Dryden. We had learned that Edward Griswold kept in his family an old negro by the name of Jack O'Liney, who had once been a slave, but who seems to have been harbored by Mr. Griswold as a subject of charity. Further investigation develops the fact that Aaron Lacy, who came to Dryden in 1799, while he resided on the Stickles corner in Willow Glen, bought and kept as a domestic servant, a slave girl by the name of Ann Wisner, remembered by some of the older people as "Black Ann," who was sent to school by her master in the Willow Glen district in those early years, and who, after her emancipation moved to Ithaca and has since then frequently revisited the family of her former master. In the will of Aaron Lacy dated in the year 1826 and recorded in the surrogate's office of Tompkins county in book B, page 69, this slave girl is bequeathed to his widow, Eliza Lacy. Perhaps other slaves were held in Dryden, but we learn of no others, and slavery was abolished in the whole state of New York early in this period, July 4, 1827.

A great change in the customs in regard to the use of alcoholic and spirituous liquors took place during this time. As we have seen, in 1824 there were five distilleries of whiskey in operation in the town and we are told that everybody in those days made use of it. Intoxicating liquor of some kind was considered a necessity to be furnished at every raising of the frame of a new building, and no farmer could commence haying without providing a supply of strong drink for the use of himself and his help during this laborious operation in those times. Tradition says that for the raising of the frame of the Presbyterian church edifice in Dryden village, which occupied a week in the year 1819, a large amount of whiskey was supplied to the volunteer workmen. Whether, as is sometimes claimed by old people, the whiskey of those days was so pure that it had none of the pernicious effects which attend the intemperate use of the modern article of the same name, is fortunately not within the province of history to determine.

In reviewing the first fifty years of Dryden's inhabitation we cannot but be impressed with the great progress and improvements which had been made, and doubtless the inhabitants of 1847 considered that the limit of progress in art and science had then almost been reached, and that but few improvements could be expected in the future. Yet at that time not a single mowing machine, reaper or family sewing machine had ever been brought into the township, the first of the for-

THE DEVELOPMENT PERIOD.

mer, an Emory mower, having been brought into town by Elias W. Cady in 1850, and of the latter the first was a Grover & Baker sewing machine presented to Mrs. John E. McElheny by her brother, Volney Aldrich, of New York, in about 1857, the cost of which was one hundred thirty dollars. At that time people came from as far as West Dryden to see a machine which could " actually sew," and that same machine is still in active use.

Up to this time not a single bushel of mineral coal ("stone coal" as it was called in those days) had ever been introduced, the first, as we learn, being a barrel of blacksmith's coal brought in from Ithaca as an experiment by Obed Lindsey and Jim Patterson in 1850. Kerosene oil had then never been heard of, and it was some time before "stone coal" was used here for heating houses, the term "coal" then being universally applied to charcoal, which was used much more commonly than now.

We believe we are safe in stating that up to this time not a single steam engine, either stationary or portable, had ever been introduced into the town except where the D. L. & W. R. R. now crosses the south-west corner. On that old road in 1840 it was attempted to use the first locomotive, but without success until it was sent back to Schenectady to be enlarged and improved. When returned it was so heavy that it wrecked one of the bridges and was abandoned until about 1847, when steam power first became a practical success on this old line of railroad.

In concluding this chapter we quote two stanzas from a centennial poem written by a lady who was born in our adjoining county of Cortland and who is a relative of the Hammond family in Dryden, as follows:

> "Where women sat beside their looms,
>   A hundred years ago,
> And wove in cloth the threads they spun
>   Of linen, wool, and tow,
> Now great King Steam, in work shops large,
>   Like some old giant elf,
> Gets up with angry puff and roar
>   And does the work himself.
>
> "The poor, old stage coach lumbered on,
>   A hundred years ago,
> O'er rugged roads and mountains steep,
>   Its progress was but slow;
> Now, through the mountain's heart, and o'er
>   Deep chasms, yawning wide,
> With iron steeds, in palace cars,
>   How fearlessly we ride."   —*Luranah Hammond.*

CHAPTER XVII.

THE CIVIL WAR PERIOD—SLAVERY.

It is with a consciousness of our inability to do the subject justice that we undertake to record the history of Dryden in connection with the War of the Rebellion and the great events which immediately preceded and followed it, occupying the third quarter of our Century Period, and extending from 1847 to 1872. It was no slight misunderstanding or sudden outburst of jealousy or anger which caused the enlightened and usually sober-minded people of our country—North and South—to engage with all their might in a fierce and bloody conflict lasting over four years, sacrificing hundreds of thousands of lives and expending billions of money, involving in its results the very existence of the nation itself. No section of the country stood more loyally by the government, freely offering up its treasure and the lives of its best citizens for the support of the Union and the cause of freedom in this desperate struggle than did the town of Dryden, and none can claim a greater interest in, or credit for, the result. In the darkest days of the conflict, when the draft riots in New York city indicated weariness of the war, and the votes of the majorities in some sections seemed ready to declare the war a failure, our people continued to roll up increasing majorities at the polls for the war party, and with a firm determination to win, promptly responded to all calls for men and money. To the extent in which she participated in it, the history of this war is the history of Dryden and will be so treated.

In the light of history it is no uncertain fact that the cause of this war was negro slavery. It was not so fully recognized as such at the time, neither party being willing to admit it, the North claiming that they were simply fighting to preserve the Union, while the South contended that they were merely seeking their independence. History removes all sham pretenses from both sides and clearly reveals the fact that the subject of the contention was the perpetuation of slavery in the United States.

As we have seen, slaves were held in Tompkins county at least as late as 1820, when the number was fifty. In the year 1799 the population of the state of New York included twenty thousand slaves, but in that year provision was made by the state government for their gradual emancipation, and on July 4, 1827, the last slave in the state was declared forever free. The colored people of the county celebrated the event at that time at Ithaca. While all the Northern States voluntarily abolished slavery within their limits early in the century, the institution flourished with increasing vigor in the South, and the antagonism between the two sections, engendered and maintained by the subject of the existence and entension of slavery, led slowly but surely to the terrible War of the Rebellion.

One of the local circumstances which early served to call attention to and agitate this subject in our county was the trial of Robert H. Hyde, the father of the late R. H. S. Hyde, Esq., of the town of Caroline, who was charged with taking to Virginia and selling a negro slave girl, Eliza, whom he had held here, in violation of the laws which provided for the gradual abolition of slavery in this state and prohibited the removal of slaves to other states to evade this law for their emancipation. In 1805 there had settled in Caroline a small colony from Virginia, including the Hyde and Speed families, who brought their slaves with them. Hyde was indicted and twice tried upon this charge at Ithaca in the year 1825. He escaped conviction, being ably defended by Ben Johnson, the most noted lawyer of the county in those years, but the affair served to stir up the rapidly growing anti-slavery sentiment in this county. While the South undertook to defend the institution of slavery as of divine origin, best calculated to subserve the highest interest of the colored race as well as that of their masters, the prevailing sentiment of the North was rapidly growing to condemn it as radically wrong. Still the mass of the Northern people were not prepared before the war to interfere with slavery in the old states where it had been established, but the question as to permitting it to be introduced and further extended in the new states and territories led to heated and bitter discussion and an increasing enmity between the two sections. The sentiment at the North was, however, divided on the subject, and there were some citizens, even in Dryden, who, up to the time of the war, openly defended negro slavery. The writer remembers that Mills Van Valkenburgh, a lawyer of Dryden and afterwards county judge, who taught the Dryden village district school in about 1855, had such pronounced views upon the subject of tolerating slavery that some of the radical abolitionists of the village, R. H. Delamater for one, refused to send their children to school under his instruction, although he was everywhere recognized as an excellent teacher and an exemplary citizen.

When John Brown in 1859 made his raid into Virginia to free the slaves and create an insurrection among them in defiance of law, the masses of people in Dryden, as well as elsewhere in the North, condemned it as a mad and foolish act. Still there was a growing sentiment in sympathy with him, which was disposed to resist the fugitive slave law requiring the return of runaway slaves to their masters, maintaining that there was a law higher than the law of the land upon that subject, and the readiness with which the soldiers of the North afterwards took up the song:

"John Brown's body lies a mouldering in the grave,
But his soul goes marching on,"

demonstrated that this sentiment was not then forgotten.

The presidential campaign of 1856, in which Fremont and Dayton were defeated by James Buchanan, was an exciting time in Dryden, only exceeded by the subsequent election of Lincoln and Hamlin in 1860. While there were never very many colored people residing in the town, the anti-slavery feeling became so intense and prevalent prior to and during the war, and the "Black Republican" majorities given in sympathy with the negroes grew to such an extent, that the town came to be known in those days as "Black Dryden."

CHAPTER XVIII.

THE WAR OF THE REBELLION.

It is now easy to see in the light of history that in their efforts to preserve and perpetuate the institution of slavery, the Southern States by their attempted secession hastened its doom to speedy abolition. Slavery might have been one of the perplexing subjects of politics to-day had not the crisis been precipitated by the commencement of hostilities in April, 1861.

It will be difficult for succeeding generations to realize with what anxiety and interest the investment and capture of Fort Sumpter and the subsequent progress of the war were watched by the people of Dryden in common with the inhabitants of all of the states of the North. No railroads or telegraph then served to deliver the war news within the town of Dryden. The only mail which was then received was brought by the daily stages from Ithaca and Cortland, meeting at Dryden village at noon. The New York daily papers of the morning would in this way reach Dryden the next day at noon, when the first news was obtained, unless, as was frequently the case, a messenger was dispatched by private contributors to Cortland, the nearest railroad and telegraph station in those times, to bring back the latest news late in the evening. Those who remember how anxiously the tidings of the war were watched for, will call to mind with what feelings of disappointment the frequent stereotyped response was received, "All quiet on the Potomac."

The capture of Fort Sumpter by the Confederates served immediately to strengthen and unite the people of the North in their determination to preserve the Union with or without slavery at first, but finally only with the complete abolition of that troublesome institution. For that purpose a large part of the Democratic party, known as "War Democrats," united with the government in its effort to preserve the Union and with that determination stood by it until the termination of the war, while the remaining Democrats, who opposed the war, or professed to be indifferent on the subject, were openly denounced and branded as "Copper-heads."

The first volunteers to go into the military service from our town joined some companies organized in Ithaca, which were afterwards united at New York with others to form the 32nd Infantry, with which they went to the front in June, 1861. Among these volunteers was Captain Sylvester H. Brown, who was killed at City Point, Va. This regiment enlisted for only two years, but saw severe service, participating in the battles of West Point, Gaines Mills, White Oak Swamp, Malvern Hill, Crompton Gap, Antietam, and Fredericksburg. After their term of two years had expired many of the survivors re-enlisted in other regiments. In the fall and winter of that year the 76th regiment was organized, of which companies F. and C. were largely recruited from the town of Dryden. This organization had an unfortunate beginning, growing out of a personal quarrel between Col. Green and one of his subordinate officers, resulting in the shooting and wounding of the latter, while they were encamped at Cortland. Afterwards the 76th, under Col. Wainwright, did valiant service and took part in the battles of Rappahannock Station, Warrenton, Gainesville, Second Bull Run, South Mountain, Antietam, Upperville, Fredericksburg, Chancellorsville, Gettysburg and Mine Run.

The early campaigns of the Union forces in Virginia were not successful. Such disasters as the battle of Bull Run served to convince the people of the North that greater efforts must be made. War meetings were held in all parts of the county, attended with bands of music and patriotic speakers. At these meetings liberal contributions were made for the aid of the families of such as should go to the front. A senatorial war committee was appointed, of which our late townsman, Jeremiah W. Dwight, was the member from this county, and a local town committee was selected, consisting of Luther Griswold,

Smith Robertson, Charles Givens, Thomas J. McElheny, and W. W. Snyder.

In the summer of 1862 the 109th regiment was organized, Company F. being largely made up of Dryden volunteers. It was mustered into service Aug. 28, 1862, but was kept on guard duty for the first year and more. Its first fight was in the terrible battle of the Wilderness when more than one hundred of its men were left upon the field of battle. Spottsylvania, Cold Harbor and the battles before Petersburg followed in quick succession, in all of which this regiment made a gallant record, but suffered severely, so that when they came to be mustered out of the service in June, 1865, there were only two hundred and fifty men left of the twelve hundred which first went into the Wilderness.

In October, 1862, the 143d regiment, of which one company was made up mostly of Dryden men under Capt. Harrison Marvin, was mustered into service. Although this regiment did not see such severe service it had an honorable record and its roll of honor bore the following inscriptions: Nansemond, Wauhatchie, Lookout Mountain, Chattanooga, Knoxville, Resaca, Dallas, Kenesaw Mountain, Culpepper Farm, Peach Tree Ridge, Atlanta and Savannah.

Capt. Geo. L. Truesdell with quite a number of other Dryden men joined early in 1864 the 15th New York Cavarly, which was organized from Aug 8, 1863, to January 14th, 1864, to serve for three years. Nine companies were recruited at Syracuse, one at Elmira, one at Cavalry Depot, Washington, D. C., and one in the state of New York at large. It was consolidated with the Sixth New York Cavalry June 17th, 1865, and the consolidated force designated the Second Provisional New York Cavalry. Col. Robert M. Richardson resigned Jan. 19, 1865, leaving in command Col. John J. Coppinger. The regiment lost by death during its service in killed during action, three officers and eighteen men; of wounds received in action, nineteen men; of disease and other causes, four officers and 129 men; a grand total of one hundred seventy men. It was at Hillsboro, Upperville, Franklin, Romney, New Market, Front Royal, Newton, Mount Jackson, Piedmont, Stanton, Waynesboro, Lexington, New London, Diamond Hill, Lynchburg, Snicker's Gap, Ashby's Gap, Winchester, Green Spring, and the Appomattox campaign.

The early enlistments were all volunteers aided and encouraged at first by liberal provisions for the families of those who should enlist, and afterwards by large bounties in addition, to the soldier himself. Only one draft was made in this town, which was executed in July,

1863, according to the terms of which the drafted man himself could hire a substitute to go in his place or, by paying three hundred dollars, the government would provide the substitute. A second and third draft was ordered but the supervisors of the county here came to the rescue and hired, at the expense of the county, enough non-resident soldiers to make up, with those who had volunteered, the full quota of the towns of Tompkins county.

We regret that we are not able to make our military record more complete, having given only a brief reference to the companies which were made up almost wholly of Dryden men. Many others were scattered through different regiments and in all branches of the service, and we supplement this brief record by the following chapter, which aims to give a complete list of the Dryden soldiers, specifying those who died or were severely wounded in the service.

CHAPTER XVIII.

PERSONAL RECORD OF DRYDEN SOLDIERS.

The preparation of this chapter has involved no small amount of labor, and great care has been taken to make it correct and complete. Still there are, doubtless, some errors and omissions; but the following data arranged in tabular form will, it is hoped, at least serve as a basis from which a more perfect record shall be made at some time in the future. If happily "grim visaged war" shall never again make its imperative demands upon the town of Dryden, its inhabitants of the rising and future generations will never fully realize what it is to have the lives of the father, brother and sons of the people of the township exposed to the hazards of camp and of battle and sacrificed in the service of their country.

Thomas J. McElheny, one of the war committee of Dryden who gave his time very fully in those years to the details of filling the quotas of soldiers required by the government from this town, relates with pardonable pride the experiences which he had in performing his arduous duties in these matters and bears witness to the liberality and patriotism manifested by the people in sustaining his efforts.

No attempt is made in this chapter to complete the record of non-resident volunteers who were induced by the liberal bounties offered by the town of Dryden to help to fill out her quota and when Dryden men had removed to other places before their enlistment their names will not be likely to be found in the following table:

HISTORY OF DRYDEN.

Name.	Co.	Reg't.	Mustered in.	Yrs.	Remarks.
Aiken, Joseph,	A	32 Inf.	June 2, '61	2	discharged at expiration of term.
Allen, Timothy,	F	15 Art.	Mar. 27, '64	3	discharged at the close of the war.
Algar, John G.,	C	76 Inf.	Sept., '61	3	transferred to Veteran Reserve Corps.
Arnold, A. S.,					non-resident.
Arnold, Chadiah,		143 Inf.			discharged with regiment.
Arnold, C. S.,					non-resident.
Arnold, John S.,					non-resident.
Arnold, John D.,					non-resident.
Arnold, Seneca S.,					non-resident.
Bachelder, Erastus,	A	127 Inf.	Aug. 15, '62	3	discharged at the close of the war.
Baker, Edwin,	E	21 Cav.	Feb. 20, '63	3	discharged at Elmira, July, '65.
Baldwin, Wm.,	I	143 Inf.	Oct. 8, '62	3	discharged at the close of the war.
Ballard, Gabriel B.,	I	143 Inf.	Oct. 8, '62	3	discharged at the close of the war.
Barber, Andrew J.,	F	109 Inf.	Aug. 27, '62	3	died of wound received at Spottsylvania, May, '64.
Bartholomew, Norman G., capt.,	F	76 Inf.	Nov. 24, '61	3	killed at Wilderness May 6, '64, buried at Etna.
Bartlett, D. Webster,	F	109 Inf.	Aug. 27, '62	3	discharged for disability, Dec., '62.
Barton, D. Webster, lt.,	F	109 Inf.	Aug. 27, '62	3	killed at Spottsylvania, May 12, '64.
Barton, Wm. H.,	F	76 Inf.	Sept., '61	3	wounded at Gainesville, died Feb., '63.
Bates, Otis A., serg.,	I	143 Inf.	Oct. 8, '62	3	discharged at the close of the war.
Bellington, Geo.,	I	143 Inf.	Oct. 8, '62	3	discharged for disability April 10, '63.
Bergin, John E., lt.,	I	109 Inf.	Aug. 27, '62	3	promoted to lieutenant U. S. Light Infantry.
Bessy, Peter,	I	143 Inf.	Oct. 8, '62	3	died of disease at Nashville, '64.
Bishop, D. C.,	E	21 Cav.	Feb. 24, '64	3	died of disease at Denver, July 8, '66.
Bloom, H. E.,	F	15 Art.	Feb. 21, '64	3	died of disease at Clarysville, Md., Jan. 15, '64.
Bosworth, Alphonso,					non-resident.
Benton, Clinton D., corp.,	F	76 Inf.	Dec. 1, '61	3	discharged at expiration of term.
Brigham, Cor. E.,					non-resident.
Brigham, Newton,	I	143 Inf.	Oct. 8, '62	3	discharged for disability.
Brown, Moses,	179 Inf.	Sept., '64	3	died of disease at Petersburg.
Brown, Orrin F.,	M	21 Cav.	Dec., '63	3	discharged at Denver, June 10, '66.
Brown, Orson C.,	I	143 Inf.	Aug. 16, '62	3	

DRYDEN SOLDIERS.

Co.	Reg.	Date		Remarks
	32 Inf.		2	killed at City Point, buried at Dryden.
F	109 Inf.		3	discharged at expiration of term.
F	109 Inf.	Aug. 27, '62	3	wounded Spottsylvania, discharged close of war.
F	109 Inf.	Aug. 27, '62	3	died of disease.
I	15 Cav.	June, '64	3	discharged at Louisville, Aug, '65.
F	109 Inf.	Aug. 27, '62	3	discharged at New York.
I	15 Cav.	Feb. 21, '64	3	discharged at Louisville, August, '65.
M	21 Cav.	Dec., '63	3	discharged at Denver, June 10, '66.
F	76 Inf.		3	pris. Wilderness, Andersonv. 7 mo., dis. close war.
E	32 Inf.	June 2, '61	2	dis. at expiration of term, re-enlisted in cavalry.
I	15 Cav.	Feb., '64	3	2 terms, 15 battles, prisoner, dis. close of war.
G	76 Inf.	July 28, '63	3	discharged at the close of the war.
F	76 Inf.	Dec., '61	3	discharged for disability, November 26, '62.
F	109 Inf.	Aug. 27, '62	3	prisoner, May 12, '64, died at Andersonville.
F	76 Inf.		3	killed at Gettysburg, July 3, '63.
F	109 Inf.	Aug. 27, '62	3	prisoner Spottsylvania, survived Andersonville. [uess, May 7, '64.
F	76 Inf.	Dec., '61	3	wounded Gettysburg, July 3, '63; killed Wilder-
I	15 Cav.	Feb. 2, '64	3	
F	109 Inf.	Aug. 27, '62	3	
F	109 Inf.	Aug. 27, '62	3	discharged for disability, July 3, '63.
			3	non-resident.
			3	non-resident.
			3	non-resident.
			3	non-resident.
	143 Inf.	Aug. 27, '62	3	discharged at Mound City, Ill., March 4, '65.
K	137 Inf.	Sept. 24, '63	3	discharged at the close of the war.
E	32 Inf.	June 2, '61	2	died of disease at New York city, June 12, '61. died before muster.
F	76 Inf.	Sept., '61	3	pro. to lt. 1863, lost leg at Gettysburg, July 3, '63.
I	143 Inf.		3	discharged for disability.

58 HISTORY OF DRYDEN.

Name.	Co.	Reg't.	Mustered.	Yrs.	Remarks.
Conklin, Nathaniel,	F	109 Inf.	Aug. 27, '62	3	discharged at the close of the war.
Cook, Enos,	I	143 Inf.	Oct. 8, '62	3	died of disease at Chattanooga, December 18, '63.
Cook, James H.,	A	10 Cav.	Dec. 31, '63	3	discharged at the close of the war.
Cook, James O.,	E	64 Inf.	Sept. 26, '61	3	discharged for disability, December 1, '62.
Cook, James O., corp.,	M	21 Cav.	Feb. 14, '64	3	discharged at Denver, July 9, '66.
Copely, James W.,		143 Inf.		3	transferred to Veteran Reserve Corps.
Cornelius, Wm.,	I	15 Cav.	Feb. 9, '64	3	discharged at Louisville at the close of the war.
Cramer, Michael,	C	76 Inf.	Dec., '61	3	discharged for disability, December, '62.
Crispell, Merritt,	F	15 Cav.	Feb. 3, '64	3	discharged at expiration of term.
Darling, Joseph,				3	non-resident.
Dart, John,	F	76 Inf.	Dec., '61	3	died of disease in Maryland.
Davenport, Chas. W.,	F	15 Cav.	Feb. 9, '64	3	discharged at expiration of term.
Davenport, D. D., corp.,	I	143 Inf.	Oct. 8, '62	3	discharged at the close of the war.
Davidson, R. G., serg.,	C	76 Inf.	Nov. 5, '61	3	discharged at expiration of term.
Decker, Rufus W.,	E	143 Inf.	Aug., '62	3	died of disease in South Carolina.
Decker, Walter,	C	76 Inf.	Dec., '61	3	discharged for disability, died soon after.
Depew, John,					
Deuel, James M.,	I	143 Inf.	Oct. 8, '62	3	discharged at expiration of term.
Denel, Thaddeus S., corp.,	E	64 Inf.	Oct., '61	3	dis. disability from accidental discharge of gun.
Devanny, Gilbert, serg.,	I	143 Inf.	Oct. 8, '62	3	discharged at the close of the war.
Deyo, Moses F.,	B	5 Art.		3	died in Dryden on furlough.
Dodge, Eugene,	F	76 Inf.	Dec., '61	3	
Dodge, Levi,	I	143 Inf.		3	
Downey, Robert,	I	109 Inf.		3	
Downey, Wm.,	F	109 Inf.	Aug. 27, '62	3	killed by accident on cars, Maryland, Oct., '62.
Draper, Egbert,	F	76 Inf.	Nov. 5, '61	3	discharged at expiration of term.
Draper, Richard,	F	76 Inf.	Nov. 5, '61	3	discharged for disability.
Durkee, Morton E.,	F	109 Inf.		3	
Dusenberry, O. G.,	I	143 Inf.	Oct. 8, '62	3	killed in skirmish Shenandoah Val., Dec. 21, '64.
Dutcher, Chas. H.,	F	109 Inf.	Aug. 27, '62	3	discharged for disability.

DRYDEN SOLDIERS.

Name	Co.	Reg.	Branch	Enlisted	Yrs	Remarks
Edsall, Stephen F.,	1	143	Inf.	Oct. 8, '62	3	non-resident from Pennsylvania.
Edsall, Wm.,	F	76	Inf.	Nov. 5, '61	3	discharged at expiration of term.
Edwards, Pattison,	C	75	Inf.		3	discharged for disability Nov. 11, '62.
Eldridge, Daniel,					3	
Ellis, Chas. B.,	F	109	Inf.	Aug. 27, '62	3	discharged at expiration of term.
Ellis, Orrin E., serg.,	F	76	Inf.	Nov. 5, '61	3	died from disease March 24, '62.
English, Thomas,	B	21	Cav.	Feb. 1, '64	3	discharged at Denver June 10, '66.
Evans, Earl, capt.,	F	76	Inf.	Sept. '61	3	re-enlisted and served thro' war, promoted capt.
Farquahr, John,	M	21	Cav.	Nov., '63	3	died from wounds March 18, '65.
Farrell, Andrew,	I	143	Inf.	Oct. 8, '62	3	
Ferris, David,	I	143	Inf.	Oct. 8, '62	3	
Ferris, John J.,	I	143	Inf.	Oct. 8, '62	3	discharged for disability June 5, '63.
Fisher, Willet,	I	143	Inf.	Oct. 8, '62	3	discharged at the close of the war.
Fitts, Chas. T.,	F	76	Inf.	Dec. 5, '61	3	discharged for disability. [dis. close war.
Fitts, Chas. T., corp,	E	179	Inf.	Sept. 17, '64	3	wounded shoulder Sept. 30, '64, head Apr. 2, '65,
Fitts, Henry W.,	I	143	Inf.	Oct. 8, '62	3	died of disease, Lookout Valley, January 11, '63.
Fogarty, John,	I	143	Inf.	Oct. 8, '62	3	discharged for disability April 20, '65.
Forrest, Cyrenus,					3	non-resident from Pennsylvania.
Fox, M. B.,	I	143	Inf.	Oct. 8, '62	3	discharged for disability August 20, '63.
Fox, Wm. C.,	A	76	Inf.	Nov. 24, '61	3	died from wounds rec'd at Gettysburg July 3, '65.
Freeman, Chas. D.,	T	143	Inf.	Oct. 8, '62	3	missed near Lookout Mountain December 20, '63.
Freese, Chauncey A.,	F	15	Cav.	Feb. 2, '64	3	discharged at the close of the war.
Freese, Henry,	C	76	Inf.	Dec. 4, '61	3	discharged at expiration of term.
Fulkerson, Henry S.,	C	76	Inf.	Nov. 5, '61	3	killed battle of Gainesville, Va., August 28, '62.
Fulkerson, John G.,	E	32	Inf.	June 6, '61	2	died of disease at Alexandria, December 12, '61.
Gee, W. Riley,	F	76	Inf.	Dec. '61	3	discharged.
George, Wm. Thomas, capt.,	A	143	Inf.	Oct. 8, '62	3	promoted capt., discharged at close of the war.
Godfrey, Chas. P.,	F	109	Inf.	Aug. 27, '62	3	lost leg May 14, '64, discharged May 25, '65.
Gorman, Cyrus B.,	F	109	Inf.	Aug. 27, '62	3	discharged at expiration of term.
Graham, Philander, serg.,	I	15	Cav.	Sept. 15, '62	3	discharged at expiration of term.
Green, Oliver H.,	1	15	Cav.	Nov. 2, '64	3	
Griffin, J. F.,						

HISTORY OF DRYDEN.

Name.	Co.	Reg't.	Mustered.	Yrs.	Remarks.
Griffin, Lewis,	F	109 Inf.	Aug. 27, '62	3	discharged June 30, '65.
Griffin, S. C.,	H	144 Inf.	Aug. '62	3	discharged at the close of the war.
Griswold, Bazaleel F.,	F	109 Inf.	Aug. 27, '62	3	died in Andersonville, July 20, '64.
Griswold, C. Dick,	E	32 Inf.	June	2	discharged at expiration of term.
Griswold, C. Dick, corp.,	K	97 Inf.	Oct. 9, '63	3	discharged at expiration of term. [17, '65.
Griswold, D. P., lt.,	C	76 Inf.	Dec. '61	3	pro. lt., wounded Petersburg, leg amp., dis. Mar.
Griswold, Nathan L., lt.,	F	109 Inf.	Aug. 26, '62	3	pro. to lt., killed before Petersburg, August 3, '64.
Hackett, John, capt.,		32 Inf.	May, '61	2	re-enlisted in Michigan regiment.
Hammond, D. B.,	I	15 Cav.	Sept. '64	3	discharged at the close of the war.
Hammond, Edwin,	F	15 Cav.	Feb. 2, '64	3	discharged at the close of the war.
Hammond, Thos. J.,	F	109 Inf.		3	re-enlisted in 179th Infantry.
Hammond, Thos. J.,	B	179 Inf.	Feb. 2, '64	3	discharged at the close of the war.
Harned, Geo.,	I	143 Inf.	Oct. 8, '62	3	died at Fortress Monroe, September 28, '63.
Hartsough, Thos. J.,	I	143 Inf.	Oct. 8, '62	3	died of disease at Chattanooga, December 8, '63.
Haskell, B. L.,	F	15 Cav.	Feb. 2, '64	3	discharged at the close of the war.
Haskell, Josiah,	F	15 Cav.	Feb. 2, '64	3	discharged at the close of the war.
Haviland, Abbott,		143 Inf.		3	discharged for disability March, '63.
Haviland, Myron,	F	76 Inf.	Sept. '61	3	discharged at the close of the war.
Hemmingway, Chauncey,	I	143 Inf.	Oct. 8, '62	3	wounded leg Sept. '64, taken pris., dis. close war.
Hemmingway, Geo. R.,	B	179 Inf.	Sept. 17, '64	3	discharged at the close of the war.
Hemmingway, Henry H., lt,	I	143 Inf.	Oct. 8, '62	3	died of disease October 18, '64.
Hemmingway, Orlando, serg.,	I	143 Inf.	Oct. 8, '62	3	discharged at New York city July 27, '65.
Hildebrant, Elihu, serg.,	E	143 Inf.	Oct. 8, '62	3	wounded at the battle of Fair Oaks.
Hildebrant, John, capt.,	E	64 Inf.	Sept. 10, '61	3	discharged for disability August 10, '62.
Hill, Osmer J., corp.,	F	76 Inf.	Nov. 5, '61	3	wounded Gainesville and died from wounds.
Hoffman, Thos. H.,	F	76 Inf.	Sept. 5, '61	3	discharged for disability March, '64.
Hollenbeck, Albert J.,	G	76 Inf.	Nov. '61	3	discharged at the close of the war.
Hollenshead, Dan'l R.,		143 Inf.		3	discharged at the close of the war.
Howard, Jerome,	B	79 Inf.	Sept. '64	3	discharged at the close of the war. [term.
Howe, Jas. T.,	I	143 Inf.	Oct. 8, '62	3	wounded and pris. Gettysburg, dis. exp. of
Howser, Chas. L., corp.,	B	9 Art.	Nov. 5, '64	3	died of wounds rec'd at Winchester, Oct. 19, '64.

DRYDEN SOLDIERS.

Name	Co.	Reg.	Yrs.	Enlisted	Remarks
Halbert, Edwin R.,	F	76 Inf.	3	Nov. 5, '61	discharged at expiration of term.
Hubslander, Wm. R.,	I	143 Inf.	3	Oct. 8, '62	discharged for disability in '62.
Hunt, Myron H.,	E	32 Inf.	3	Oct., '62	prisoner Fair Oaks, discharged for disability '63.
Hurd, Albert,					no record.
Hurd, John W.,	I	143 Inf.	3	Oct. 8, '62	discharged for disability September 30, '63.
Harley, Elisha, Jr., corp.,	I	143 Inf.	3	Oct. 17, '62	discharged for disability August 7, '64.
Huson, Bowker,	F	109 Inf.			did not enter the service.
Hyde, Benjamin,	F	109 Inf.	3	Aug. 27, '62	killed at Spottsylvania May 12, '64.
Hyde, Chas. W.,	C	76 Inf.	3		discharged at Washington before actual service.
Hyde, Norman,	C	76 Inf.	3		discharged for disability before actual service.
Jackson, Jefferson,					no record.
Jagger, Frank, corp.,	I	143 Inf.	3	Oct. 8, '62	discharged at expiration of term.
Jones, Lyman,	F	109 Inf.	3	Aug. 27, '62	discharged at expiration of term.
Kane, Chas.,	A	179 Inf.	3	Aug. 22, '64	discharged at the close of the war.
Kelly, John,					no record.
Kennedy, Wm. W., lt.,	F	109 Inf.	3	Aug. 27, '62	pro. 1st serg., 1st lt., w'nded twice, dis. close war.
Kingsley, Monroe,					no record. (wounds Chattanooga Aug., '64.
Kiser, Albert A.,	I	143 Inf.	3	Oct. 8, '62	wounded Peach Tree Creek, July 20, '64, died of
Kiser, Jacob,					no record.
Kline, Philip,	E	21 Cav.	3		no record.
Knickerbocker, Clay,	I	143 Inf.	3	Oct. 8, '62	discharged for disability.
Lacy, Geo. L.,	F	76 Inf.	3	'61	no record.
Lacy, Geo. L.,	I	15 Cav.	3	Dec. 2, '64	taken prisoner, discharged at close of the war.
Lambertson, Jas. E.,	I	143 Inf.	3	Oct. 8, '62	discharged for disability, April 10, '63.
Lambertson, John N.,	C	76 Inf.	3	Dec. 28, '61	discharged for disability, October 28, '62.
Lambertson, Wm.,	I	143 Inf.	3	Oct. 8, '62	discharged for injuries received on cars.
Lamont, Wm.,	B	179 Inf.	3	Sept. 30, '64	discharged at the close of the war.
Lawson, Daniel,	M	21 Cav.	3	June 2, '64	discharged at Fort Leavenworth, August 9, '65.
Lent, Hiram B.,					non-resident from Pennsylvania.
Lester, Wm. H., serg.,	B	8 Col.	3	Nov. 14, '63	discharged at Brownsville, Tex., at close of war.
Lindsey, John,	F	76 Inf.	3	Nov. 5, '61	died of disease at Fredericksburg, June 27, '62.
Lindsey, Obed H.,	I	15 Cav.	3	Feb. 2, '64	discharged at the close of the war.

HISTORY OF DRYDEN.

Name.	Co.	Reg'l.	Mustered.	Yrs.	Remarks.
Loper, Lucien,					non-resident from Pennsylvania.
Lormore, Jas. C., serg.,	I	103 Inf.	Mar. 7, '62	3	discharged at the close of the war.
Luckey, A. B.,					non-resident from Pennsylvania.
Luddington, Flixton,	F	109 Inf.	Aug. 27, '62	3	discharged at the close of the war.
Lyke, Rufus F.,					non-resident from Pennsylvania.
Lyon, Warren H.,	F	109 Inf.	Aug. 27, '62	3	discharged at the close of the war, June 4, '65.
McDermott, James,	F	155 Inf.	Aug. 17, '62	3	wounded Cold Harbor, May 3, '65, died of w'nds soon after.
McDonald, Robert,				3	non-resident from Pennsylvania.
McElheny, Marion F., corp.,	I	32 Inf.	June 2, '61	2	dis. for disability Jan., '62, re-enlisted 109 Inf.
McElheny, Marion F., corp.,	F	109 Inf.	Aug. 27, '62	3	wounded at Spottsylvania.
McGregor, Clinton D.,	F	76 Inf.	Nov. 14, '61	3	discharged at expiration of term.
McGregor, Clinton D., serg.,	1st V. R. C.		May 7, '64	3	wounded at Gainesville, discharged close of war.
McGregor, Daniel,	F	76 Inf.	Nov. 14, '61	3	wounded Gainesville, died of disease Jan. 28, '63.
McHue, James,				3	non-resident from Pennsylvania.
McKee, David,	E	32 Inf.	June 9, '61	2	discharged at expiration of term.
McKee, David,	I	15 Cav.	Feb. 2, '64	3	discharged at expiration of term.
McKinney, Wm.,	A	179 Inf.	Sept. 17, '64	3	discharged at the close of the war.
McLean, Conrad,	F	109 Inf.	Aug. 27, '62	3	wounded at Petersburg, discharged close of war.
McWhorter, J. T., serg.,	I	143 Inf.	Oct. 8, '62	3	discharged for disability, June, '64.
Mack, Halsey,	I	15 Cav.	Feb. 2, '64	3	discharged at the close of the war.
Manchester, J.,				3	non-resident from Pennsylvania.
Maricle, Cornelius,	G	76 Inf.	Sept. 3, '61	2	discharged for disability November, '61.
Marsh, Augustus,	I	15 Cav.	Sept. 3, '63	3	discharged at the close of the war.
Marvin, Harrison, capt.,	I	143 Inf.	Oct. 8, '62	3	discharged at the close of the war.
Mastin, Britton,	F	75 Inf.	Dec., '61	3	discharged February 24, '62.
Mastin, Britton,	I	15 Cav.	Feb. 2, '64	3	discharged at the close of the war.
Matson, James H.,	F	109 Inf.	Aug. 13, '61	3	discharged at the close of the war, June 4, '65.
Matson, John C.,	I	143 Inf.	Oct. 8, '62	3	discharged at the close of the war.
Mattison, David,	C	76 Inf.	Sept., '61	3	taken prisoner at Wilderness, died Andersonville.
Mattison, Geo. L.,				3	non-resident from Pennsylvania.
Maxwell, Edward,	I	143 Inf.	Oct., '62	3	trans. Vet. Res. Corps, disch'g'd at close of war.

DRYDEN SOLDIERS.

Name	Co.	Reg.	Enlisted	Age	Remarks
Mead, Elias A., lt.,	C	76 Inf.	Sept., '61	3	wounded at Antietam, honorably discharged.
Miller, Albert W.,		V. R. C.		3	discharged at close of the war.
Miller, Frank	F	76 Inf.	Nov. 14, '61	3	killed at 2nd Bull Run, Aug. 28, '63.
Moffat, Wm., lt.,	I	143 Inf.	Oct. 8, '62	3	resigned.
Monroe, Milo, serg.,	F	109 Inf.	Aug. 8, '62	3	discharged at Denver, June 10, '66.
Monroe, Wm.,	I	15 Cav.	Feb. 2, '64	3	killed at Newmarket, and buried on the field.
Montgomery, Daniel R.,	F	76 Inf.	Nov. 14, '61	3	wounded at Gettysburg, dis. expiration of term.
Montgomery, J. J.,			July 9, '64	3	Medical Cadet U. S. A.
Morey, Wm. A.,	L	143 Inf.	Oct. 8, '62	3	died of disease in Georgia.
Morgan, John,	F	109 Inf.	Aug. 27, '62	3	
Morgan, R. S.	C	76 Inf.	Dec., '61	3	also 3d U. S. Cav., discharged at close of the war.
Mosely, Chas. D.,	A	32 Inf.	May 15, '61	2	discharged from disability Sept. 29, '62.
Mosely, Chas. D.,	F	15 Cav.	Aug. 26, '61	3	discharged at close of the war.
Mosely, Edwin T.,	I	15 Cav.	Feb. 2, '64	3	died of disease at Fairfax Seminary, July 14, '65.
Mosher, Philip D.,	I	143 Inf.	Oct. 8, '62	3	died of disease at Washington.
Mosher, Wm. A.,	C	76 Inf.	Nov. 5, '61	3	no record.
Mynard, Cortland,	B	179 Inf.	Sept. 17, '64	3	discharged at close of the war.
Nash, David,	I	143 Inf.	Oct. 8, '62	3	discharged at close of the war.
Nash, Philander,	I	15 Cav.	Feb. 2, '64	3	
Norton, Wm. D.,	C	76 Inf.	Dec., '61	3	died before actual service.
Nugent, John,	E	155 Inf.	Sept., '62	3	discharged at close of the war.
Obert, Eli A.,	F	109 Inf.	Aug. 27, '62	3	killed in battle on Weldon R. R., August 21, '64.
Odell, George,	I	15 Cav.		3	discharged at the close of war, died soon after.
Ostrander, Myron,	F	15 Cav.	Feb. 2, '64	3	wounded and lost leg, discharged August, '65.
Overacker, Isaac,	I	143 Inf.	Nov. 8, '62	3	died of disease April 4, '64.
Owen, Daniel J.,				3	died of disease in service.
O'Wrighter, Marion,					non-resident from Pennsylvania.
Paine, John,	I	143 Inf.	Oct. 8, '62	3	discharged for disability July 20, '63.
Peak, Seth R.,	F	15 Cav.	Feb. 2, '64	3	discharged at the close of the war.
Pease, Almon,	I	143 Inf.	Oct. 8, '62	3	discharged at Washington before actual service.
Pelham, Benjamin,					non-resident from Pennsylvania.
Pendleton, Geo. L.,					

Name.	Co.	Reg't.	Mustered.	Vis.	Remarks.
Perrigo, Chas. M.,	I	143 Inf.	Oct. 8, '62	3	dis. for disability, leg amputated Sept. 17, '63.
Pettengill, F., corp.,	I	143 Inf.	Oct. 8, '62	3	died of disease in Columbia Hosp., Washington.
Pettigrove, John,					no record.
Pratt, Samuel,	I	143 Inf.	Oct. 8, '62	3	discharged at expiration of term.
Price, Chas. H.,	E	32 Inf.	June 2, '61	2	discharged at the close of the war.
Puderbaugh, John A.,	F	109 Inf.	Aug. 27, '62	3	dis. at expiration of term, re-enlisted in 143 Inf.
Puderbaugh, Theo. J.,	E	32 Inf.	June 3, '61	2	discharged at the close of the war.
Robinson, John L.,	I	15 Cav.	Feb. 2, '64	3	discharged at expiration of term.
Robinson, Joseph,	E	32 Inf.	June 3, '61	2	discharged at expiration of term.
Roe, Wm. M., serg,	I	143 Inf.	Oct. 8, '62	3	discharged at the close of war, died soon after.
Root, Horace L., lt.,	I	143 Inf.	Oct. 8, '62	3	wounded at Peach Tree Creek, dis. close of war.
Rulison, Geo. P.,	F	109 Inf.	Aug. 27, '62	3	wounded Petersburg, July 30, '64, arm amp.
Russel, D. E.,	F	109 Inf.	Aug. 27, '62	3	discharged at the close of the war.
Ryder, Wm.,					non-resident from Pennsylvania.
Schutt, Jeremiah,	I	143 Inf.	Oct. 8, '62	3	discharged at the close of the war.
Schutt, Monroe,	E	32 Inf.	June 2, '62	2	wounded 1st Bull Run, dis. disability July 2, '62.
Schutt, Socrates,	F	109 Inf.	Aug. 27, '62	3	discharged at the close of the war.
Scott, Chas.,	I	143 Inf.	Oct. 8, '62	3	died of disease April 6, '63.
Seaman, Ephraim,	I	15 Cav.	Feb. 2, '64	3	discharged at the close of the war.
Seaman, Peter, serg,	I	15 Cav.	Feb. 2, '64	3	prisoner Newmarket, dis. Louisville close of war.
Seaman, Wm.	I	143 Inf.	Oct. 8, '62	3	discharged at the close of the war.
Selby, Henry,	B	26 Col.	June 14, '63	3	no record.
Shaver, John W.,	I	143 Inf.	Oct. 8, '62	3	discharged at the close of the war.
Shaw, Henry,	I	143 Inf.	Oct. 8, '62	3	discharged at the close of the war.
Shaw, Wm.,	I	143 Inf.	Oct. 8, '62	3	discharged for disability.
Shepard, Wm. C.				3	no record.
Sherwood, Emerson,	F	109 Inf.	Aug. 27, '62	3	discharged at the close of the war.
Sherwood, John,	I	143 Inf.	Oct. 8, '62	3	discharged for disability March 10, '63.
Sherwood, Lafayette,					no record.
Sherwood, Morgan,	I	143 Inf.	Oct. 8, '62	3	died at Bridgeport, Alabama.

DRYDEN SOLDIERS.

Name	Co.	Regt.	Branch	Date	Age	Remarks
Sherwood, W. P.,	I	143	Inf.	Oct. 8, '62	3	died at Nashville, Tenn.
Simons, Daniel P., serg.	F	109	Inf.	Aug. 27, '62	3	wounded at Spottsylvania, dis. at close of war.
Simons, Seneca A.,	F	109	Inf.	Aug. 27, '62	3	no record.
Skillman, Geo. F.,	F	109	Inf.	Aug. 27, '62	3	dis. for disability April 8, '63, died August, '65.
Skillman, Jas. M.,	I	143	Inf.	Oct. 8, '62	3	non-resident, from Pennsylvania.
Smalley, W. R.,						
Smith, Edwin W.,	M	21	Cav.	Feb., '64	3	discharged at the close of the war.
Smith, L. D.,	I	143	Inf.	Oct. 8, '62	3	killed at Atlanta, July 30, '64.
Snyder, Ezra,	F	109	Inf.	Aug. 27, '62	3	discharged for disability, no date.
Snyder, Henry J.,	I	143	Inf.	Oct. 8, '62	3	discharged at Cincinnati, April, '64.
Sorrell, Edward,	B	U. S. Col.		June 14, '63	3	killed on picket Graham's Neck, S. C., Dec., '64.
Sorrell, John H.,	B	26	Inf.	Dec. 24, '63	3	discharged at the close of the war.
Spear, M. L. G., lt.	F	109	Inf.	Aug. 27, '62	3	resigned February 1, '64.
Stanton, Wm. A.,	F	109	Inf.	Aug. 27, '62	3	discharged for disability.
Starr, B. Peter, corp.,	I	143	Inf.	Oct. 8, '62	3	discharged at the close of the war.
Stevens, Chas.,						no record.
Straight, Hiram,						
Strong, B. G.,	F	109	Inf.	Aug. 27, '62	3	discharged at the close of the war.
Strong, C. L., corp.,	F	109	Inf.	Aug. 27, '62	3	discharged at the close of the war.
Strong, Philemon B.,	L	15	Cav.	Feb., '64	3	died of disease at Baltimore.
Stubbs, Wm. A.,	C	76	Inf.		3	discharged at expiration of term.
Suttin, Geo. W.,	L	15	Cav.	Aug. 31, '64	3	discharged at the close of the war.
Suttin, Nathaniel D.,	I	32	Inf.	June 2, '61	2	dis. for disability Sept. 10, '62, died soon after.
Sweet, A. C.,	B	94		Aug. 15, '64	3	discharged at the close of the war.
Sweet, A. Cole,	E	32	Inf.	June 2, '61		wounded Gainesville, South M'nt'n, dis. ex. term.
Sweet, A. Cole,	F	15	Cav.	Feb. 2, '64	3	discharged at the close of the war.
Sweet, A. Lewis,	F	76	Inf.	Nov. 2, '61	3	discharged for disability, July 14, '62.
Sykes, Jonathan H.,	F	109	Inf.	Aug. 27, '62	3	discharged at the close of the war.
Tanner, Garrett S.,	I	143	Cav.	Aug. 2, '64	3	
Tanner, Lyman,	E	32	Inf.	June 2, '61	2	discharged at expiration of term.
Tanner, Lyman, serg.	L	15	Cav.	Feb. 2, '64	3	promoted to q. m. serg., discharged close of war.
Teeter, Edward H.,	C	76	Inf.	Nov. 5, '61	3	discharged disability Aug. 20, '62.

Name.	Co.	Reg't.	Mustered.	Yrs.	Remarks.
Teeter, Edward H.,	F	9 Art.	Aug., '64	3	discharged at close of the war.
Thomas, Theodore F.,	I	15 Cav.	Aug., '64	3	discharged at close of the war.
Tomlinson, Robert,		155 Inf.		3	discharged at close of the war.
Tripp, John D., corp.,	F	76 Inf.	Dec., '61	3	dis. for disability, Apr., '62; afterward med. cad.
Tripp, Wm. C.,	I	15 Cav.	Feb. 2, '64	3	discharged at Louisville at close of the war.
Truesdell, Geo. L., capt.,	L	15 Cav.	Feb. 2, '64	3	pro. May 8, '65; discharged at close of the war.
Tucker, John,	F	15 Cav.	Feb. 26, '64	3	discharged at close of the war.
Tucker, Orrin,	F	109 Inf.	Aug. 27, '62	3	discharged for disability, March 28, '64.
Tyler, Jas. V.,	F	109 Inf.	Aug. 27, '62	3	died of disease, July 16, '64.
Underwood, Nathan,	F	109 Inf.		3	
Underwood, Ogden G.,	F	109 Inf.		3	
Vail, Samuel J., serg.,	F	109 Inf.	Aug. 27, '62	3	wounded Wilderness; died of disease Oct. 4, '64.
Valuschamp, Abraham,				3	non-resident.
Vanderpool, John W.,	F	76 Inf.	Nov. 5, '61	3	discharged at expiration of term.
Vanderpool, Simon,	F	76 Inf.	Nov. 5, '61	3	
Van Horn, Nathaniel,				3	non-resident.
Van Horn, Samuel,				3	non-resident.
Van Natta, Theodore,	F	15 Cav.	July 13, '64	3	discharged at close of the war.
Van Order, Eugene,		32 Inf.		3	
Van Order, Fred,		32 Inf.		2	
Van Valkenburgh, Eugene, corp.,	F	109 Inf.	Aug. 27, '62	3	discharged for wounds received at Spottsylvania.
Wagoner, Alonzo B., serg.,	F	76 Inf.	July 26, '64	3	two terms same reg't; discharged at close of war.
Wagoner, Garrett,	F	76 Inf.	Nov. 5, '61	3	
Waite, Andrew,	I	143 Inf.	Oct. 8, '62	3	dis. disability Dec. 13, '62; re-enlisted 21 Cav.
Waite, Andrew,	M	21 Cav.	Feb. 20, '64	3	discharged at close of the war.
Waite, Henry B.,	F	143 Inf.	Oct. 8, '62	3	discharged at close of the war.
Waite, James,	I	143 Inf.	Oct. 8, '62	3	
Wallace, J. Henry,	G	15 Art.	Sept. 5, '63	3	w'ded Lacey Springs, Va., Dec., '64, dis. close war.
Wallace, Wm. L.,	F	109 Inf.	Aug. 27, '62	3	killed before Petersburg, Aug. 27, '64.
Ward, Ai,	I	143 Inf.	Oct. 8, '62	3	discharged for disability March, '63.
Weaver, Henry D., corp.,	C	76 Inf.	Oct., '61	3	killed at Gettysburg, July 1, '63.

Welch, James,	F	143 Inf.	Oct. 8, '62	discharged at close of the war.
West, Albert M.,	F	109 Inf.	Aug. 27, '62	died of disease Sept. 12, '63.
White, John A.,	C	76 Inf.	Nov. 5, '61	died of disease in Virginia, Aug. 27, '62.
White, Wm. R., corp.,	F	109 Inf.	Aug. 27, '62	killed at Spottsylvania, May 12, '64.
Wickham, George,	F	143 Inf.	Aug. 10, '64	discharged at close of the war.
Wilcox, Geo. R.,	I	15 Cav.	June, '64	discharged at close of the war.
Wilcox, Joseph L.,	F	15 Cav.	June, '64	
Wilcox, Lyman,	F	143 Inf.	Oct. 8, '62	discharged on account of age, Nov. 9, '62.
Wilcox, Marion,	F	76 Inf.	Nov. 5, '61	discharged before actual service.
Willey, Samuel M.,	I	185		
Williamson, Clark,	F	15 Cav.	June, '64	discharged at the close of the war.
Wilson, Henry,	F	76 Inf.	Nov. 5, '61	transferred to Vet. Res. Corps; dis. close of war.
Woodmancy, Geo., corp.,	I	143 Inf.	Oct. 8, '62	discharged at the close of the war.
Wright, Geo. W.,	I	143 Inf.		

Women, as well as men, gave their services to the country in this time of need, and Mrs. Julia A. Cook, whose husband, Enos, had already died in the service, and whose only son, James H., served throughout the war, volunteered as a nurse and was on duty in the hospitals at Washington in June, 1864, until her own sickness compelled her to return. As an inland town Dryden could not be expected to contribute much to the naval forces of the country, but an incident which interested the people of Dryden village and enlisted their deepest sympathy at the time, should be here mentioned. Jared Boorom, a relative of a Dryden family, had been a sailor and in his wanderings had married a little Spanish woman whom he had met in the West India Islands. Upon the breaking out of the war he brought her and their little daughter to Dryden, where he provided for them with his relatives while he enlisted as a gunner on the Galena, a gunboat of the U. S. Navy. Mrs. Boorom could speak but very little English, but with her peculiar Spanish ways she was a subject of great interest to Dryden people, among whom she made many friends. But suddenly there came news that Boorom was wounded by the explosion of a shell in an attack on Fort Fisher in the James River, May 16, 1862, and a day or two later that he was dead. The grief of the poor young widow knew no bounds and excited the deepest sympathy from all who had known and heard of her. The remains of her husband were brought to Dryden and laid in the Green Hills cemetery, where a monument to-day marks his grave. His wife soon after returned to her native country.

CHAPTER XX.

INTERNAL IMPROVEMENTS.

While the period of the war involved great loss of life and property to the North as well as to the South, it was, to our section of the country, in some respects a time of unusual prosperity. The money which was freely paid out by the government for services and supplies came into ready circulation among the people, and the prices of everything went up to high figures, so that those people who remained at home and formed the producing class were able to secure enormous prices for their products. Wheat brought $2.50 per bushel; wool one dollar per pound; while butter was sold for sixty cents and at some times even more than that per pound. Real estate, as well as other property, was booming, and everybody holding property of any kind was agreeably surprised upon finding himself richer than he had previously supposed himself to be. This increase in wealth was in a measure imaginary, and to some extent, at least, due to a depreciated currency by which the value of things was then estimated. When the currency was brought up to a par value with gold, some time after the close of the war, the delusion began to be dispelled, and the value of property has ever since then seemed to depreciate.

Still there were people during the war, as there always have been and always will be, who were continually complaining of the hard times, and suggesting that if ever the war should cease then they might accomplish something, while those who then went to work and made their efforts productive, accumulated property more rapidly than it was possible to do in the same length of time either before or since that period.

The apparent prosperity which then prevailed in business matters stimulated local enterprises, and the first railroad to furnish means of transportation within the town, at first known as the Southern Central, was opened for travel between Owego and Auburn in the year 1869. Such a project had long been dreamed of and hoped for by the people of the town, and we find on an old map of Tompkins county published in 1838, a copy of which is in the possession of Dr. Mary Briggs of Dryden village, a railway projected from Ithaca to Auburn by way of Etna and Freeville, over almost the same route now occupied by the branches of the Lehigh Valley. The old Ithaca and Cortland railroad, known in those days as the "Shoo Fly," was opened as far as Cortland running diagonally through the centre of the town of

Dryden, in 1871. A great effort was made by and in behalf of Dryden people, especially those living in and about Dryden village, to secure the constructtion of the Southern Central. Many other towns along the proposed line were bonded to furnish means with which to construct it, but the town of Dryden was never obligated in that way. The citizens, however, believed that only by very liberal subscriptions to the stock of the company could the road be secured, and a subscription amounting to nearly two hundred thousand dollas was obtained from the people, only about one half of which materialized, Many under the strong influence brought to bear upon them and out of a sense of duty to the public interests of the town, agreed to take more stock than they afterwards felt able to pay for, and subsequent developments indicated that the road would have been finally built without so great a sacrifice on the part of the people. Those towns, however, which bonded themselves fared the worst, for their bonds were paid when times were harder and property had greatly depreciated in value. The Midland Railroad Company projected a road in this period from Freeville to Auburn by way of West Dryden and Lansing, which was not completed until 1880, and after being operated for about ten years was absorbed by the Lehigh Valley Company and discontinued. The telegraph accompanied the railroads, or in the case of the Southern Central preceded it by a few years. Thus the town from being wholly destitute of railroad privileges up to 1869, has ever since been traversed by at least two lines of railroad, crossing each other at nearly right angles near the centre of the township, providing five railroad and telegraph stations within its borders.

Near the end of this period, and about the year 1870, attention was called to the fact that Dryden was holding rather more than her full share (in fact nearly all) of the political honors of the county. It so happened at that time that Hon. Richard Marvin, as Supreme Court Justice, then residing in Chautauqua county but brought up as a Dryden boy, was assigned to hold a term of Supreme Court at Ithaca. Mills Van Valkenburg was then serving as county judge and surrogate, elected from Dryden; Horace L. Root was serving as sheriff, as well as Thomas J. McElheny as county clerk, both elected from Dryden; while Benjamin F. Squires, the court crier had formerly been a Dryden merchant. With Milo Goodrich, of Dryden, then a member of congress from this district and a prominent figure at the bar of that court it was conceded that for a country town Dryden then had a claim upon at least her full share of the offices of that court and of the county.

CHAPTER XXI.

THE PERIOD OF MATURITY.

By applying the term "maturity" to this present time, the last quarter of the Century Period of our history, we do not intend to imply that it is a time when perfection has been reached, or that further developments of a progressive nature may not be expected in the future history of our town. It is regarded by us as mature only as we view it from the standpoint of the present as compared with the primitive conditions of the past, while to those who may review it one hundred years hence, the present time will doubtless appear, in some respects at least, as a period of rude development. This period will be treated of here very briefly, as it is not yet ripe as a subject for history, and it is rather to give those who shall come after us and who may chance to peruse our efforts, some idea as to how our times appear to us to-day than for any other purpose that we complete our general history of the town of Dryden with this chapter.

There are some few respects in which great progress has been made during the past hundred years where it would seem that but little improvement need be expected or asked for in the future. One of them is in the matter of highway bridges, of which our town is required to maintain many, although none of extraordinary dimensions. In the Pioneer Period it is presumed that there were no bridges of any account, the inhabitants then being required to ford the streams in summer and cross them on the ice in winter. In the Second Period pole bridges were constructed, rude affairs—many of which were carried away with every spring flood. These were replaced in the War Period with comparatively substantial structures of wood, of the truss pattern, but they were subject to decay, the life of such a bridge, however well constructed and protected, being less than twenty years. But now all or very nearly all of them have been replaced during the past twenty-five years by substantial iron structures, supplied by the town at considerable expense, placed upon solid piers of masonry or iron piles, in such a manner that they seem to be almost indestructible and imperishable.

Another respect in which great progress has been made and apparently the limit of perfection almost reached is in the matter of educational advantages. Common school education for the young is now not only free, but in a measure compulsory, and there can be but little hope for the children of to-day who do not readily improve the

THE MATURITY PERIOD.   71

superior advantages now afforded them by our schools. If we compare the school buildings of to-day with those of twenty-five years ago, and then again with those of fifty and seventy-five years ago, we shall be impressed with the degree of comfort and elegance which our own times afford in comparison.

The dwelling houses and farm buildings of the present time are not to be compared with the rude habitations of fifty and seventy-five years ago. It was not then considered necessary to winter cattle under cover except in the worst storms, and then the poorest shed was supposed to furnish ample protection. When the country was mostly covered with forests the severity of winter was not felt by man or beast as it is now, and we are told that in the Pioneer Period snow drifts were unknown. Now the cattle barn of the Dryden farmer is usually larger and often more expensive than the house in which he lives, which is itself a palace in points of convenience and elegance as compared with the homes of his ancestors.

The methods of dairy farming as practiced in the town have met with a wonderful change, since fifty years ago. Then the milk was all made up into butter and cheese at home, while now all that which is not consumed in fattening calves for the city markets is, in most localities, taken to the railroad stations to be shipped on the milk train, or to the nearest of the cheese or butter factories which are distributed throughout the township.

We should not pass over the present time without mentioning the now omnipresent "bicycle," which within the past twenty-five years has developed from its first appearance as the old "velocipede" and within the past few years has come into very general use as a means of pleasure and convenience even in the country. It promises at least to compel the farmers to build and maintain better roads, which will result greatly to their own advantage and profit in the end.

In one respect there is some reason to complain of our times and that is in regard to the depreciation in the market value of real estate within the past twenty-five years. In the Pioneer Period, as we have seen, land was purchased for a few dollars per acre. For the first seventy-five years and until about the close of the War Period the value of real estate had a steady and constant upward tendency, until good farms in the town were readily sold at from sixty to one hundred dollars per acre. The young farmer who had invested in land and lived during that time, as old age came on often discovered that his increased wealth was as much due to the natural increase in the value of his farm as to the crops which he had raised and sold off from it, while the farmer of to-day, who invested his resources in land twenty-five years ago, finds to his sorrow that the depreciation in the market value of his farm often counterbalances the labor and efforts of a lifetime expended upon it. The actual market value of the real estate of the town during that time, in spite of improved buildings, has depreciated nearly, if not quite, one half. From this tendency of the times, which was unforseen and unexpected, many, and especially those who had invested beyond their means in real estate, have suffered severely; but in other respects these times are propitious. It is the abundance and cheapness of the necessities of life which now surround us, and not their scarcity as it was in the year 1816. In spite of this plenteous supply of its various products, labor itself is in good demand and well paid, and at no time, it is safe to say, within the century would the same amount of well directed labor purchase so much good common food or clothing as at present. The very prosperous times which have immediately preceded the present have unfortunately stimulated extravagance, and to this more than to any other cause is due the complaint of hard times so commonly heard.

As an illustration of this the writer remembers that about fifty years ago old Esquire Tanner used to keep in his postoffice at Dryden village, in two small glass jars with tin covers, and four square red boxes with sliding glass fronts, the stock of sugar candy which supplied the children of the village and surrounding country, more numerous then than now. One jar contained lemon drops—thirteen for a penny; another jackson balls, at a cent apiece; and the four others contained stick candy of different kinds. His total sales of that commodity could not have exceeded twenty-five dollars per annum. Now the merchants tell us that the retail trade in candy in Dryden village exceeds one thousand dollars per annum, and is more than equalled by the sale of southern grown fruit, which fifty years ago was unknown to us. Not only is extravagance exhibited in such kinds of food, much of which is worse than useless, but so extravagant have people become in these "hard times" in the matter of superfluous clothing throughout the country, that during the past winter the Legislature of the great State of New York has in its wisdom enacted a law requiring the ladies who insist upon displaying such a profusion of flowers, ribbons and feathers in their head-gear as to eclipse the view of everything else, to remove their hats when attending entertainments, and at the same time we believe an amendment was offered but lost limiting the number of yards of cloth which might be wasted by the ladies in making up their puffed sleeves.

But in spite of the so-called hard times, useless extravagance and the depreciation in the value of real estate, there are many respects in which marked improvement has been made throughout the country with prospects of still greater advancement.

We read of many of the earlier settlers who lost the land which they had under many hardships and with much difficulty paid for, without any fault of their own, through defective and fraudulent titles, which were then very common. Now the system of recorded land titles is so perfect that very seldom does any such loss occur, and even then it results from gross carelessness.

We learn that in early times there was a great deal of local litigation, and that a number of pettifogging lawyers were kept busy in every hamlet of the township settling the disputes of neighbors by contested law-suits in Justice's Court over horse trades, dog fights, and other foolish matters. This state of things has almost entirely disappeared.

We are told by old people that in those "good old times" there was never a town meeting held without more or less fighting being witnessed. These were not wrestling contests or boxing matches, but real bloody, brutal fights, in which the "bullies" of the town exhibited their powers of inflicting and enduring blows to the crowd of their assembled townsmen. Now happily such an exhibition would not be tolerated at our town meetings or elsewhere, and the most noted of pugilists are obliged to seek a refuge as far away as New Orleans or Nevada in which to exhibit themselves in their contests.

It is said that in the early days of Dryden the Lacy and Knapp families were noted for their pugilistic contests with each other in dead earnest. Think of the family from which our very exemplary late lamented John C. Lacy descended, being noted for its brutal fighting qualities, frequently exhibited at town meetings, and then tell us whether the times and the manners have not greatly improved during the century.

CHAPTER XXII.

DRYDEN VILLAGE IN THE PIONEER PERIOD.

We now return from our general survey of the whole town to take up each separate locality, giving to each its own particular local history, commencing with Dryden village, where, as we have seen, the first settlement was made. There were then no corporate limits and we shall include with the village in these times all of the events and families naturally connected with it without regard to definite boundaries

After the settlement of the Amos Sweet family on Lot No. 39, as we have seen, in 1797, the next to locate upon the site of Dryden village appears to have been Dr. Nathaniel Sheldon, who was the first physician of the town and who built the first frame house on the corner now occupied by the brick store of D. T. Wheeler & Co. Ruloff Whitney, who, as we have seen, assisted Col. Hopkins, of Homer, to build the first saw-mill of the town on Fall Creek near Willow Glen in 1800, soon after had a saw-mill of his own where the Dryden Woolen Mill now stands, but the exact dates of these events cannot be given. Serren H. Jagger, Sr., built one of the first frame houses on the premises since owned by D. J. Baker, where his oldest daughter, Betsey, was born in 1805, who afterwards became the second wife of John Southworth, and the grandmother or great-grandmother of nearly all of his living descendants. Mr. Jagger was a tanner and currier by trade and then operated a small tannery in the rear of his residence. The five Lacy brothers located in and about Dryden village in 1801, and the Seth Wheeler family from New Hampshire and the Edward Griswold family from Connecticut in 1802, as the former accounts have it; but some investigation leads us to believe that it was about two years later.

The first postoffice in the town and the only one for some time after, was established at Dryden village, as shown by the department records at Washington, October 1, 1811, with Jonathan Stout as postmaster. He was, however, succeeded on July, 1812, by Parley Whitmore, who retained the office for a long time.

The most vivid and reliable pen picture which we can give of Dryden village in this period is afforded by the dercription of the late John C. Lacy, furnished for publication by him on his eightieth birthday, October 21, 1888, and from which we quote as follows:

"MR. EDITOR—Having some recollection of the situation of things in this village and vicinity seventy or more years ago, and as this is the eightieth anniversary of my birth and residence here, I thought I could in no better way notice the event, than to state briefly some of my recollections of these times, to wit:

"There were but two roads in the village, and crossing at right angles, forming the four corners as now. They were rough and crooked, the one running north and south was difficult of travel and was noted for the frequency in which teamsters became *mired* with their loads of lumber and produce bound for the Homer and Syracuse markets and returning with salt, which sold at five dollars per barrel. A brook ran across the east and west road near D. J. Baker's (now Henry Thomas's) over which was a pole bridge. A branch of Virgil Creek crossed the road near the late Wm. West's (now D. T. Wheeler's) residence, over which was a bridge, under which I have caught fish; where Mr. Rockwell's factory (the Woolen Mill) now stands was a saw-mill owned by a man by the name of Whitney, and afterwards by Jason Ellis. Near this mill was a little shop where a man by the name of Ballard made nails by hand, which he sold at eighteen pence per pound. Where Mill street now is there was nothing but a foot-path, and the crossing of the streams was over trees that had fallen across them. The highway then ran on the west side of Whitney's pond (or Rockwell's) and entered the village road where Mr. Rockwell's wool house now is. On this road was a log house where different families had lived for several years before the road was discontinued, to wit: R. Whitney, Joseph Thomas, and Stephen B. Lounsberry. James, Union, Pleasant, Lewis, George, Rochester, Marsh, and Elm streets were either in the state of nature or under cultivation by the farmer. The village was small, the houses small, few and scattering; one small tavern where the Blodgett House stood, one store where C. Green's tailor shop is, one school house near H. Cliff's residence gotten up by private subscription, in shares—some took more and some less. (Benjamin Lacy had about one-fourth of the stock.) For a sample of the houses, I would cite you to the house on Rochester street, of which unknown miscreants made a bonfire on the Fourth of July not long since. This house, in its best days, stood where E. Rockwell now resides. With this exception there were no houses between J. Cole's and the creek. The other side of the road was equally vacant of buildings from D. J. Baker's down to the creek. Where Dr. Montgomery's office now stands there was a log distillery in full blast, and on the site of the Geo. Hill block was a small cabinet shop. The best house was on the Moore lot, built and owned by Dr. John W. Phillips,—since having been moved and now owned by John McKeon. The four corners of the village, comprising six rods square each, were not then built upon, but remained a public green, as was intended by the several *donors* who gave them to the good people of the town for that purpose.

"All was in a rude state—the farms but partially cleared, stumps, straggling and girdled trees all over, swamps not drained. The people worked and suffered many privations and hardships, unaided by modern labor-saving machines; the work of both men and women was done by hand—the haying, with the scythe, the harvesting, with the sickle and the grain cradle, and the threshing with the flail. The wearing apparel was spun and woven by the women on the hand wheels, and on the hand looms. This, in addition to their household work, made it doubly hard for them. When they rode out they either rode on horseback or in lumber wagons and sleds, but oftener went on foot; if to parties or to get married, all the same. No fine carriages or railroad coaches, no mowing machines, no reapers, horse pitchforks, sulky rakes or sulky plows, no threshing machines, no Woolen Factory, no meeting houses, no grist-mill or tannery, no newspaper, no Dryden Springs Place. The mineral springs were discovered by the Lacy brothers while digging and prospecting for salt in 1820-21. No. free school. The boy that went to school a few days in the year furnished his own wood and paid his own tuition. No two-cent postage on letters; a letter to a friend five hundred miles away required eighteen pence postage, and for friends to separate such a distance was almost equal to separating forever; for the parties had but little time to write and still less money to pay the heavy postage and telephoning and telegraphing were not then thought of, so they would lose track of one another altogether. Money was hardly thought of in *deal*, except to pay taxes, the payment of which was one of the most important matters that annually perplexed and disturbed the people, money was so hard to be got. Barter was the order of the times. A bushel of corn was the price of a common laborer's day's work, and a bushel of wheat the mechanic's.

"The cold seasons of 1818, '19 were times that tried the men's souls. Corn was entirely cut off by the frosts, wheat and other products were scarce and dear, eighteen to twenty shillings per bushel for wheat, little or no money to buy with. If it were better in older and larger places the transportation of produce was so difficult and expensive it did them no good. This is the time when Capt. Geo. Robertson, then a well-known citizen of another part of the town, refused to sell his grain to men who had money, but sold it to those who had no money, on the ground that those who had could get it somewhere else, (in Lansing.) This is the time one of my neighbor's boys told me he "lived three days on two cold potatoes, and nothing under Heavens else," and another neighbor's little girl told me she had had nothing to eat for two days and was as weak as a little frog. This was a time, too, when a dollar to a man was more than a pound sterling would be to-day. The snows and frosts of those years have never since been equalled here for severity."

DRYDEN VILLAGE. 77

We think that Mr. Lacy was mistaken as to the years of the famine, which were 1816, '17 instead of 1818, '19.

As corroboration of the six rods square from each of the four corners intended as a public common referred to by Mr. Lacy, we find on the county records a deed bearing date May 18, 1812, executed by "Abram Griswold, Nathan Goddard, John Taylor, and Joshua Holt, all of Dryden, Cayuga Co.," to "The Good People of the town of Dryden," purporting to convey six rods square from each corner, constituting 144 square rods, nearly an acre, in the exact center of the village. As a matter of law "The Good People of the Town" constituted a grantee too indefinite to hold the property, and each corner was afterward appropriated for private use, except the M. E. church corner, which was afterward conveyed with other premises to the Presbyterian society subject to the rights granted to "The Good People" as aforesaid.

In this period there was an earnest rivalry between this settlement and Willow Glen as to which should become the metropolis of the town, and from the active part which Edward Griswold, Sr., took in it, giving a blacksmith forty acres of land off from his lot in order to induce him to locate here, and from his successful efforts through his son Abram to establish the Presbyterian church with other enterprises here, as well as the gift, through his son, of the corner to "The Good People" and the knoll to the east for a cemetery, we believe he is entitled to be regarded as the "Father" of the village as Captain Robertson was of the town. In addition to the description by Mr. Lacy of the village in the early times, we can say that in the year 1816 Hooker Ballard kept the tavern, Joshua Holt had a grocery store, and afterwards manufactured chairs at the old oil mill on South street. Parley Whitmore kept a store as well as the postoffice near where the M. E. church now stands. James H. Hurd and Timothy Stowe were cabinet makers. Thomas L. Bishop had a saw-mill west of the village; Jesse B. Bartholomew was a distiller on Main street; and Ebenezer Tuttle was a carpenter and builder. Of the farmers, Seth Wheeler, Edward Griswold and Selden Marvin lived north of the village; David Foote, Abram Griswold, Nathan Goddard and Nehemiah Tucker east; Michael Thomas, Daniel and Thomas Lacy and James Bowlby south; and Benjamin and Richard Lacy west. Jedidiah Phelps was a brick maker, and John Phillips as well as John Taylor and Nathaniel Shelden were the physicians.

As Mr. Lacy remarks there were no streets then in Dryden village except the two main roads crossing at right angles and forming the four corners, and the place, for the want of another name, was for a long time called "Dryden Corners."

CHAPTER XXIII.

PIONEER FAMILIES OF DRYDEN VILLAGE.

It is recognized that this chapter and other similar memoranda of the pioneer families is incomplete, there being others which deserve a place among the pioneers of Dryden village if we only could have obtained the material out of which to have written their early history.

BAKER, DAVID J., was born at Great Bend, Pa., March 3, 1795, but when he was two months old his father's family moved to Homer, N. Y., the mother and child being conveyed from one place to the other in a canoe on the Tioughnioga River, there being no roads at that time for transportation. There he lived until eighteen years of age, when he went to Aurora, and a few years later (1816) he came to Dryden. Here he soon built a house on the premises now owned by his son Albert and his daughter, Mrs. Thomas, where he continued to live until his recent death at the age of ninety-five years. On Nov. 10, 1823, he married Samantha, daughter of Hooker Ballard, whose hotel at that time was located just west of where the stone block has since been built. Mr. and Mrs. Baker occupied the same house on Main street in Dryden village for nearly seventy years and he was a member of the Masonic order for nearly seventy-five years, being at his death the oldest Mason in the state. In about 1832, he organized a fine cavalry company in the old state militia, of which he was captain, and he afterwards held the rank of major. His death occurred January 11, 1890, his wife surviving him less than two years. Of their five children all survive except their daughter Samantha, who died recently, and all of the remainder are residents of Dryden village except Mrs. Helen A. Frost, of Wheatland, Iowa.

Mr. and Mrs. Baker are among the few residents of Dryden who, by their long and useful lives, were able to connect the Pioneer Period with the present time. Both were too well known to the present generation to require any extended history to be given here. They were very exemplary citizens in their domestic as well as in their social and public relations, she being always a devoted, industrious and dignified wife and mother as well as a leading and active member of the M. E. church, and he being a prominent, public spirited and prosperous business man.

BOWLBY, JAMES, came with other early settlers between 1805 and 1810 and located upon two hundred eight acres where Martin E. Tripp now resides south of the village. Of his nine children all early went west or to Bath, N. Y., where some of them still reside, except Nancy A., wife of Henry H. Ferguson, who still resides here in the town where she was born in 1816. She recollects many interesting incidents of the old times. Her father was drafted here in the War of 1812 and her mother to help raise money to hire a substitute to go in his place sold her wedding dress, the most valuable article of clothing which she had. Mrs. Ferguson recollects the old log distillery in Dryden village referred to by Mr. Lacy, and says that at one time when her father emptied out the barrel to be taken to the distillery to be refilled, he threw out some cherries which had been kept in the liquor to give it flavor, and that she and the other small children after eating some of the fruit which was well preserved and very nice, felt a very peculiar sensation from the effects of which for a time they could not see, and they did not know what was the matter of them. Perhaps those who have had some similar experiences with the products of the modern "still" can appreciate what was the trouble. When she was about twenty years of age her father and mother and the rest of his family moved to Bath where he died.

BURCH, JOHN, SR., settled in Dryden as early as 1810, coming here from Lewis county, but originally from Connecticut. Soon after locating in Dryden he married Betsey Topping, and their oldest son, John, who is the ancestor of the members of the Burch family now living in Dryden, was born here in 1811. In 1812 John Burch, Sr., joined the army and served near Sackett's Harbor. He was afterwards a pensioner by reason of that service and died in Dryden about twenty years ago. His son, John, Jr., was a captain of militia and is also dead. His daughter Nancy, widow of Thomas Lormor, is still living in Dryden, and his daughters, Martha Burch and Mary Winship, are living at Newark Valley, N. Y. Many of his descendants are living in the West.

GRISWOLD, CAPTAIN EDWARD, is the ancestor of a now numerous Dryden family. He was early a sea captain residing at Killingworth, Connecticut. Having served in the War of the Revolution, his wife, Asenath (Hurd), prevailed upon him, after peace was declared, to abandon his sea-faring life and cast his fortunes in the undeveloped West, which then included a large part of New York state. They first settled in Fairfield, Herkimer county, from which so many Dryden pioneers came, where they sojourned several years and where their younger children were born. They are said to have come to Dryden in 1802. The deed to Edward Griswold of Lot 39, including the northeast quarter of Dryden village, is dated October 16, 1805, conveying six hundred forty acres for a consideration of $2,250.00. He must have been a man of considerable means for those days and was prosperous. He was short and thick-set in his make-up and honorable and upright in his character. There is no evidence that he ever built a log cabin, but he early constructed near the center of his lot the little red house, not far from where the Dryden village reservoir is now located, in which he lived. He died at the age of 84, his wife surviving him to the age of 95.

Their children were: Abram, who married Margaret Givens, leaving many descendants, among whom are A. G. Hunter and Mrs. Lafayette Sweetland, both of Dryden; Polly, who married Timothy Stowe, having no descendants; Asenath, who married William Hoagland, leaving a number of descendants; Nancy, who married George Carr, and left descendants all now non-residents; Charles, who married Hannah Tanner, leaving many descendants including the late Leonard and Luther Griswold; Jerusha, who married Daniel Bartholomew, and after his death, Jesse Topping, leaving descendants of whom one is our present Daniel Bartholomew; Edward, who married Polly Tyler, leaving numerous descendants, mostly non-residents; and Nathan, who married Patience Lindsey, and left descendants, among whom are Benjamin Griswold and Mrs. Chester Carmer, of Dryden.

HURD, JAMES H., migrated from Killingworth, Conn., to Seneca county, N. Y., in the year 1800, and a few years later he moved to Dryden, where he built, in the year 1817, what is still known as the Hurd house, now occupied by Benjamin Griswold on East Main street. He was a cabinet maker and for many years the undertaker of Dryden, like all undertakers of those days, manufacturing usually to order in his own shop as well as trimming, staining and varnishing the coffins which he sold. They were usually made of pine, the price of such an article being from five to nine dollars, some undertakers charging one dollar per foot for the box, according to its length. Being hastily made after the death of the person for whom they were designed they were freshly varnished and thus the odor of varnish was always associated with the grief of the mourners at funerals of the olden times. Among the children of Mr. Hurd were Denison, the father of Mrs. J. H. Pratt, late of Dryden but now deceased; Clementine, the wife of Jesse Givens, and Laura, the only child surviving, who is the wife of Benjamin Griswold. James street was laid out through some of the land of Mr. Hurd and was named from him. He was at one time captain of a Dryden company of light infantry and was for a long time a man of prominence in the town.

JAGGER, SERREN HALSEY, was one of the very early settlers, coming to Dryden about the year 1800 from "between the lakes," probably from Ovid. It is claimed that he built one of the first frame dwellings in Dryden village, located on the lot between the present residences of Albert J. Baker and Henry Thomas. Here his oldest daughter, Betsey, who became the second wife of John Southworth, was born in 1805. He was a tanner and currier as well as a shoemaker and had a small tannery back of his residence where he employed at least one man, by the name of John Welch. This must have been one of the earliest mechanical industries instituted at Dryden Corners. Another daughter, Mrs. Prudence Stevens, now of New Woodstock, N. Y., was born here in 1816, and is one of the oldest survivors of those who were born in Dryden now living. She joined the Presbyterian church at Dryden in 1835. Another younger daughter is Mrs. Harriet Shepard, of Homer, N. Y. There were two sons, Serren H., Jr., and Matthew, both of whom have died leaving families.

LACY, JOHN C. (See special biography.)

LARABEE, ELIAS, was one of the original lot owners, who drew by ballot Lot No. 49 of Dryden, including what is now the southeast quarter of Dryden village. He served in the fourth regiment of New York Continental troops and drew a pension of forty-eight dollars per annum under the act of 1818. In September, 1825, he was indicted for the murder of Amasa Barnes and after trial in December following was convicted of manslaughter and sentenced to fourteen years in the State Prison. This incident grew out of his shooting at some persons who were hanging about his house at night, and in the darkness he fatally wounded Barnes, who was a friend of his. This, so far as we know, was the only act of homicide ever committed in Dryden village, and occurred on the Goodwin lot just east of the Kennedy bridge. Shortly afterwards in view of the circumstances and his services as a soldier, Larabee received a pardon, after which he lived in Dryden village and on the Carty place near the Lake, until near 1850, when he died, over eighty years of age. The Corrington and Lawson families are descendants of his.

MARVIN, SELDEN, in the winter of 1808-9 moved, himself, wife (Charlotte Pratt Marvin, formerly of Saybrook, Ct.), and five children, from Fairfield, Herkimer county, N. Y., on a sled—tradition says an ox sled—to Dryden, and settled on the hundred acres since known as the

Albright farm north of the village. Some six or eight acres had been chopped over and partly cleared before his arrival. He was hospitably received and entertained by Mr. and Mrs. Barclay, who lived in a log house across the road and a little south. The Barclays were then elderly people, and although they had children, their names seem to have disappeared long since from among the descendants of the town. Mr. Marvin soon had his little log house built and his family moved into it. It was much like other log houses of the time—having a loft or garret above, and two rooms below, in one of which was a large, open fire-place built mostly of stones and without jambs. After a few years a lean-to was added in which there was a bed, a hand-loom and spinning wheels. His struggles to clear up his farm and at the same time to feed, clothe and educate his children, were like those of his neighbors around him, who undertook a big job when they, poor as they were and with scarcely any kind of labor-saving machinery, possessing but few agricultural implements, and these poor both in kind and quality, settled down upon lands covered by dense forests and undertook to clear them up and get their living out of them. Their faith was truly sublime!

Mr. Marvin had cleared up the greater part of the hundred acres and built a frame barn upon it in about 1824 or '25. He sold it to Elisha Albright in 1832, and moved himself and family to Chautauqua county. He was induced to take this step in part by a revival in him of the old pioneer spirit of adventure and change, and in part by his desire to buy land to make farms for his younger children, and to be settled nearer his two sons—Erastus the elder, who had settled at Kennedyville, in Chautauqua county, and Richard at Jamestown.

But man proposes and God disposes. Mr. Marvin never realized either one of these objects. He had journeyed, with his wife and seven little children in an old-fashioned two-horse lumber wagon, over a rough and long road and arrived safely and all well at his son's house in Kennedyville. But before he had had time to explore the country or buy a single acre of land, either for himself or his children, his son Erastus was taken sick and died of a fever and he himself and his wife died soon after. The three died within a month with the same fever and in the same house. Their remains repose in the cemetery at Jamestown. Such was the sad ending of Mr. Marvin's unadvised and ill-judged last attempt to establish a new home in a new country. He died at the age of fifty-nine years.

It is not to be doubted that a special providence cares for orphans. Seven small children, the oldest not yet fourteen, were here suddenly deprived of both parents. In this emergency their elder brother, William, then twenty-four years old, took charge of the estate, moderate in amount, and the children. He found homes for four of them, Henry, Harrison, Wesley and Harriet (Tanner), among friends of their father and mother in Dryden. Homes were found for the others among friends elsewhere. The seven all grew up, married and settled in life. All became, too, by various means, well educated and have made useful and highly respectable citizens.

Mary Hibbard, the widow of Erastus, returned to her parental home in Homer carrying with her a baby boy. He died in New Haven, at the age of eighteen, while attending Yale college.

Mr. Marvin was born in Lyme, Ct., and was twice married. His first wife died in 1816. She was buried in the old burying ground in or near the village of Dryden. By her he had seven children. One of them, Richard, represented Cattaraugus and Chautauqua counties in Congress for several years, and was afterwards one of the judges of the Supreme Court in the Eighth Judicial District for twenty-four years. His home was in Jamestown, where he died in 1892.

Another son, William, was appointed U. S. District Attorney for the Southern District of Florida by President Jackson in 1835, and afterwards judge of the same district by President Polk. After the civil war he was appointed Provisional Governor of that state by President Johnson. He is still living in good health at Skaneateles, N. Y., and celebrated his eighty-ninth birthday last April, (1897.)

[For further particulars concerning Richard and William Marvin, and their portraits, see a subsequent chapter of this volume.]

By his second wife (the widow Vandenburgh whom he married in Truxton, from which place he brought her and her three children to Dryden in the bottom of an old fashioned sleigh) Selden Marvin had seven children, one of whom, George W., is a lawyer in Norwich, N. Y., and another, Harrison, has served several years as supervisor of our town and president of Dryden village, being now in the employ of the State Government at Albany.

Selden Marvin was a public spirited citizen, who generally attended the town and district school meetings. He was quite often elected a commissioner of highways and was for a considerable number of years trustee of the gospel and school lot. In politics he was a Federalist, but he was known less for his civic virtues than for his religious characteristics. He was a Methodist—a class leader and exhorter. The few Methodists in and about the village, consisting of Mr. Marvin, John Guinnip, Mr. Hunting, old Father Holt, and a few others whose names are not recalled, used to meet together on Sundays, sometimes in private houses, but more often in the old school house in the village. At these meetings the faithful prayed and sang hymns together. Mr. Marvin was their leader. He used to pray and exhort with great earnestness and power and in a loud voice which was often heard over half the village. A great number of persons in that day declared that they had been converted or greatly strengthened and comforted by his prayers and exhortations. His memory is still fragrant in the minds of a few persons yet living. He was an honest, simple hearted, humble minded, God fearing man, inoffensive and much beloved by his friends and neighbors.

SWEETLAND, BOWEN and JAMES, brothers, came from Vermont as young men early in the century and together owned and operated a saw-mill on the creek about twenty rods below the Woolen Mill, where the banks of the old mill pond can still be seen in the pasture lot of D. Bartholomew. Afterwards Bowen kept hotel where the Blodgett hotel was built later. The old building where Sweetland served as landlord, having been moved off and remodeled, is believed to be the house where Thomas Tamlin now resides on Union street, having been first occupied after its removal by Esquire E. H. Sweet, the nurseryman and shoemaker. Bowen Sweetland finally owned and occupied the Burlingame farm, one-half mile north of the village, where he died March 13, 1859, 72 years of age. His seven children all settled in the West except Bowen, Jr., who died in Dryden a few years ago, and Lucinda, who married Alanson Burlingame, Sr., and died in Dryden about thirty-five years ago.

James, after leaving the saw-mill, purchased the farm a mile east of the village which he afterwards sold to Bradshaw, and then removed to the Layton farm near the Lake, where he died in 1862, aged 74 years. His wife was Frances Wakely and his eight children all found homes in the West except two sons, George and Lafayette, still residents of Dryden, and Sarah (Hiles), who recently died here.

TANNER, ABRAHAM and WILLIAM T., two brothers, from Petersburgh, Rensselaer county, N. Y., after serving in the War of 1812, came to Dryden. Their younger sister, Hannah (Griswold), had preceded them, she having come with Amos Lewis, and it was a visit to her which resulted in the early settlement here of her brothers. They were blacksmiths and opened a shop together near where the Bradshaw house is now located, one mile east of the village, but Abraham, on account of his health, was obliged to seek lighter work, and, after some experience as a merchant, which was not altogether successful and as hotel keeper where James Lormor, Sr., recently resided, he became postmaster and justice of the peace, offices which he held for more than twenty-five years, and in administering which he gave very general satisfaction. His first wife, whom he married in 1818, was Asenath Wakely, after whose death he married for his second wife Betsey Lum, by both of whom he left descendants.

William T. continued in the blacksmith business and afterwards with his sons embarked too largely in the manufacture of wagons, and failed. In 1820 he married Polly West, who survived him, and by whom he had a large family of children. Both of these brothers were men of excellent character and good common sense, but both seemed to have been wanting in some of the sterner qualities which go to make up a thoroughly successful business man.

THOMAS, MICHAEL, left the state of New Jersey in the summer of 1811, traveling northwest, seeking a home in the wilds of New York. After prospecting some time among the lakes he came to Dryden Sept. 11, 1811, and bought one hundred six acres in the south-east corner of Lot No. 48, for which he paid $430.23 in sound money of the State of New York and received a good warranty deed, still in possession of the family, from Egbert Benson, executor of John Lawrence, who died a resident of New York city but who had been an extensive dealer in Dryden real estate. Four cows, two span of horses, two covered wagons well filled and one thousand dollars in money then constituted his worldly possessions in addition to his land.

His family at that time consisted of seven children, the youngest one of whom was the only child of his second wife, who accompanied them. Four more children were born to them in Dryden. The oldest, Martha, or Mattie, was already married to the ancestor of the Space family in Dryden, Jacob Space, who at this time accompanied his father-in-law in his migration from New Jersey, and located where his son William now lives. Eliza married Sanford Bouton and moved to Virgil. Fannie married Edward Cole and died in Freeville. Polly married William Sutfin and lived in Freeville. John married Sophia Bowlby and moved to Bath. Joseph married and lived in New Jersey. Michael married for his first wife Catharine Trapp, and for his second wife Ellen Swart, and lived near Dryden Lake, where he died in March, 1897, 87 years of age. Anna married twice and is still living near the Black River in the northern part of the state. Charlotte married George Bouton, a clergyman of the M. E. church, and became the mother of Ex-Mayor C. D. Bouton, of Ithaca. William married Catharine Caswell and is still living in the house originally built by his father in 1824, and in which he was born a year later, the house having since been extensively enlarged and repaired. Malvina, the youngest of the family, married Almond Trapp, who was the youngest of a family of eleven children, and both are living near McLean.

Grandma Thomas, as she was, in her old age, familiarly called, had a good memory and often told amusing and interesting incidents of this journey from New Jersey to Dryden and described many instances of the privations and hardships of pioneer life. The south half of Lot No. 48, with the exception of a small clearing where the wagon house on the Thomas farm now stands, was then covered with a heavy growth of timber. Fish and game were plenty, bears being common, and it was no unfrequent sight to see deer in cold weather when the snow was deep feeding with the cows near the barn. A jug is still preserved in the family which was used in the pioneer journey to carry milk for the children, it being over one hundred years old.

South street was then located where is now the lane to the barnyard, west of the clearing, which contained a log house and barn and a grove of small elm trees. One of these elm saplings which is described as being, when the Thomas family came there, "no larger than a chair post," has grown with the growth of Dryden, the trunk of which is now sixteen feet in circumference near the ground and is one of the largest if not the oldest elm tree in the township.

Michael Thomas and his wife worked hard in clearing up their farm and lived long to enjoy the fruits of their labor, he having died in 1858 at the ripe age of 92, while she, being thirty-two years his junior, survived him twenty-seven years.

THOMAS, JOSEPH, SR., a brother of Michael, was an early pioneer of Dryden from the same family in New Jersey, among whose children were Joseph, Jr., and John Thomas, who resided only a few years ago near where Walter Thomas, the son of John, now lives, and Mrs. Abram Carmer and Mrs. George Tripp, all of whom are represented by numerous living descendants.

WEST, JOHN, and wife lived in Rhode Island in 1798, where their son Gardner was born May 7th of that year. In some way they caught the "Western fever" of those days and with a brother, Mason, came as far as Fairfield, Herkimer county, N. Y., where they bought a home together and where their daughter Mary (Aunt Polly Tanner) was born July 21st, 1803. The partnership between the two brothers was not entirely satisfactory, as is usually the case under such circumstances, and in 1805 John came out to Dryden prospecting for a new home still further west. As the result he sold out his possessions in

Herkimer county to his brother and moved his family to Dryden, where they arrived in February, 1806, with all their goods on an ox-sled. They stopped temporarily in a log house which stood in the orchard near the house where Harrison Hiles now lives, which was then, or shortly after, the home of Joshua Holt, known also as "old Father Holt." Together with Benjamin Tucker they purchased the greater part of Lot 28, one mile and more north from Dryden village, and Mr. West built for himself a log house, where his son, William West, was born May 18, 1806. Their next eldest child, Percy Hiles, was born there June 12th, 1808, on the same farm where she now resides with her son John, the log house being located where the orchard now is. She will therefore be ninety years old next June and is able to furnish more details of the early events of those years than most other old people now living. One brother (Nathan West) and three sisters (Sally M. Draper, Flavilla Hiles and Lovina Clark) were afterwards born. A frame house was built where the house of her son, John W. Hiles, is now located, when she was ten years old (1818), and up to that time her father, John West, had nothing but an ox team. Some time after, he purchased one horse, but Aunt Percy says that the roads were not suitable for horses to travel on in those days. Nearly all of the children of John West will be recognized as familiar characters to the people of Dryden village, and his descendants now living here are numerous.

WHEELER, DEACON SETH, served in the War of the Revolution, at the close of which he married Rebecca Eliott, of Boston, and lived in Croydon, N. H. In the spring of 1804, he, with his oldest daughter, Rebecca, and son John, came to Dryden, prospecting for a new home in the West. Being pleased with the country Seth and his son returned in the fall for the rest of the family, which included, in all, his wife and ten children. They came with one ox team, three horses, and two wagons, carrying all their worldly goods, including about one thousand dollars in money, with which was purchased one hundred eighty acres of land one mile north of Dryden village on both sides of the highway still known as the "Wheeler road," being premises now owned by S. C. Fulkerson, James McDermott, and E. P. Wheeler. In 1822 a commodious frame house was built, replacing the log cabin which had accommodated the family until that time. Seth Wheeler was a fluent talker, a man of marked ability, deacon in the Baptist church, an earnest exhorter, holding meetings frequently in the neighboring school districts. He died in 1828 aged 72, and was buried with his wife, whose death preceded his, in the old cemetery east of the village, where a double slate slab still marks the location of their graves.

Of their children, Rebecca married Eliseph Sanford and moved to Greenwood, Steuben county, N. Y. Betsey married Jared Todd, of West Dryden, and afterwards, with eight children, moved to a new place in Michigan, named from them Toddville, where their descendants are now numerous. Susan married John Pettigrove and moved to Owego, some of their descendants now living in Ithaca. Lucy and Polly died unmarried. Seth, Jr., married Amantha Lacy, lived on the east part of the farm and died without surviving issue. Enos, the ancestor of the most of the family still living in Dryden, married Mary Blair, and was a successful farmer, a genial and public spirited citizen, a school trustee and an active member of the Presbyterian society of Dryden. He died in 1867. John also left descendants living in Dryden, married Eliza Blair, was a Methodist, and moved from Dryden before his death. Salinda, born in 1799, is still living, at the age of 98 years, with her son in Litchfield, Mich. [Since the foregoing was in type for printing this book, news is received of her death in February, 1898.] She married William Marsden Blair, and one of their daughters is the wife of Representative Flickinger, of Ohio. Anna, the tenth child, married Anson Cook and moved to Michigan, where their descendants still reside.

WHITMORE, PARLEY, was Dryden's early merchant, druggist, postmaster, justice of the peace, and scrivener. No History of the town would be complete which did not take notice of him, although our data concerning him are very incomplete. He came to Dryden early, was postmaster in 1812, and in his latter years here he lived on South street about where the I. P. Ferguson house now stands, and his store was on what is now the church corner. He seems to have been, financially, somewhat dependent upon Capt. Edward Griswold, who furnished, to a great extent, the capital stock invested in his business, his goods being brought by teams from Albany, on the return trip from marketing loads of pioneer produce. Those who knew him say that he was a valuable man in a new country, although he seems to have been too easy and indulgent to become a successful merchant. He was somewhat more intelligent and better acquainted with the rules of law and ways of business than the farmers about him. He administered justice among them very fairly and settled many of their disputes without suit, drawing up for them their contracts and other papers. Old Dryden village deeds and contracts are usually acknowledged before or witnessed by him. We are not able to learn that the town supported any lawyers in the Pioneer Period and still, strange as it may seem, (?) under such guidance as Squire Whitmore gave them, the people lived and prospered. He had two sons, Philo, who long ago married and settled in Corning, and George, who married and lived in Ithaca, but we are unable to learn of them now and it seems that we shall be obliged to confess that Dryden has lost trace of the race of one of its earliest citizens and benefactors, Esquire Whitmore.

CHAPTER XXIV.

DRYDEN VILLAGE IN THE DEVELOPMENT PERIOD.

Whitney's saw-mill, located on the site of the present Woolen Mill, must have called into existence the first use of water power in the village. Its origin was very early in the century and it remained in use as late as 1845, very nearly up to the time when the stone walls of the new Woolen Mill were erected in about the year 1850 by A. L. Bushnell. The origin of the Woolen Mill dates back to 1819 when the first "clothing works," as they were then called, were established by Benjamin Lacy. A flume from the saw-mill pond carried water to drive the carding-machine, fulling-mill and cloth dresser of those times, which constituted the "clothing works," the yarn being spun and the cloth woven on the hand wheels and looms of the neighboring farmers. Such cloth finishing machinery, used to finish the homemade cloth of that period, was quite frequently met with throughout the country. Ethel Barnum, who first came to Dryden with his brother-in-law, Samuel Williams, in the year 1818, and was the father of our Ralph W. Barnum, became the proprietor of this enterprise after the death of Mr. Lacy, but he died soon after, in 1823. It was not until after the property was sold to Bennett & Gillett, about 1844, that cloth was actually woven there, a brand of "sheep's gray" cloth being manufactured by them which had a local reputation for good quality among the farmers.

The village had no grist-mill until 1831, but Benjamin Bennett came down from Locke the year before and, after carefully looking over the ground and measuring the fall of water which could be obtained for power by combining the lake outlet with Virgil Creek, selected the site of the present stone mill, upon which a wooden building was then erected for a grist-mill. Edward Davidson, a brother-in-law to Bennett, became a partner with him in the enterprise. They purchased of

Cyrus Rummer the right to construct and maintain a raceway from Virgil Creek over his premises and sold to Tabor & Blakeslee a water privilege where the Kennedy tannery is now located. They were obliged to purchase of Michael Thomas and John C. and Garrett Lacy rights to conduct in a raceway the water from both streams across their premises, and thus the present grist-mill water privilege had its origin in 1831. Lyman Corbin afterwards purchased the property and in 1845 replaced the wooden grist-mill by building the present stone structure.

About the year 1824 there came from Middletown, Conn., Asa Phillips, a young man of some prominence in Dryden's history, whose brothers were Dr. John W. Phillips, of Dryden, and Dr. George W. Phillips, of Ithaca, both registered at Ithaca in the years 1820 and 1821 respectively. He first came as a school teacher, married in 1828 a niece of Daniel J. Shaw, who had been a Dryden merchant, and became postmaster under the appointment of President Andrew Jackson on March 3, 1831—a position which he held until his death, July 4, 1843. He was a partner with Moses Brown in the mercantile business and was an influential member of the M. E. church of the village, for which the first church edifice was erected in these times. His son Robert A. Phillips, now a real estate dealer of Washington, D. C., was born in Dryden village in 1833, and has contributed some interesting data derived from his residence here, which continued until 1850. He relates that within his recollection the United States mail was brought into Dryden Corners daily in a four-horse thoroughbrace coach, the driver blowing a long tin horn as he entered, loud enough so that it was heard throughout the whole settlement. The postage on a single letter was then eighteen pence ($18\frac{3}{4}$ cents). Eggs were then received at the store in exchange for goods at five cents per dozen, and butter at from ten to twelve cents per pound, but wheat was higher then than now, the average price being about $1.50 per bushel.

Amos Lewis, who lived east from the village, was a great horse dealer in those times, carefully matching and training horses for the New York market to which he took them, sometimes realizing as high as one thousand dollars for a pair of horses thus prepared by him.

In the year 1836 John Southworth built his brick house on North street and the original section of the brick block on the southwest of the Dryden four corners. In later years (about 1850) Hiram W. Sears, who came to Dryden from Madison county about 1845, extended the original brick store in front as seen in the accompanying cut produced from an old photograph of that time taken by Dr. F. S.

Howe, whose gallery was opposite, and later (about 1865) Merritt Baucus constructed the addition on the west side, the original building being less than one-third of its present dimensions. While his house and store were being built Mr. Southworth lived in the little house on East Main street now occupied by Will Mespell, where his first wife had died in 1830, and which it is suspected had been removed from the site of the brick store to make room for it; if so it is the oldest house now existing in town, being the first frame house built by Dr. Sheldon about 1800. This supposition is supported by the fact that it has two sets of sills under it, indicating that it has been moved to

THE OLD BRICK STORE.

its present location, and the additional fact that there never was any plastering on some of the walls and the partitions are made of wide, rough, but clear pine boards such as would naturally be very abundant when lumber first began to be manufactured. The roof, cornice and outside covering are doubtless of a later date.

In 1840 Joseph McGraw, Jr., built the brick store on the opposite, southeast corner known as the hardware block, where he for some years after carried on business as a merchant. At about this time two of the best dwellings in the village in those days were erected on Main street; one, now occupied by E. Banfield and formerly owned by Esquire Tyler, was built by Bradford Potter, and remains very much as it was originally built, and the other, the Dr. Montgomery house on the opposite side of the street, was built by a Mr. Putnam, and a third story has since been added. Both are said to have been raised on the same day, one with the use of liquor for the workmen, which was the established custom on those occasions, but at the other raising a supper was substituted, being the first effort to promote the cause of temperance which we are able to record in Dryden village. Thus it is seen that the building of the village was materially advanced in this period.

In these days there had come to the village from the farms on the neighboring hillsides, three young men who were all destined afterwards to become Dryden merchants, and one of them to take a leading part in the public affairs of the town and county. All were of humble but respectable parentage and all had been obliged to spend their boyhood at work upon the farms of the backwoods, so to speak, of a lumbering town, with very scanty means of education. But all were entering manhood possessed of excellent habits and had within them the elements of true gentlemen with all which that term implies, as was afterwards developed in their lives, but neither of them otherwise possessed any apparent advantage over the ordinary farmer boy who goes to town to seek his fortune. They were John McGraw and Jeremiah W. Dwight, both from the rather forbidding South Hill neighborhood, and Edwin Fitts from near Willow Glen. From small beginnings in their business careers the two former accumulated large fortunes, Mr. Dwight in his latter years adding political honors to his business success, while the latter, though no less a gentleman and esteemed and respected by all who knew him, lacked those sterner qualities which are essential to make up the successful man of business. It is said that Mr. McGraw commenced his business apprenticeship with the early Dryden merchant, Daniel J. Shaw, and afterwards served as a clerk in the brick store then kept by his older brother, Thomas McGraw, and John Southworth, and upon the death of Thomas, about 1838, he succeeded to his interest. Mr. Dwight, who was four years younger than McGraw, commenced his clerkship in the year 1838 in the store of Alanson Benjamin, which stood near where Charles Green's shop is now located, and soon afterwards became a partner with A. L. Bushnell in the brick store since known as the hardware block. The subsequent careers of these two Dryden boys will be treated of hereafter in special biographies. Mr. Fitts, who was between the others in age, after a clerkship with McGraw & Phillips (Joseph McGraw, Jr., and George W. Phillips) in the brick store, carried on business for himself in the Blodgett Block, and failed.

He was afterwards employed in the custom house in New York.

We would like to impress upon the ambitious young men of the rising generation that although the use of intoxicating drink and tobacco was much more universal then than now, the women as well as the men of those days freely enjoying the use of the pipe as well as the snuff-box, and a bottle or jug of "spirits," if in no larger quantities, being considered a necessity for frequent use in every household, neither of these young men ever indulged in the use of intoxicating beverages and the two of them most successful never acquired the habit of the use of tobacco in any form whatever.

At this stage of its development Dryden began to possess legal talent, the first full fledged attorney to reside here being Corydon Tyler, whose home and office were both located on Main street opposite to where is now the Grove Hotel. His office was a nice little building, still interesting to the writer, which was afterwards moved up-town and located on the Pratt corner, where it was used by Milo Goodrich in 1850 for his postoffice, on the exact spot to which the present postoffice has recently been removed, and is now, in its old age, annexed in the rear to the Pratt row of business places. Esquire Tyler seems to have been a man of character and ability; although from some anecdotes told of him we surmise that he was almost too aristocratic in his nature and too hasty in his temper to be able to adapt himself entirely to the requirements of his profession in a new country town. He had law students under him, one of whom was Harvey A. Dowe, a native of Dryden village, who afterward made Ithaca his home. Hiram Bouton was also a local attorney of considerable ability and tact, who took up his abode here as early as 1833, and held the office of justice of the peace as late as 1872.

Milo Goodrich, then a young man without reputation or fortune, located here with his wife soon after their marriage in 1844, renting rooms for house-keeping of Thomas Lewis in the building on Main street which has since been enlarged and converted into the Grove Hotel.

The local physicians of this period included John W. Phillips and Michael Phillips, registered in 1820; James W. Montgomery, and Daniel D. Page, in 1828; Isaac S. Briggs and Edwin P. Healey, in 1841. Dr. Page resided on what is known as the John C. Lacy corner, and there in his orchard, on the corner of Main and Mill streets, according to so good an authority on pomology as Charles Downing, originated the Bunker Hill apple, still greatly prized in this locality where it is well known.

Dr. Montgomery, who was a man of social and literary standing as well as of professional ability, having twice represented Dryden in the Legislature at Albany, as well as being an active member of the local reading and debating society of that time, lived where his son and daughter still reside on Main street.

Dr. Briggs was also a man of literary as well as of professional ability and an excellent citizen.

At or near the close of this period a terrible scourge, known here and remembered as the Dryden fever, swept over the new country and was particularly fatal in the village and its vicinity. It is now said to have been a species of malignant typhoid fever, developed perhaps by the rapid changes in the condition of the lowlands so recently deprived of their natural covering of foliage and not yet reclaimed by artificial drainage.

CHAPTER XXIV.

DRYDEN VILLAGE IN THE WAR PERIOD.

While the town and rural districts have been decreasing in population ever since 1836, the village of Dryden has had a slow but steady and continuous growth from the beginning of its settlement. Perhaps, however, at no time was that growth so rapid as at the commencement of this period. The building of the stone Woolen Mill by A. L. Bushnell at this time afforded a promise of future business prosperity to the village, but if its somewhat checkered career, involving at least two failures, and two fires, in one of which all of the combustible material was destroyed, could have been foreseen, the high hopes based upon its success would have vanished. Still in its periods of prosperity it has been a source of great advantage to the village, giving employment to a considerable number of inhabitants, and at no time has it been capable of yielding products of so much value as at present.

The building of the stone block in 1852-3 by Jeremiah W. Dwight was a great undertaking for a young business man in a small village, but under his efficient direction and management it has always been a success, affording a good and continuous income from the investment.

At about the same time P. M. Blodgett built next west of the stone block the three-story wooden building known as the Blodgett block, which was not so successful, and which was destroyed by fire about

1866. Stimulated by these improvements Col. Lewis Barton, who kept the old hotel opposite the stone block, enlarged it by adding a third story at this time, (1855.)

Col. Barton was a very popular landlord and a public spirited citizen, serving as president of the village in 1860, and as marshal on various occasions, one of which was a large temperance parade. He came to Dryden from Virgil early in this period and died in 1863. Among his descendants were Lieutenant Daniel W. Barton, who was killed in the battle of Spottsylvania, May 12, '64; Chas. W. Barton,

DRYDEN WOOLEN MILL.

whose surviving son, Daniel W., resides at Elizabeth, N. J.; Mrs. Mary E. Hiles, whose surviving son was recently engaged here in tracing out the annals of the Hiles family, and Lucy Ette Spiece, of Ardmore, Pa., who is now the only surviving child of Col. Lewis Barton.

The first newspaper published in the village came from the handpress of H. D. Rumsey, in 1856, and was first known as "Rumsey's Companion." After several changes in the name and ownership it was discontinued, within two years after it commenced publication. It had, however, fortunately for us, published and thus preserved under the title of the "Old Man in the Clouds," the series of articles which have been of great aid in the preservation of the early history of Dryden. In July, 1858, it was revived under the name of "The Dryden Weekly News," by Asahel Clapp, who continued its publication successfully until 1871, when he removed it to Ithaca where it is still published by his son as The Weekly Ithacan. Soon after, a new paper was published at Dryden village under the name of The Dryden Herald, which, after changing hands several times, was greatly enlarged and improved under the management and ownership of A. M. Ford and now under the proprietorship of his son, J. Giles Ford, is one of the most enterprising local papers to be found issued in a country village.

The war itself left but very little impress upon the village, and, as already stated in the town history, it was from a business point of view a time of unusual prosperity.

The advent of the Southern Central railroad in 1869 has already been referred to and produced no great immediate change in the affairs of the village. To the merchants the advantage of reduced freight rates and quicker transportation was offset by the ease and frequency with which their customers sought places in larger towns to do their trading. To the farmers, because it offered a better and nearer market, especially for such bulky articles of produce as potatoes and hay, the permanent benefit of the railroad has been considerable, and without railroad facilities to-day our condition would indeed be deplorable. A proposition was made when the Ithaca & Cortland railroad was being built that by raising the sum of twenty-five thousand dollars, the junction could be secured within the limits of Dryden village, and at almost any other time it would have been seriously entertained, but at this time the village had almost exhausted itself in the effort to secure the Southern Central, and affected with the reaction already being experienced from the decline of the unusual prosperity of the preceding years, the people were content to let the opportunity pass by.

The merchants of this period included J. W. Dwight & Co., (the company including E. S. Farnham, Isaac P. Ferguson, and A. F. Tanner) in the stone block, George L. Truesdell and William H. Sears, in the Exchange block, and Hiram W. Sears, Eli A. Spear, and later Merritt Baucus, in the brick block. Hiram W. Sears, who married a daughter of John Southworth, for a number of years carried on an extensive business in packing pork, buying wool and other mercantile enterprises.

Cyrus French developed a flourishing business in the hardware block. G. H. Sperry and Alanson Burlingame inaugurated the coal and lime business at the railroad station. H. F. Pierce conducted a moderate furniture and undertaking business, while Harrison Marvin and Otis Murdock conducted the boot and shoe business.

The Woolen Mill flourished in the hands of E. Rockwell, the tannery was greatly enlarged and improved by the Kennedy Brothers, and the grist-mill was managed by John Perrigo, assisted later by his son, Charles M.

The medical profession was reinforced during this time by the arrival of Dr. Wm. Fitch, from Virgil; and Dr. J. J. Montgomery succeeded to the practice of his father.

The old hotel passed from the proprietorship of Col. Lewis Barton to Deuel & Jagger, then to Jagger alone, and afterwards into the hands of Peter Mineah, whose co-partner at one time in the business was Ex-Sheriff John D. Benton, while James H. Cole developed the Grove Hotel after the Blodgett House was destroyed by fire. Mills Van Valkenburgh, Garry E. Chambers, W. W. Hare and Silas S. Montgomery developed into lawyers from law students in the office of Milo Goodrich.

A literary society, existing sometimes in the form of a reading circle and at others as a debating club, flourished in these days and many of the older citizens will remember with what earnestness and zeal Dr. Briggs, J. W. Dwight, T. J. McElheny, John C. Lacy, and many others maintained the affirmative or negative of numerous questions in debate at the old school house. Our attention has recently been called by one of the old members of this literary organization, to the beneficial results which were seen in the subsequent careers of some of its members, and a little reflection should awaken in us of the present generation an appreciation of such means of self-culture.

In the year 1857 Dryden village was incorporated, the population then being about four hundred and the corporate limits including 999¼ acres. The petition for incorporation was signed by Thomas J. McElheny, Isaac P. Ferguson, George Schenck, Lewis Barton, Freeman Stebbins, Hiram W. Sears, William W. Tanner, David J. Baker, N. L. Bates, Abraham Tanner, Jeremiah W. Dwight and fifty-eight others, and upon the vote taken upon the question of incorporation one hundred and twelve ballots were cast, of which seventy-eight were in the affirmative. In 1865 the village was re-incorporated under a special charter (chapter 320 of the laws of 1865) prepared with great care by Mills Van Valkenburgh, then an attorney residing in the village and afterward county judge.

HISTORY OF DRYDEN.

The first officers elected in 1857 were as follows: Trustees, David P. Goodhue, Rochester Marsh, William W. Tanner, John B. Sweetland, and Isaac H. Ford; assessors, Augustus H. Phillips, Orrin W. Wheeler, and John C. Lacy; collector and poundmaster, Godfrey Sharp; treasurer, Horace G. Fitts; clerk, Thomas J. McElheny.

The following table gives the names of the presidents and clerks of the village to the present time:

PRESIDENTS.

David P. Goodhue,	1857-8	Harrison Marvin,	1876
Freeman Stebbins,	1859	George E. Goodrich,	1877
Lewis Barton,	1860	J. E. McElheny,	1878
Freeman Stebbins,	1861	John H. Pratt,	1879-80
John C Lacy,	1862	John H. Kennedy,	1881
John Perrigo,	1863	Erastus H. Lord,	1882-3
John W. Phillips,	1864	D. R. Montgomery,	1884-5
Rochester Marsh,	1865-6	Albert J. Baker,	1886
Eli A. Spear,	1867	John H. Kennedy,	1887-8
D. Bartholomew,	1868	D. R. Montgomery,	1889-90
G. H. Washburn,	1869	George E. Goodrich,	1891-4
Alvin Cole,	1870	C. D. Williams,	1895
John H. Kennedy,	1871-2	George Sutfin,	1896
Rochester Marsh,	1873	E. Davis Allen,	1897
G. H. Sperry,	1874-5		

CLERKS.

T. J. McElheny,	1857	S. S. Montgomery,	1867
M. Van Valkenburgh,	1858	C. D. Bouton,	1868
Harrison Marvin,	1859	S. S. Montgomery,	1869-70
William H. Sears,	1860	George E. Goodrich,	1871-2
I. P. Ferguson,	1861	William E. Osmun,	1873-5
Mott L. Spear,	1862	George E. Goodrich,	1876
William H. Sears,	1863-4	W. H. Goodwin, Jr.,	1877-80
C. D. Bouton,	1865	L. D. Mallery,	1881-2
M. Van Valkenburgh,	1865	D. T. Wheeler,	1883-94
William H. Sears,	1866	E. D. Branch,	1895-97

CHAPTER XXVI.

DRYDEN VILLAGE IN THE MATURITY PERIOD.

Near the beginning of this time (1872 to 1897) the outlook for the business prosperity of the village was not encouraging. Asahel Clapp had moved his printing office and newspaper from Dryden to Ithaca;

Jackson Graves, who had maintained a flourishing select school, the old Dryden Academy, was about giving up the enterprise, and portions of the Blodgett lot where the large hotel building was burned in 1866 had not yet been rebuilt. In fact there had been and was for a few years to come but very little new building in the village; the time of unusual prosperity had passed and the future was unpromising.

In these dark times for the village, the first sign of returning confidence was seen in the establishment of a Union Graded Free School to take the place of the old District School and defunct Academy. The writer well remembers the meeting at the old school house on Main street, where D. Bartholomew now resides, at which this change was made which seemed to be a turning point in Dryden's future prosperity as a village. Nearly every voter was present at the meeting, including such conservative taxpayers as John Southworth, John C. Lacy and Alpheus F. Houpt, to oppose the measure, and the more confident, progressive citizens, such as Harrison Marvin, Merritt Baucus and Barnum S. Tanner, to favor it. The attendance was full, the discussion excited, and the result for a time doubtful. The successful issue of the matter was supposed to have been brought about by a little strategy practiced by Harrison Marvin, whose duty it was, as clerk of the district, to prepare a list of the voters who answered upon the call of their names to the question, "yes" or "no." Mr. Marvin placed at the head of the list those who were most likely to favor the measure and the responsive "yes" came so frequently at the beginning of the call that the opponents were disheartened and the doubtful voters joined the majority.

In the year 1876, under the leadership of Capt. Marvin as president, the Village Hall was built on South street at an expense of about sixteen hundred dollars, furnishing accomodations for a fire department and fire extinguishing apparatus as well as a lock-up, and a public hall above. A hand engine was purchased and cisterns were constructed in different parts of the village as resesvoirs of water for fire extinguishing purposes, but fortunately their practical utility was never very much put to the test.

The business failures during this period included John and Chas. M. Perrigo, at the Grist Mill; Sears & Baucus, at the Brick Store; the Rockwell Bros., at the Woolen Mill; and finally Kennedy Bros., at the Tannery, which, following in too quick succession, combined to depress further business enterprises.

In 1892 another crisis in the public affairs of the village was reached when the question of bonding the village for a gravity system of waterworks was submitted to the taxpayers, who, after considerable discussion and much opposition on the part of the more conservative element, decided by a majority of twelve upon a full vote, to issue the bonds and undertake the work, which was completed in the two years following. The system was put in at an expense of about twenty-five thousand dollars, and has since had one practical test in extinguishing a fire under full headway in the third story of the Woolen Mill, and it is now believed that this important step in the progress of the village, supplying excellent water permanently for all purposes, although involving a considerable expense for a small village, will never be regretted.

PARK AND M. E. CHURCH.

Stimulated by this enterprise and by an offer on the part of a former citizen, Hon. Andrew Albright, of Newark, N. J., to present to the village an elaborate ornamental fountain as a memorial to his parents, who were early residents of the town, upon the condition that citizens would provide for the removal of the church sheds which then occupied a part of the village "green" and prepare a suitable foundation and surroundings for such a fountain, this improvement was also undertaken, and at an expense of upwards of fifteen hundred dollars, mostly provided by voluntary contributions, additional land was purchased to furnish sites for the sheds of both church organizations, which were then removed to the rear; the "green" was enlarged and graded so as to be worthy to be called the village "park," and the fountain was accepted and connected with the village system of waterworks.

About the same time another public enterprise, designed to provide a suitable hall for public meetings and entertainments, was instituted by the citizens under the leadership of John W. Dwight, who was the most liberal contributor and most efficient promoter and manager of the undertaking. A stock company was organized under the name of the Dryden Opera House Co., and a building erected on the new Library street in the year 1893 at an expense of about three thousand five hundred dollars, which does credit to the village and to those who contributed the stock as a public benefit, not expecting any immediate dividends on the stock as an investment.

An effort was also made at this time to revive the manufacturing industry at the Woolen Mill, which had been idle for a number of years, and Hugo Dolge, whose brother, Alfred Dolge, built up the manufacturing interests in Herkimer county, was induced to locate here by a loan of five thousand dollars, contributed equally by the mill owners and citizens, to be used as capital in carrying on the business. In spite of the business depression which has paralyzed almost all manufacturing concerns during the past two years, the mill has been put in much better condition than ever before and its products seem to be finding ready market, with prospects of increasing success as the times improve.

As a result of these efforts, in the year 1895 a dozen or more new houses were constructed in the village, as many as had been built in the dozen years preceding, and the prospects of Dryden as a flourishing country village were very much improved.

The building of the Southworth Library at this time will be considered in a separate chapter.

The thorough and systematic lighting of the streets is a public improvement recently inaugurated by the board of village officers, which is already much appreciated and completes our list in the review of recent public improvements of the village.

As business developments of this period in our village worthy of note here, we should mention the prosperous marble and granite works of Williams & Bower and the furniture business of the French Bros., both originating in a small way and now much exceeding similar concerns in most country towns. The grocery business, as conducted by the Baker Bros., in the stone block, will compare favorably in the variety and quality of its stock with any similar concern in the county.

The medical fraternity of the village has been reinforced in these later years by Doctors E. Davis Allen, Frank S. Jennings, and Mary L. Briggs, while the lawyers consist of George E. Monroe, George E. Goodrich, and L. D. Mallery, Esquire J. Dolph Ross officiating as town and village magistrate.

Mention should here be made of the Dryden Springs Sanitarium, built up and conducted by Miss S. S. Nivison, M. D., during the last half of the Century Period, just outside of the village limits. A hotel building was first erected on this site early in the forties by Uncle Thomas Lewis and by him rented to different parties who conducted it as a hotel and water cure. The medicinal spring waters which were here developed or discovered early in the century by the Lacy Brothers while prospecting for salt, have always been esteemed and made use of by the people of the community and have recently been carefully analyzed for Dr. Nivison with the following results:

MAGNETIC SPRING.

Total solids, 11.5 grains per gallon.

Residue consists of Lime, Soda, Patassium, trace of Iron—as Sulphates and Carbonates.

Carbon Dioxide free and combined, 13.00 grains per gallon.

Lithia, traces.

SULPHUR SPRING.

Total solids, 22.00 grains per gallon.

Residue consists of Lime, Soda, Magnesia, Iron in form of Carbonates and Sulphates, also Chlorides.

Carbon Dioxide free and combined, 6.5 grains per gallon.

Calcium Carbonate, 5.8 grains per gallon.

Hydrochloric Acid combined, 4.0 grains per gallon.

Silica, 0.55 grains per gallon.

Lithia, traces.

As in reviewing the town, so in closing the village history we cannot but compare some of the present conditions with those of the earlier times.

For instance the shoemakers of one hundred years ago were "traveling men," not "drummers," as the term "traveling men" would now imply, but men who with their kit of shoemaking tools went about from house to house in the new settlements, making up the farmers' leather into footwear for the family, enough to last for a year, when the shoemaker would again visit them. T. S. Deuel, whose grandfather, Reuben Deuel, was one of these traveling shoemakers, has the old account book of his ancestor, in which are charged in shillings and pence the work which he did in each family as he visited them one hundred years ago. Fifty years ago instead of traveling shoemakers the work was done in the shop in the village, and W. S. Moffat used to keep in his shop on East Main street at least half a dozen men constantly employed in making boots and shoes to order, and every person who was about to need some footwear was required first to go to the shop and have his foot measured. All is now changed and the boots and shoes of to-day are nearly all manufactured in the large cities and distributed through the traveling drummer and local salesman.

Dryden village to-day supports two excellent meat markets, supplied with refrigerators, power meat choppers propelled by motors connected with the village system of waterworks, and furnished with all other modern conveniences in that line. Nearly fifty years ago old Uncle John Wilder and Godfrey Sharp undertook to carry on a meat market in the basement of the stone block, promising to butcher and furnish fresh meat of some kind during certain days of each week, but, as we remember it, the enterprise was given up as a bad job, until it was afterwards successfully revived by Levi Messenger. The difficulty in those days with the meat market was that everybody was supplied with salt beef and pork which was laid down in barrels for each family in the fall or early winter as regularly as we now provide potatoes for the year, and fresh meat was a luxury not often thought of.

The first permanent barber to locate in Dryden was Wm. H. Lester, who, when a young man twenty years of age, opened a shop July 1, 1858, in the southeast room of Barton's Hotel. Prior to that time Dryden men either shaved themselves or let their beards grow in the natural way, as was quite often done. Now the village supports two very creditable barber shops with four men constantly employed.

Thus we are able to see how times have changed with us during the past hundred years.

MAIN STREET, DRYDEN.

RYDEN VILLAGE.

13 Mrs. C. Rummer,
19 E. E. Bannell.

Wall Street.
1 J. D. Ross,
4 C. J. Bailey,
8 J. D. Ross.

Lewis Street.
1 D. D. Edwards,
2 Abram Hutchings,
4 George Hart,
5 Fred Sherwood,
6 D. R. Montgomery,
7 D. Bartholomew,
8 D. C. McGregor,
10 A. C. Rockefeller,
15 Wm. W. Ellas,
19 Joseph Basil,
20 Abram Hunter,
23 Mrs. Sidney Sorrell,
24 James Graham,
25 29, M. Tripp,
32 R. H. Newsome,
40 Mrs. John Hunter.

Mill Street.
2 H. A. Lormor,
4 Arnold Hopkins,
6 O. Coleman,
7 George Bradley,
8 Barney Tyler,
10 Mrs. Harriet Carpenter,
14 I. D. Jenks,
18 E. D. Branch,
26 Dryden Stone Mill,
28 Guy Chew,
29 A. Marsh,
34 Chas. Lormor.

Lake Street.
9 John McKeon,
11 I. P. Ferguson estate,
13 Edward Swart,
17 Hiram Pugsley,
21 John Swart,
22 John Swart, cidermill,
25 John Goodwin,
40 David O'Dell,
48 J. H. Kennedy,
50 P. E. Kennedy,
52 Dryden Tannery.

Montgomery Street.
5 Wm. Wheeler,
11 John Sandwick.

James Street.
8 D. S. Messenger,
12 Thomas Tamlin,
16 R. E. Stilwell,
21 W. Pond,
25 B. Bishop estate,
31 Charlie Ballard,
33 Carson Vunk,
35 A. P. Brown,
37 Irving Brown,
43 Wm. H. Moore.

South Street.
1 Weyant & Kingsbury, hardware,
3 Mrs. W. H. Moore,
5 W. H. Moore, shoes,
6 Wheeler & Co., storehouse,
7 W. H. Moore, residence,
8 Wheeler & Co., storehouse,
9 George Cole, residence,
10 M. Tyler, carriages,
12 Bailey & Ellison, bl'ksmiths
13 H. Marvin,
14 S. W. Daniels, shop,
15 Ellery Vunk,
16 Firemen's Hall,
18 Chas. Tanner,
19 Mrs. I. P. Ferguson,
21 Chas. Williams,
22 R. C. Rummer,
23 J. E. McElheny,
24 Wm. Tanner,
25 Geo. E. Goodrich,
26 Mrs. Chas. LaBarr,
27 Mrs. A. Hill,
28 James E. Lormor,
36 Mrs. Anna Stewart,
38 Mrs. A. Collings,
42 Truman Parker,
46 W. F. Miller,
47 Dr. Mary Briggs,
48 S. M. Stanton,
58 Henry Small,
64 F. & F. Caswell,
68 Mrs. Catharine Mellon,
70 Orris Church estate.

Miscellaneous.
a Frank Stout,
b J. B. Wilson,
c S. S. Nivison,
d Barney Weber,
e Daniel Lawson,
f Southworth estate,
g Depot,
h Milk Depot,
i Rockwell's Coal Yard,
j Chappuis' Coal Yard,
k Hart's Stock Yard,
p Old Griswold House.

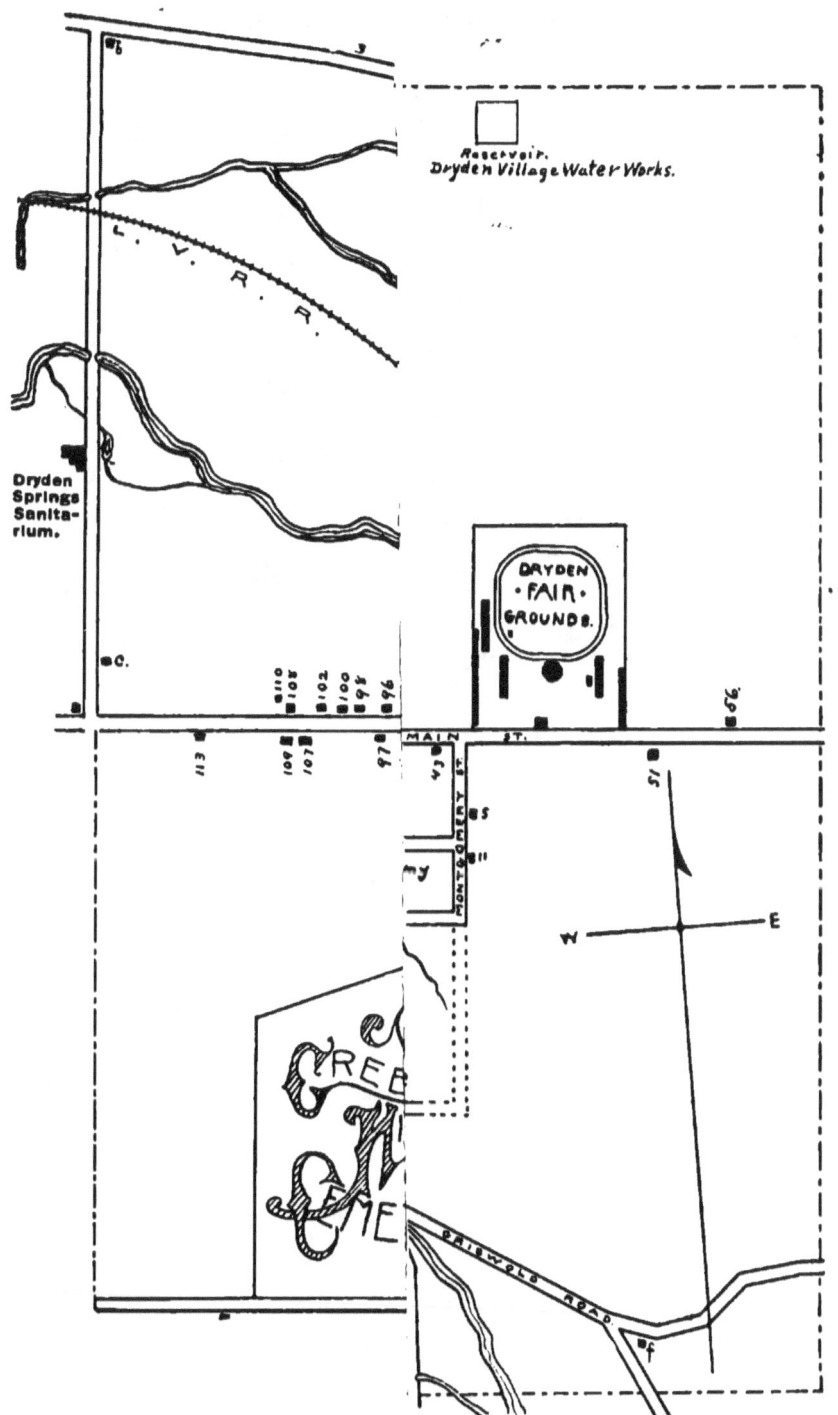

KEY TO THE MAP OF DRYDEN VILLAGE.

West Main Street.
1 D. T. Wheeler & Co., store
2 Post-office
3 W. E. Vunk, store
4 J. H. Pratt, harness
5 Wavle's Hotel
6 Wm. Mespell, market
8 J. H. Pratt, store
10 M. Little, market
12 W. H. Baker, grocery
14 L. A. Niver, barber
16 G. Rummer & Son, shoes
17 C. H. Seamau, grocery
18 J. B. Fulkerson, store
19 Vunk & Tanner, bl'ksmiths
20 Q. J. Hill, store
22 A. T. Niver, tailor
23 A. T. Niver, billiards
23 J. C. Lormore, clothing
23 J. G. Clark, drugs
25 W. W. Adams, hardware
26 J. G. Clark, residence
27 G. C. Sweet, undertaker
28 Library
29 Ira R. Boun, jewelry
31 Chas. F. Mason, jewelry
33 Henry Thomas, residence
34 D. McLachlan
36 R. L. Weaver
37 A. J. Baker
38 Lucien Weaver, drugs
39 P. S. Howe
40 Isabelle Lormior
41 J. B. Fulkerson
44 Dr. J. J. Montgomery, office
43 J. R. French
44 Dr. J. J. Montgomery
45 E. Banfield
46 Grove Hotel
53 Mrs. D. F. Van Vleet
54 L. D. Mallery
56 Chas. M. Perrigo
57 Misses S. & L. Tanner
59 D. S. Messenger
60 G. M. Rockwell
61 D. P. Bartholomew
63 G. C. Sweet
66 Mrs. M. L. Kevney
67 Mrs. Mary Hyde
68 Mrs. Abram Hutchings
70 L. T. Wheeler
71 Geo. W. Bailey
73 R. M. West
75 George Wickham
76 A. Bailey
77 Miss P. Smith
78 Henley Hunter
79 George W. Sutfin

80 J. D. Ross
81 Hugo Polge
82 Hugo Polge, residence
83 Mrs. M. A. Deno
84, 85, 86 Hugo Polge
87, 89, 91, 93 Dryden Woolen Mill
88 Hugo Polge, woolen mill office
90 W. W. King, planing mill
93 A. Houpt estate
96 W. W. King
97 George F. Monroe
98 Mrs. Mary Swift
100 Horace Pitts
102 Casper Sherwood
107 Robert Schutt
108 Sylvester Foster
109 Charles Meade
110 Miss S. S. Nivison
113 T. S. Deuel

East Main Street.
1 Weyant & Kingsbury, hardware
7 M. E. Church
5 Porter & Sutfin, und'takers
7 French Bros., furniture
9 Mrs. R. A. Dwight
11 H. H. Ferguson
13 Chapman Strong
15 Wm. Kespell
16 John Muncey
21 A. Burlingame estate
23 Frank Hutchinson
24 Dr. E. D. Allen
26 Dr. E. D. Allen, office
28 C. H. Seamans
30 C. H. Seamans, bl'ksmith
33 B. R. Bower
34 Benjamin Griswold
39 Mrs. Wm. Dupee
43 Mrs Caroline Beattie
51 Harrison Manning
56 James Steele

North Street.
2 Will H Silcox, photo
4 Williams & Bower, marble
6 J. H. Pratt
10 J. H. Pratt
11 Presbyterian Church
14 M. C. Loomis
16 Mrs. Fred Ward
18 Mrs. Lovina Lord
21 Southworth estate
22 A. M. Clark
24 A. M. Clark
32 M. P. Pratt

54 A. D. Burlingame
35 Mrs. Mary Burlingame

Elm Street.
4 { J. Giles Ford,
  { Wm. A. Glazier
8 Geo. P. Hatch
10 John Tripp
12 Mrs. Martha Tyler
31 Dryden Herald

Library Street.
4 Opera House
6 John Ellis
7 R. P. Chappuis
8 Dr. F. S. Jennings
14 Mrs. Geo. Pratt

George Street
1 Chas. Burghardt
2 John D. Lamont
4 Merritt Tyler
5 Lyman Smith
8 H. Witty
17 Mrs. F. Dutcher
21 George Calver

Union Street.
1 Charles Williams
2 J. C. Lormore
3 E. Williams
4 J. D. Lamont
5 C. J. Sperry
6 Aaron Albright
7 Mrs. Mary Tucker
8 Darius Givens
9 W. H. Sandwick
10 Presbyterian parsonage
14 Mrs. A. Lombard

Pleasant Street.
1 G. J. Sweetland
3 J. A. O'Field
4 O. H. Sperry
5 John Carpenter
6 A. J. Fortner
7 Miss A. Mineah
8 Mrs. S. Bellard
10 Delos Mahan
11 Miss Anna Dunley
14 Scott estate

Rochester Street.
1 Mrs. Abram Hutchings
3 C. J. Sperry
5 Hubbard Lask
7 J. C. Vanderhoef
10 W. W. French
11 Leander Hutchings

13 Mrs. C. Rummer
19 E. E. Bassell

Wall Street.
1 J. D. Ross
4 C. J. Bailey
8 J. D. Ross

Lewis Street.
1 D. D. Edwards
3 Abram Hutchings
4 George Hart
5 Fred Sherwood
7 D. R. Montgomery
7 D. Bartholomew
8 D. C. McGregor
10 A. C. Rockefeller
15 Wm. W. Ellis
19 Joseph Basil
20 Abram Hunter
21 Mrs. Sidney Sorrell
22 James Graham
23 29, M. Tripp
33 R. H. Newsome
40 Mrs. John Hunter

Mill Street.
2 H. A. Lormor
4 Arnold Hopkins
6 O. Coleman
7 George Bradley
9 Barney Tyler
10 Mrs. Harriet Carpenter
14 I. D. Jenks
18 R. D. Branch
20 Dryden Stone Mill
28 Guy Chew
29 A. Marsh
34 Chas. Lormor

Lake Street.
9 John McKeon
11 P. Ferguson estate
13 Edward Swart
17 Hiram Pugsley
21 John Swart
22 John Swart, cidermill
25 John Goodwin
29 David O'Del
31 J. H. Kennedy
30 F. R. Kennedy
52 Dryden Tannery

Montgomery Street.
5 Wm. Wheeler
11 John Sandwick

James Street.
8 D. S. Messenger
12 Thomas Tamlin
16 R. E. Stilwell

21 W. Pond
25 R. Bishop estate
31 Charlie Ballard
32 Carson Vunk
35 A. F. Brown
37 Irving Brown
43 Wm. H. Moore

South Street.
1 Weyant & Kingsbury, hardware
3 Mrs. W. H. Moore
5 W. H. Moore, shoes
7 Wheeler & Co., storehouse
7 W. H. Moore, residence
8 Wheeler & Co., storehouse
9 George Cole, residence
10 M. Tyler, carriages
12 Bailey & Ellison, bl'ksmiths
13 H. Marvin
14 S. W. Daniels, shop
15 Ellery Vunk
16 Firemen's Hall
18 Chas. Tanner
19 Mrs. L. P. Ferguson
21 Chas. Williams
22 R. C. Rummer
23 E. McElheny
24 Wm. Tanner
25 Geo. E. Goodrich
26 Mrs. Chas. LaBarr
27 Mrs. A. Hill
28 James E. Lormor
29 Mrs. Anna Stewart
38 Mrs. A. Collings
42 Truman Parker
46 W. F. Miller
47 Dr. Mary Briggs
48 S. M. Stanton
58 Henry Small
64 F. & P. Caswell
66 Mrs. Catharine Mellon
70 Orvis Church estate

Miscellaneous.
a Frank Stont
b J. B. Wilson
c S. S. Nivison
d Barney Weiher
e Daniel Lawson
f Southworth estate
g Depot
h Milk Depot
i Rockwell's Coal Yard
j Chappuis' Coal Yard
k Hart's Stock Yard
p Old Griswold House

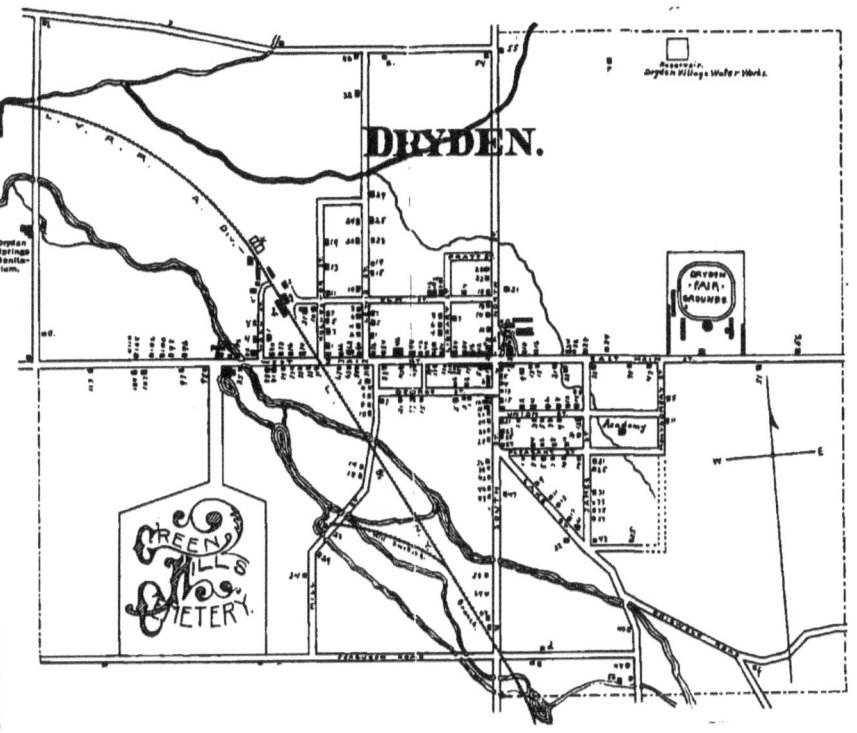

CHAPTER XXVII.

ANECDOTES OF DRYDEN VILLAGE.

It was the privilege of the writer some years ago to spend an evening in a small company of former Dryden men at Fargo, North Dakota, with John Benton, formerly sheriff of Cortland county, and afterwards for a few years one of the proprietors of the Dryden Hotel as a partner with Peter Mineah. On that evening Mr. Benton entertained the company very agreeably by telling Dryden stories, which he can do to perfection, and after keeping his hearers in convulsions of laughter for an hour, he concluded by saying that there was no place on earth where he had ever been which furnished such a fund of anecdotes as Dryden, and among his many excellent characters for humorous stories he placed John Tucker, of Dryden, with his innocent smile and stammering tongue, head and shoulders above all others. If my readers could have listened to the genial ex-sheriff on the evening in question while he was giving his recollections of some of the humorous incidents of his sojourn in Dryden village, I think they would readily accede to the truth of his conclusions.

It is designed in this chapter briefly to give a very few samples of some of the true anecdotes which are connected with the history of Dryden village.

The first one concerns Parley Whitmore, who, as we have seen, was the postmaster and justice of the peace located at the "Corners" in pioneer times. Among the numerous attendants at his court upon the occasion in question were the two McKee brothers, James and Robert, who lived north of the village and who are the ancestors of many of the present inhabitants of Dryden. In some way these two brothers were very much displeased with something which occurred before the justice at this time and they had not much ability or disposition to conceal their displeasure. So excited did Jimmy become that in giving vent to his feelings upon the subject he used profane language in the very presence of the court. This could not be tolerated or overlooked, and the justice arraigned the culprit on the spot, imposing a fine of one dollar upon Jimmy for contempt of court. This produced quiet in the court room, but the two brothers were more angry than ever, fairly ready to burst with suppressed indignation, when Robert, who had the most money but who was the less fluent in his speech of the two, stepped forward and laid down on the table before the court one dollar in payment of the fine, and started to put up his pocket-book; but upon second thought he opened it again, taking out this time a five-dollar bill which he plumped down before the court and turned triumphantly to his brother, saying, "Now, Jimmy, swear your fill."

It was before the same Justice Whitmore that at one time in the early days of Dryden a rather pompous individual whom we will call Mr. T., stepped up in the presence of a crowd of spectators and asked, "'Squire how much will it cost me to knock down Jim Beam?" Justice Whitmore, who seems to have had some common sense as well as a knowledge of the rules of justice, answered rather officiously somewhat as follows; "It would be improper, Mr. T., for me to fix in advance the penalty for such an offense, but I will say that in my judgment an attempt on your part to commit the crime which you mention would cost you among other things a good threshing."

As illustrating the state of school discipline in our early times, which we are happy to be able to say has sustained some improvement since then, we relate an incident which occurred in the old schoolhouse on Mill street, which was located where the John Gress house now stands. A "man" teacher was commonly employed in the winter term, whose duty it was to train the older boys, many of whom could attend only in the winter season, and lucky indeed was the teacher who was not turned out of the schoolhouse before the first warm days of spring called them back to their work on the farm.

One winter over fifty years ago Nehemiah Curtis was the name of the teacher, and so faithful had been his work and so gentlemanly his bearing that all the scholars liked him and the last day of school approached without any serious difficulty. In view of the fact it was decided to have some special exercises upon the last day and the scholars on the day before trimmed up the school room with evergreens procured from the woods, which were then not far away. But on the morning in question when the teacher and pupils, dressed in their best apparel for the occasion, entered the schoolhouse they were met at the door by two cows, one belonging to Abraham Tanner and the other to James Patterson, which had been locked in over night and had browsed and trampled down the trimmings and mussed up the school room generally. The good-natured teacher's high hopes of ending the term prosperously were thus suddenly crushed and he was about to give up in disgust when the better disposed pupils offered to take hold and repair the damage so far as possible and clean out the school room for the exercises, which they did. Of course no one knew who the guilty culprits were who caused the mischief, although great efforts were made at the time to ascertain, but one of our present peace officers of the town now admits that he then persuaded his "best girl" to falsely represent to his inquiring parents that he spent the evening in question with her in order to shield him from the suspicion of having been among those who introduced the cows into the schoolhouse.

One short story must be told of John Tucker as a sample of his ready wit and stammering tongue, although we cannot undertake to convey to the reader who has not seen it an adequate conception of the innocent smile which lights up his countenance upon these occasions. The incident which we shall attempt to relate has in its repetition been associated with different individuals, which is immaterial, for in all versions of it the part of the essential character, John, is the same. For the benefit of those readers who are not acquainted with him it must be stated that John is a great trapper and his favorite game is the skunk. He is thoroughly acquainted with the haunts and habits of these peculiar animals and derives no little revenue annually from the sale of their pelts which he thus collects and which are quite valuable for fur.

One day in the spring when John was looking over his stock of skins in company with a friend, his next neighbor, Mrs. Dupee, happened out at the back door near where they were and inquired incidentally of John how many skunks he had caught that season, to which he replied, "Twenty." She went in-doors and a few minutes later her husband, William Dupee, came along and he asked John how many skunks he had caught that season, to which he readily replied, "F-f-forty-five." After William had disappeared his friend remonstrated with John for showing such disregard for the truth and giving such contradictory statements concerning the result of his winter's trapping, when he replied with an innocent smile on his face, "Why, B-b-ill can stand more s-s-skunks than she can!"

CHAPTER XXVIII.

SCHOOLS, CHURCHES, AND CEMETERIES OF DRYDEN VILLAGE.

As we have already seen, the pioneer log cabin of the township, after it had ceased to be used as a place of habitation by Amos Sweet, became its first schoolhouse in the year 1804, with Daniel Lacy serving in it as the first schoolmaster of Dryden. Imagine the children of the pioneers who first settled about "Dryden Corners" coming together to receive their first school education and congregating in a room ten feet square inside, with one door and one window without sash or glass, and no stove, but a fire-place made of a few hardhead stones placed together, and no chimney but a hole in the roof for the smoke to pass out. The next teacher at the "Corners," of which we have any note, was Charles Grinnell, who came from Columbia county early in the century and taught school, boarding with John Southworth before he built his brick house in 1836. But the first account which we are able to give of the schoolhouses of the village brings us down to near the middle of the century, when there were two public school buildings, one being a wood-colored house on South street where the Marvin house is now located and the other a red schoolhouse on Mill street, which has since been remodeled where it stood, into what is now known as the John Gress house.

There was also another school building which stood on the site now occupied by the residence of Charles Perrigo, on the corner of Main and Lewis streets, but this accommodated a private school and here the celebrated criminal, Ruloff, in the year 1842, served as a teacher for a short time, and here, over fifty years ago, a very capable teacher by the name of Burhans trained the youth of the village.

This building had a belfrey and bell but was afterward used as a shop and was finally destroyed by fire. About the year 1850 a new union school house was built, taking the place of the others, on the lot now occupied by Daniel Bartholomew as a residence. The upright part of this building, which was an imposing edifice at the time, now serves as the plaster and lime storehouse of G. M. Rockwell, near the railroad depot, and one of its wings is the Wall house on Wall street. Here various principals of the district school ably presided and succeeded each other, including a Mr. Starr, Mills Van Valkenburgh and finally George E. Monroe, Esq., who continued to teach there until the Union Free School District was organized in 1872.

About the year 1860 Jackson Graves from Pottsville, Pa., who had then recently married Mary J. Bishop, who was a very capable and an excellent Dryden teacher, purchased the site of the present public school property in Dryden village, and erected the present academy building, which was known as the Dryden Seminary, conducting it as a private school enterprise under their efficient management for about ten years, when the property was purchased by the school district and has since been maintained as a public Union Free School and Academy. Prof. Graves had in the meantime been elected School

Commissioner of the second district of Tompkins county, and has since resided in the town of Danby, his first wife having died in 1892. Mr. and Mrs. Graves will long be remembered by the present generation of Dryden village as faithful and efficient teachers.

Since the establishment of the Union Free School the standard of educational advantages in the village has not been allowed to fall, and many excellent teachers have served the district, including Charles A. Fowler, afterwards principal of the Binghamton city schools, Francis J. Cheney, Ph. D., now principal of the Normal School at Cortland, and Herbert M. Lovell, since principal of the Elmira Academy and now an attorney and counselor of that city. Dr. Wm. Fitch, George E. Goodrich and George E. Monroe have successively served as presidents of the Board of Education.

THE PRESBYTERIAN CHURCH.

The First Presbyterian society of Dryden was organized February 17th, 1808, with the following charter members: John Terpenning, Juliana Terpenning, James Wood, Sarah Wood, Stephen Myrch, Rebecca Myrch, Benjamin Simons, Isabel Simons, Derick Sutfin, Elizabeth Topping, Abram Griswold, Asenath Griswold and Jerusha Taylor. The first services were held at the home of Mr. Serren H. Jagger, a shoemaker in Dryden village, and in the barns of Thomas Southworth and Elias W. Cady at Willow Glen. The church edifice was commenced in 1819 and completed in 1824 under great difficulties.

It was extensively repaired in 1847 and again in 1861, and with some recent improvements now appears as represented in the accompanying view. In the year 1851 a town clock was purchased by subscription and placed in the tower of this building and we are, fortunately, able to give from the old suscription paper the names of the subscribers and amounts contributed for that purpose, which are as follows:

Thomas Lewis,	$4 00	Hiram Bouton,	$2 00	Timothy Cross,	$ 50
John C. Lacy,	3 00	D. J. Baker,	3 00	Lewis Barton,	4 00
Enos Wheeler,	5 00	W. S. Moffat,	1 50	Wm. Ercanbrack,	50
Bowen Sweetland,	2 00	Joseph McGraw,	1 00	Darius Givens,	1 50
Daken & Stebbins,	2 00	Michael Butts,	2 00	Wm. H. Miller,	2 00
Thomas Jameson,	3 50	Geo. Truesdell,	1 00	T. Burr,	1 00
Briggs & Goodyear,	1 00	Orrin Wheeler,	1 00	Isaac Ferguson,	1 00
Collin Robinson,	2 00	D. P. Goodhue,	50	J. W. Montgomery	3 00
John Southworth,	10 00	G. D. Pratt,	4 00	Pardon Tabor,	5 00
Jacob Stickles,	1 00	Otis Murdock,	1 00	Abram Emory,	1 00
S. Cleveland,	1 00	Wm. Hazlett,	1 00	P. M. Blodgett,	5 00
Ralph Barnum,	1 00	L. J. L. Bates,	1 00	A. Foster,	10 00
Wm. Holmes,	2 00	Amos Lewis,	2 00	L. B. Corbin,	4 00
H. H. Ferguson,	1 00	A. H. Phillips,	1 00	J. H. Hurd,	3 00
Milo Goodrich,	1 00	Willet Ellis,	2 00	E. A. Givens,	1 00
S. Goddard,	1 00	J. W. Dwight,	2 00	A. L. Bushnell,	5 00
Leonard Griswold,	50	I. P. Ferguson,	1 00	Wm. F. Tanner,	1 00
Bradford Kennedy,	1 00	John Ercanbrack	1 00	S. S. Bunnel,	2 00
Joel Bishop,	3 00	Gordon Johnson,	1 00	S. & C. Bradshaw,	2 00
Abraham Tanner,	1 00	Stickle Hamblin,	50	Gardner West,	50
B. W. Squires,	2 00	Stephen Emory,	1 00	S. T. Wilson,	2 00
Wyatt Allen,	2 00	D. Bartholomew,	1 00	Jesse Givens,	2 00
John R. Lacy,	3 00	H. C. Beach,	1 00	Jacob Prame,	1 00

We are thus able to give the names of the public spirited citizens who resided in and about Dryden village about fifty years ago, recalling to the memory of old residents many familiar faces, only a very few of which can be seen among us to-day.

The list of the ministers who have succeeded each other at this church is also here given and is as follows:

Nathan B. Darrow,	Luther Clark,	Geo. R. Smith,
William Williston,	George W. Pruden,	Anson G. Chester,
Joshua Lane,	H. P. Crozier,	Charles Ray,
Timothy Tuttle,	R. S. Eggleston,	E. W. Root,
William Miller,	F. Hendricks,	G. H. Dunning,
Samuel Parker,	Charles Kidder,	C. O. Hanmer,
Elnathan Walker,	A. V. H. Powell,	G. V. Reichel,
Reuben Hurd,	W. G. Hubbard,	Fred L. Hiller,
Isaac Patterson,	A. McDougall,	Oliver T. Mather.
Samuel Robertson,	J. V. C. Nellis,	

DRYDEN VILLAGE. 111

A Methodist Episcopal class was first organized at Dryden Corners about the year 1816, with Selden Marvin, Edward Hunting, and Abraham Tanner among the original members. They had no church building until about 1832 when a church society was organized with the following charter members:

Parley Whitmore,	Selden Marvin,	Asa Phillips,
J. W. Montgomery,	Robert Dier,	George Carr,
Daniel Godfrey,	M. C. Brown,	Erastus Bement,
Philo Godfrey,	Elias Ferguson,	Abraham Tanner,
Daniel Coleman,	Andrew Guile,	Pardon Tabor.

Their church edifice erected in 1832 was destroyed by fire in 1873, while being repaired and enlarged, and the present building, a view of which is given on page 10, was erected in the following year at an expense of about eleven thousand dollars.

The clergymen who have supplied this church are as follows:

J. T. Peck,	O. M. McDowell,	David Keppel,
Wm. Bailey,	S. B. Porter,	I. Harris,
M. Westcott,	O. Hesler,	James Gutsell,
P. R. Kinne,	E. Owen,	W. H. Goodwin, L. L. D.
M. Adams,	L. D. Tryon,	M. S. Wells,
M. W. Rundell,	S. Minier,	David Keppel,
C. W. Harris,	M. M. Tooke,	Robert Townsend,
W. H. Pearne,	E. G. Curtis,	S. S. Barter,
H. E. Luther,	T. D. Wire,	James R. Drake,
D. Lamkins,	J. H. Barnard,	R. N. Leake,
George Parsons,	E. Owen,	J. H. Ross,
W. W. Rundell,	B. Shove,	A. C. Willey,
A. Cross,	L. Hartsough,	Worth M. Tippy,
—— Hagar,	A. L. Lusk,	J. W. Terry,
Wm. C. Cobb,	Selah Stocking,	George Britten,
C. W. Harris,	H. Meeker,	C. W. Walker.

The first death in Dryden village was probably of some member of the family of Amos Sweet, all of whom are said to be buried in the grounds opposite to the Dryden Springs Sanitarium. Tradition informs us that a grave-yard was early started near the corner of Main and Mill streets and some evidence of this fact was recently found when the village water pipes were being laid in that locality. The early habit of using private family burying grounds has already been referred to and the first public ground of which we have any record in the village was located on the gravel knoll west of the fair-grounds. How early this site was in use we are unable to determine, but a deed from Abram Griswold to the Trustees of the First Presbyterian Society of Dryden of an acre of land in this locality bears date February 10, 1830, and contains this commendable statement from the grantor: "The true intent and meaning of this indenture of said piece of land is that all sects and denominations have the privilege of burying their dead and using the same as a burying ground." Probably the use of this site as a burial ground for the inhabitants of the village antedated this public dedication of it for that purpose. More land was afterwards added but no incorporation was perfected, and the locality is now neglected and abandoned as a cemetery, and has grown up to a second wilderness; some graves marked by dilapidated stones remain, while numerous pit-holes here and there show where the remains of others have been taken up to be removed to more modern cemeteries. A visit to this locality, where many of the pioneers of Dryden still lie buried, will afford striking suggestions of the brevity of human life and of the rapidity with which after death our mortal remains will be absorbed by mother earth, and the places which once knew us will know us no more. The gravel from the parts of this knoll which have not been used for burial purposes is now being rapidly removed for filling and grading purposes and the existence of a burial place there is likely to be entirely forgotten.

In the year 1863 the people of the village united to organize a cemetery association and to purchase a new site for a permanent cemetery. The Green Hills cemetery is the result, located in the southwest section of the village and comprising nearly fifty acres of land, only a small part of which has yet been used for burial purposes. The site is upon the highest ground in the corporate limits of the village, so that the home of the dead commands a beautiful view of the homes and business places of the living. The association has been somewhat crippled in its operations by a considerable indebtedness incurred in the purchase of its extensive grounds, but this debt is now being paid off and great improvements have been made in opening and grading its main avenue, to the site, which is remarkably adapted by nature for this purpose and which will in time be so improved as to be one of the most commodious and beautiful cemeteries to be found in a country village.

CHAPTER XXIX.

THE SOUTHWORTH LIBRARY.

JENNIE McGRAW-FISKE.

If any one could have claimed to unite in her veins the flow of the blue blood of Dryden pioneer aristocracy, that person was Jennie McGraw-Fiske. Her great-grandfather was Judge Ellis, " King of Dryden " in its early years. Her grandfather was John Southworth, Dryden's millionaire farmer, while her father was John McGraw, Dryden's barefooted farmer boy in 1827, who soon after commenced his business career as a clerk in a Dryden store at eight dollars per month, becoming later a Dryden merchant, and after a life of great business activity and success died possessed of an estate worth two millions.

She was born in the house on North street in Dryden village now owned and occupied by Mrs. E. H. Lord, nearly opposite to the Southworth homestead, in September, 1840. Her mother died and her father moved from Dryden before she was ten years of age. She was educated at Canandaigua and at a school in Westchester county. Her health being always delicate, she was encouraged to gratify her taste for foreign travel, which she did, first visiting Europe when about twenty years of age, and several times afterwards.

Of her marriage to Prof. Willard Fiske in 1880 and her death in the following year, which was subsequently followed by the celebrated litigation as the result of which the bequest of the bulk of her estate to Cornell University was defeated, we need not speak here at length.

In the distribution of the estate of her grandfather, John Southworth, she received a share as representing her deceased mother, and it seems to have been her desire to return to Dryden village a substantial memorial to her grandfather out of this portion of her estate, for in her will she makes the following provision:

"I give and bequeath unto Jeremiah W. Dwight, John E. McElheny and Dr. J. J. Montgomery, all of Dryden, N. Y., the sum of thirty thousand dollars, in trust, for the following uses and purposes, to wit: I desire that they, with such associates as they may select, shall procure, under the laws of the State of New York, a corporation or association to be organized at Dryden aforesaid under the name of The Southworth Library Association, the object and purpose whereof shall be the building, support and maintenance of a public library in the said village of Dryden; that said trustees shall transfer said trust funds to said association upon the trust and condition that not more than fifteen thousand dollars of said sum shall be expended in real estate, buildings and furniture, and that the remainder shall constitute a fund to be invested and the interest or income thereof to be applied to the purchase of books and other necessary expenses of said association, excluding, however, salaries of officers and pay of servants thereof.

"If this purpose be not accomplished within three years after my death the trust shall cease and the fund shall be paid to and distributed with my residuary estate."

In pursuance of this bequest the Southworth Library Association was incorporated April 22, 1883, with Jeremiah W. Dwight, John E. McElheny, John J. Montgomery, Henry B. Napier and Erastus S. Rockwell as incorporators. In the following year the Baucus property on the corner of South and Union streets was purchased and remodeled so as to afford temporary accommodations for the Library, and here it was first opened to the public September 25, 1884.

For about ten years the Library was accommodated in a portion of this building, the rent of the remainder, which was leased for a dwelling, being used to pay the expense of employing a librarian.

In the meantime a permanent site was purchased on the new corner on Main street formed by opening Library street, and a fine, substantial building here erected of which we are able to give the accompanying pictorial illustration.

It is constructed of Ohio sandstone in a very thorough and substantial manner at an expense of about fifteen thousand dollars. The building is fire-proof and includes commodious and elegant reading rooms. Here the trustees intend, among other things, to provide for a collection of historical relics, which will be securely preserved for future generations. The structure was completed in the year 1894, since which time there has been presented to the association and placed in the tower of the building, a Seth Thomas clock, the gift of Mrs. D. F. Van Vleet, of Ithaca, as a memorial of her parents, Mr. and Mrs. John C. Lacy, who were for a long time residents of Dryden.

Some unhappy differences of opinion among the citizens of the village as to the intention of Mrs. Fiske in excluding from the purposes for which the funds of her gift could be used "the salaries of officers and servants thereof" has caused the building to be closed for some

THE SOUTHWORTH LIBRARY.

portion of the time, for the lack of a provision, as the trustees claim, for the employment and pay of a janitor and librarian, and these questions are not yet settled to the satisfaction of all; but it is believed that these matters will soon be determined by the courts or otherwise.

According to the last report of the librarian, in the month of April, 1897, the number of volumes in the Library was 6994. These volumes comprise a careful selection of the best works in the whole field of literature, including the latest editions of all standard authorities. The invested interest-bearing funds of the association now amount to about seventeen thousand dollars, the income from which is to be devoted principally to the purchase of books and will continue to supply the reading matter best adapted to the wants of the people in ever-increasing accumulations of the best works of the best authors. Prof. Willard Fiske, although sojourning in Italy for the past few years, has been made a trustee of the association and has shown his interest in the institution by presenting to the Library a valuable and unique set of the complete works of the bard, John Dryden. The following is a list of the present officers and trustees of the association:

TRUSTEES.

John E. McElheny, President,
Dr. J. J. Montgomery, Vice-President,
Dr. F. S. Jennings, Secretary,
              Willard Fiske.

D. R. Montgomery,
John W. Dwight,
D. E. Bower,

Treasurer, - - - - - H. B. Lord

CHAPTER XXX.

WILLOW GLEN.

A stranger now passing through the quiet locality of our town which formerly was known as "Stickles's Corners," but latterly called by the more romantic name of "Willow Glen," upon looking about him would naturally inquire, "Where are the willows and where is the glen?" for both are at present a little obscure. It is said, however, that over fifty years ago, when this name was first applied to the locality by one of its inhabitants, Miss Huldah Phillips, the banks of the little stream which flows down through the "Corners" from the hillside were lined with large willow trees, forming with them a glen which made the name very appropriate.

As we have already seen, the settlement of Willow Glen dates back as early as 1798, when three of the very earliest pioneer families of the town located there, and during all of the Pioneer Period it was a formidable rival of Dryden village. During that time it contained a tannery upon what was afterwards the Phillips corner, a grist mill (one of the earliest in town), and two saw-mills (one of which was *the* earliest in town, being completed in 1802), upon Virgil Creek, two stores, two distilleries, one hotel, a blacksmith shop, an ashery and a large wagon shop, all constituting a good business equipment for a new country settlement. One by one these elements of business have disappeared, and all which now remains in that line is the old blacksmith shop, converted in these latter days into the factory and storehouse of Mosso's Tempering Compound, and the wagon shop across the way conducted by Andrew Simons. Willow Glen has always had and still maintains a good school, and with it is connected an incident which is still remembered by some of the oldest inhabitants, who were children when the events took place. It is the "Story of the Bison" and reads as follows:

On a certain autumnal Saturday afternoon about seventy-five or more years ago two men entered Willow Glen by the highway from the west, leading between them a wild, shaggy animal, a buffalo recently captured on the prairies, being the first one seen in this part of the country. They stopped at the hotel, then kept by William Wigton, in whose barn they exhibited the buffalo to those who would pay ten cents for the opportunity of seeing him. During the afternoon the school was let out—Saturday was a school day in those times—and some of the scholars had ten cents with which to purchase the privilege of seeing the exhibition, but many others did not, and as an inducement to the owners of the animal the older school boys proposed that those who could should pay, but that all of the school children should see the buffalo; but the proposition was not accepted and none of the scholars were admitted to the barn. As night approached, Mr. Wigton, who had overheard some plans among the boys, who were displeased with the rejection of their proposition, informed the proprietors that he would lock up the barn at night but he would not be responsible for what might happen to the buffalo. They replied that there was no danger that any one would molest the animal for it was all that they could do to manage him and no one else would venture to undertake it.

Matters were left in this way, but in the morning the barn doors were open and the buffalo was gone, no one knew where. There was a long watering trough which extended into the barn and some one during the night had drawn the plug, letting the water out so that he could enter the barn through the empty trough and unfasten the doors from within. The proprietors in vain spent the morning looking after the source of their income, but no track or trace of him could be found.

Early that morning Darius J. Clement, the old gentleman who died a few years ago in Dryden village, but who was then a boy living with his parents where John Card now resides, went out before it was fairly daylight to the barn to do the milking. He returned soon after saying to his parents that he believed the Evil One himself had taken possession of the barn during the night, for such pawing and bellowing, by a large animal with short horns, a large shaggy head, fierce, glaring eyes and a long tail, he had never seen or heard of before. Mr. Clement, who was a very religious man, decided that the Sabbath was no time to investigate the matter and directed that nothing should be done with the animal until the next day. But the news began to be circulated that the buffalo was in the barn of Mr. Clement and the people from all about began to congregate so that by noon all the men and boys from the neighborhood were assembled, and Mr. Clement was very willing that the cause of the disturbance should be removed. Some of the boys, presumably the same who had brought him there in the night, readily undertook the task of removing him and in so doing they led him through a clearing in which a vicious bull was being pastured. No sooner did the bull see the intruder of something like his own species approaching than he came rushing toward them ready for a contest for supremacy. Those who then had charge of the buffalo were very willing to let go their hold, which they did, thereby having the fun of witnessing a Sunday bull fight. The result proved that the buffalo, with his short horns and wild, vigorous habits, was too much for his domesticated cousin, who was compelled to recognize the superiority of the intruder. The fun being over the boys returned the buffalo to his owners, who went on their way sadder if not wiser men.

Willow Glen, as well as the northwest corner of the township, claims a share in the invention of the power threshing machine, an inventive genius by the name of Miller having there developed one of the first threshing machines ever seen, which, with subsequent improvements, has revolutionized that part of the farmer's labor.

We have as yet failed to secure very satisfactory notes of the pioneer families of Willow Glen. Of the first three families to locate there in 1798, so far as we are able to learn, the Clausons have no descendants now residing in town, while Ezekiel Sanford and David Foote are the ancestors of quite a number of the present inhabitants. John Southworth, whose father, Thomas Southworth, came to Willow Glen in 1806, will be the subject of a separate chapter. Joshua Phillips, who owned and perhaps built the tannery on the now vacant corner of Willow Glen, was early a prominent citizen, being a Member of Assembly from this county in 1820 and a supervisor of the town in 1839. He came to Dryden from Nassau, Rensselaer county, about

1806, or, as some say, in 1811, and was a major in the State Militia. His wife, whom he married in Rensselaer county, was Huldah Bramhall, a very estimable wife and mother. They had no daughters, but twelve sons, one of whom, Archibald, now resides on the former homestead of his father-in-law, Peter Mulks, near Slaterville, and another, Albert, who married into the Twogood family, is still living at Merton, Waukesha county, Wis., 91 years of age, with another brother, Henry, whose age is 80. Among the others was George W. Phillips, who was once prominent in business in Dryden village. Joseph Bramhall, a brother of Mrs. Phillips, was a carpenter and an early resident of Willow Glen, leaving children who still perpetuate from him the name of Bramhall. He was an assessor of the town at the time of his death, which resulted from consumption. His widow afterwards married Israel Hart and became the mother of Chas. I. Hart, of Dryden. We have already mentioned Elias W. Cady as a prominent citizen in public affairs, Member of Assembly, supervisor and first president of the Dryden Agricultural Society, who died in 1883 at the age of ninety-one years. He came here from Columbia county in 1816, and also married into the Bramhall family. His oldest son, Oliver, recently died, but his youngest son, Charles Cady, of Auburn, N. Y., and daughters, Rebecca A. (Dwight), Harriet S. (Ferguson), and Mary Cady, all of Dryden village, are still living. His daughter Sarah (Wilson) died, leaving numerous descendants now residing in the town. Aaron Foster was not a pioneer of Dryden, but settled in the year 1829 upon the farm which he sold to Joseph McGraw, where, for a number of years, he operated the lumber and grist mills of Willow Glen, there still being no grist mill in Dryden village, and later he removed to the village. His daughter was the wife of Geo. D. Pratt and his son, A. H. Foster, of Superior, Wis., was one of our guests at the Centennial Celebration.

Aaron Lacy, from New Jersey, settled on the Stickles corner in 1799. His only surviving child, John R. Lacy, afterwards lived and died on the corner still held by his family one mile north of Dryden village.

Willow Glen has had no churches, but the barn of Elias W. Cady afforded the Presbyterian society accommodations for preaching and communion service before their building was completed in Dryden village.

The inhabitants have suffered somewhat from religious fanatics, the first visitation being from a band of some fifty "Pilgrims," as they called themselves, who came from Vermont in 1818, and are thus described by the "Old Man in the Clouds:" "When they moved in they had several wagons, some of which were drawn by four horses. One team carried the large tent beneath which the entire family was housed in all kinds of weather. The name of their Prophet was Thaddeus Cummins, a very stout, healthy and well proportioned man, with sandy hair, and about thirty-five years of age. The name of the woman whom he brought as his wife was Lucy. A priest also accompanied the Prophet, whose name was Joseph Ball. There were some two or three brothers by the name of Slack; the rest of the company was made up of the off-scourings of wretched humanity. When the Prophet and his followers arrived near the residence of David Foote they pitched their tent and rested over night, but moved the next day into the woods then on the Stickles farm, where they remained a week, when they again moved upon the north bank of Fall Creek near the former residence of Jacob Updike. Here this singular people remained for fully six weeks, practicing all kinds of deviltry upon themselves and the people in the neighborhood. They had no beds, but slept in nests of straw, each sex in common with the other, they having no belief in or respect for the marriage ceremony. They did not believe in beds, chairs, or tables. They stood up to eat and sucked food through a goose quill, and could not be persuaded to eat in any other way. They wore large white cloths upon their backs, which, as they said, were marks for the Devil to shoot at. Their antipathy against the Devil was very great and every morning early they might be heard howling and yelling like a parcel of wolves for two miles around, driving the Devil out of their camp."

When they left town they went to an island in the Mississippi river, unfortunately inducing some Dryden and more Lansing people to follow them, where they finally disbanded. They should not be confounded with the "Taylorites," who flourished here later and some of whom afterwards joined the Shakers.

There is perhaps no better index of the degree of thrift and refinement which exists in a community than the condition of its graveyards. The principal burial place now used by the people of Dryden at large is the Willow Glen Cemetery, located very near the center of the town, the Green Hill Cemetery in Dryden village being patronized more especially by the residents of that village. Both are laid out and maintained in a manner indicative of the prosperity and intellectual culture of the people of the township. The former, which we now consider, has been especially fortunate in its financial management and the devotion which its officers and friends have shown in its development. It already has a surplus fund of over three thousand dollars, invested at interest, and this surplus has been for the past few years rapidly increasing from the sale of lots. The interest from this money, with such contributions as are added to it, enables the officers to keep its beautiful grounds, consisting of about thirteen acres, in excellent condition, and for a country burying ground it has few rivals either in the natural beauty and extent of its grounds or in the good taste exhibited in its adornment.

The older section was used as a burial place early in the century, some inscriptions recording deaths as early as 1816, and in this section the remains of Judge Ellis and Esquire McElheny, whose deaths occurred in 1846 and 1836, and Aaron Lacy, the original owner, who died and was buried there in 1826, were deposited before the present extension of its territory was contemplated. But in 1864 the friends of the enterprise perfected an organization, and subscribed, as a fund for purchasing additional ground, about one thousand dollars, which was contributed by the following inhabitants:

Wm. Hanford,	$100	Samuel Rowland,	100
Geo. A. Ellis,	100	Thos. Jameson, Sr.,	100
Mrs. Olive Lewis,	50	Jonathan Rowland,	50
Huldah Stickles,	50	Geo. Hanford,	50
Anson Stickles,	50	Zephaniah Lupton,	50
Fred Hanford,	50	Artemas Smiley,	75
Amos Lewis,	50	John R. Lacy,	50
Darius J. Clement,	50		

All these sums have since been repaid by the sale of lots or in other ways so that the society is now entirely out of debt with the surplus above indicated and considerable territory still available for the sale of lots. The principal officers at present are, Moses Rowland, president; Theron Johnson, treasurer; Geo. E. Hanford, secretary.

CHAPTER XXXI.

WEST DRYDEN.

Some statements contained in "The Landmarks of Tompkins County" would seem to indicate that the earliest settler located at West Dryden before the year 1800. The proximity of this part of the town to Lansing, which, from its location on the lake, was reached by the pioneers some years before Dryden was accessible, gave plausibility to these statements, but a patient and careful investigation of the subject establishes the fact that the pioneer first to locate at "Fox's Corners," as it was known in early times, was Evert Mount, who came in the year 1801 or 1802. He was followed by Jacob Primrose and Samuel Fox. Mr. Mount, who was a blacksmith, built his cabin and shop on the southwest corner, while Primrose first occupied the southeast and Fox located on the northwest corner a few rods from where the church now stands. Some rivalry is said to have existed among this trio of pioneers as to which should give the new settlement its name, Mr. Mount suggesting "Mount Pleasant," and Primrose, "Primrose Hill," but Fox carried off the honors and "Fox's Corners" it was called until a postoffice was established under the name of West Dryden, December 23, 1825. Many, however, still know it best by its original name, which still clings to it, and letters yet occasionally find their way to the postoffice addressed "Fox's Corners, N. Y."

It is remembered that before the postoffice was established here the mail was delivered from house to house, being brought from Ithaca once a week by a man named Hagin, who made his trips on horseback, and who finally while performing this duty was thrown from his horse and killed.

From 1816 to 1840 West Dryden was a business place of some note, supporting good stores, shops, hotels and the like. It is supposed that Daniel C. Carr kept the first store, carrying on in connection with it an "ashery" at which "pearlash," a crude form of saleratus, was manufactured. Lumber, shingles, ashes and barter of all kinds were taken in exchange for "store goods," and the space surrounding a country store in those days had much the appearance of latter day lumber yards. Carr was succeeded by Israel Hoy, who became the first postmaster in 1825, and built and kept the first hotel, dealing largely in lumber. As store-keeper he was followed by Reed & Sanders, after whom came Robert T. Shaw and Parley Guinnip and later Lykin & Hance, Lykin & George and H. H. George.

Charles W. Sanders, author of Sanders's series of school books, resided at West Dryden several years, during which time he completed his "First Speller." John Barber did a large carriage making business at an early day and James Youngs manufactured large quantities of broad and narrow axes, adzes, chisels, augers, etc., besides furnishing the usual products of a smith's shop.

The first physician was Dr. Harvey Harris, registered at Ithaca in 1828, who was followed by Doctors Baldwin, White, Barker, Howell and Pelton, all of whom were here prior to 1840.

The first school house was a log building located one-half mile west

WEST DRYDEN.

of the "Corners" directly across the road from where A. W. George now lives. This was built in 1806 or 1807. No roads had as yet been opened to many of the settlers' cabins, and children had often to find their way to school a long distance through a dense forest by means of blazed trees. In a few years, the school was removed to the corners and a large frame building erected which was used for school purposes on week days and for church service on Sunday. This was soon followed by a building on the northeast corner and later by one on the present site. The present school building is the fifth which has been used for school purposes since the settlement of the place.

WEST DRYDEN M. E. CHURCH.

The first Methodist society in the town of Dryden was organized at West Dryden in 1811 by Rev. Geo. W. Densmore. The members of the first class were Samuel Fox and wife, David Case and wife, Selden Andrus and wife, and one other whose name is not known. Densmore was succeeded by Revs. James Kelsey, Isaac Puffer, John Kimberlin and other old time circuit riders. Meetings were held at the houses of members of the class and other places until about 1815, when a large building was erected on the corner where the blacksmith shop now stands. This was used for both church and school purposes for a few years and was the only church here until the present edifice, constituting with its white dome one of the most prominent and familiar landmarks of the township, was built in 1832 by Peter Conover at a cost of twenty-two hundred dollars. It has sittings for three hundred people.

The first trustees were Lemuel Sperry, Thomas George and William George. The pastors of the society since 1845, include Revs. W. N.

Pearne, D. Lamkin, D. Cobb, A. Cross, W. N. Cobb, S. Minier, E. Hoxsie, J. M. Searles, F. Reed, R. C. Fox, J. B. Hyde, F. M. Warner, J. V. Benham, A. M. Lake, L. R. Pendle, W. E. York, E. D. Thurston, L. T. Hawkins, J. E. Rhodes, Philo Cowles, W. M. Sharp, A. S. Durling, George Britten, G. D. Walker, J. A. Roberts, T. C. Roskelly, F. E. Spence.

Among the pioneer families of West Dryden, which, for the purpose of this chapter, is considered as including the four town lots which corner here, are:

CASE, DAVID, who was a native of Hartford county, Conn., and came to Truxton, N. Y., about 1798 and to Dryden in 1808 or 1809. He purchased fifty acres of land on Lot 12, where he lived until he died. He was in the War of 1812 and was buried on the farm of A. W. George. No stone marks the place where he and other pioneers there lie. Soon after coming to Dryden his wife died and he afterwards married the widow of Burnett Cook, who was also an early pioneer. Susan (Cook) Case was a daughter of John Morris, whose will was the first one recorded and proven after the formation of Tompkins county. One son of the second wife, Eleazer Case, is now living in Ithaca aged 80 years. David Case and wife were members of the first Methodist class formed at West Dryden in 1811.

FOX, GEORGE, was also a native of Hartford county, Conn., coming as far west as Truxton in 1798 and to West Dryden in 1808 or 1809, when he purchased fifty acres of land on Lot 12, where he remained until he died. He was also in the War of 1812 in the company of Capt. Bassett of Col. Bloom's regiment. He was buried on the farm now owned by A. W. George with no stone to mark his final resting place. His only son was Palmer B. Fox, well known throughout the county, and who left descendants, including Aretas Fox, still a resident of West Dryden.

FOX, SAMUEL, became a resident of West Dryden in 1804, coming from Fabius, Onondaga county, to which place he had emigrated fourteen years previously from East Hartford, Conn., where he was born in 1756. He had served seven years in the Revolutionary War, enlisting in May, 1775. In July, 1780, he was sent to the command of La-Fayette in Virginia, where he was in the battle at the mouth of the James River, the siege of Yorktown, and at the surrender of Lord Cornwallis. He was one of the first settlers of Fox's Corners and from him the place derived this name by which it was first known. He built his first log house a few rods west of where the M. E. church now stands and was one of seven to form the first Methodist class in the township.

WEST DRYDEN.

To Samuel Fox and his wife, Mabel (Webster), were born eleven children, of whom three died unmarried. Edmund returned to Fabius, N. Y., Julius removed to and died in Wisconsin, but the remaining six, including Anna (who married Ephraim Bloom), Samuel, Jonathan, Eunice (who married Harris Roe and afterward Francis White), Asa (who married Eunice Dodge), and Chester (who married Julia Spafford), all settled in and about West Dryden.

Samuel Fox died in West Dryden Oct. 10, 1844, 88 years of age. His farm of about fifty acres is still included in that of his grandson, James A. Fox, to whom we are indebted for some interesting incidents of the hardships endured by the pioneers and their families. When his father, Asa, was a boy trying to keep up with the men in hoeing corn, his grandfather, Samuel, to encourage his son sent to Ludlowville by a neighbor who happened to be going down, for a hat, the first the boy had ever had. When it was brought back the father placed it upon his son's bare head, but after he had hoed once around with it on, the boy took it off and laid it by under the fence, saying that he was not used to it and it made his head ache. He had his first pair of boots when he was eighteen years of age, children going barefooted like colts until that age, and he secured a pair of shirts by splitting one thousand rails. When he bought his farm there was a mortgage on it held by a man in New Jersey, where he went twice on foot to make his payments.

When the eldest son, Edmund, went by himself he had a pair of oxen and a cow, constituting his stock and team. When his season's work was half done one of his oxen died and his only recourse was to yoke the cow in with the other ox to carry on the work of the farm, the cow being thus required to furnish the family with milk and butter and at the same time do half of the team work. We should hear but little about the present bad times if people now realized the extremities to which the pioneers were often reduced.

FULKERSON, BENJAMIN, JOSIAH and CHAPMAN, brothers, were originally from New Jersey, coming to Lansing soon after 1790. They came to Dryden in 1805, Benjamin purchasing in that year all of Lot 22 except the survey fifty acres and paying for it two thousand dollars. He bought fifty acres which is now included in the farm of J. H. George. On this he built his cabin, but soon after died. His wife, who was Sally Giles, survived him many years and was married to Simeon Van Nortwick, also an early pioneer. Benjamin and Sally Fulkerson had one son, Benjamin, Jr., and one daughter, Phoebe, who married Henry White, son of Daniel White. Benjamin, Jr., married

Emily Douglas, who is now living with her daughter, Mrs. J. B. George, at the age of 86.

Josiah Fulkerson bought of his brother the south half of Lot 22, building his house where his great-grandson, Lamont Fulkerson, now lives. His wife was Polly Cook and his family consisted of five sons, Burnett C., Silas, Benjamin, Lot and Calvin. The daughters were Sally, who was married to John George; Ann, to Sheldon Sharp; Jane, to Hiram Snyder; and Maria, to James Snyder, the latter being the only one now living.

Another brother, Chapman, who came to the town from Lansing soon after, also settled on Lot 22. He was born in New Jersey in 1785, and his wife, Hester Brown, two years later. They were married and settled on a farm half a mile south of West Dryden in 1807. The first winter they kept their stock on browse and a few ears of corn each day, and wolves killed several sheep. Mrs. Fulkerson rode horseback and carried a child twelve miles to Teetertown, now Lansingville, to church during the first few years of their married life. Their first child was Betsey, who married Dayton Primrose and lived at West Dryden; she left children. Sarah married Philip Robertson and settled in the western part of Pennsylvania; she is still living and has three children. Miranda did not marry; Stephen B. lives on the old homestead. Malvina married Albert Twogood; they moved to Marion, Iowa, and left six children. Daniel removed to the West. Sophia married Abram Anthony; they settled in Iowa and have a family of six. Samuel C. married Lucinda Hill, has always lived in the town of Dryden, and has five children. Louisa married Elliott Fortner and left three children. John lives in Iowa. Chapman Fulkerson died December 24, '49, aged 64 years. Hester Fulkerson died January 21, '69, aged 81 years.

GEORGE, DAVID, was born near Monmouth Court House (now Freehold), Monmouth county, N. J., in the year 1769. He was nearly ten years old when the battle of Monmouth occurred near his home, June 28th, 1778. He carried water all day to the soldiers wounded in that bloody battle of the Revolution; and at night nearly fell with exhaustion. In 1793 Mr. George married Alletta Sheppard, whose father and grandfather both were officers of note in the Continental Army in the Revolution; both of them were taken prisoners in 1781 and carried to New York by the British, undergoing much suffering at their hands. Mr. George moved into the town of Dryden with his family in the year 1804, and settled three fourths of a mile east of West Dryden upon a farm of one hundred acres, a portion of which is now owned and occupied by a Mr. Lathrop. Some parts of the buildings now on such portion were built by Mr. George during his lifetime. The family passed through all the hardships of the pioneer settlers of the town. The forest was almost unbroken, while the clearings already made were few and far apart. He was a weaver by trade, weaving coverlets, blankets, cloth and linen, and there are persons in the town now who have some of his work.

MRS. ALLETTA GEORGE.

In spite of their hardships and surroundings Mr. and Mrs. George raised a family of twelve children, namely: Thomas, who settled in Syracuse when it was a small village, and always lived there; Alletta, who always lived in the town, until her death; Rachel, who married George Conrad and after living a few years in Cattaraugus county, N. Y., moved west. One of her sons, Hon. W. F. Conrad, lives at Des Moines, Iowa, and is a prominent Judge of that state. Elisha, too, settled in Syracuse and always lived there. Joel with his family settled in Joliet, Illinois; Peter and his family settled in Steuben county, N. Y.; Sarah lived at Niagara Falls. Mary married Peter Grover; one of their sons, Andrew J. Grover, is still remembered by many in this section, and after him the G. A. R. Post at Cortland is named. Hannah married Solomon Silver, and lived for a number of years at Peruville, in this county; Eliza late in life married Dr. Isaac Carpenter and settled at Auburn, N. Y. She is at present living at Jamestown, N. Y. Adaline married William L. Fessenden and is living at Candor, N. Y. Harvey married Susan Van Horn, for a while was a merchant at West Dryden and later moved to Kansas and died there about ten years ago.

Mr. George continued to live upon the farm where he settled, until his death, which occurred October 3rd, 1848. His widow survived him twenty-one years; her death took place September 12th, 1869, she being ninety-one years of age. She could remember seeing the British soldiers of the Revolutionary War pass her father's house on their way through the Jerseys.

None of their descendants now reside in Tompkins county; but a grandson, Dilworth M. Silver, an attorney of Buffalo, N. Y., has devoted himself to tracing out the history of this branch of the George family, and has materially aided us with the results of his researches, being able to trace his grandmother's ancestry back to the year 1654, which was the date when the first of her ancestors came to America.

GEORGE, JOEL, an elder brother of David, was born in Monmouth county, New Jersey, in the year 1767. He married Mary Toan, and all of their older children were born in New Jersey, but about the year 1798 they migrated "West" and after sojourning for about six years at Scipio, N. Y., located in Dryden on land now owned by Andrew Baker, about the year 1804. He bought three hundred acres, which included the farm now owned by S. M. George. His sons were Thomas, John and William T. The daughters were married—Sally to William Van Nortwick; Elizabeth to Thomas Hance, Jr., afterwards to Judge Joshua North; Clarissa to Peter Conover. Joel was the first blacksmith in that part of the town, carrying on the business many years. Among his grandchildren are S. M. George, James H. and Almanzo W. George, all still residing in West Dryden and representing the three male branches of their common ancestor, Joel.

KIMBERLIN, REV. JOHN, who had traveled thousands of miles on horseback through the wilds of New York, Pennsylvania and Ohio as an early Methodist circuit rider, came to Dryden about the year 1815, and bought of Selden Andrus the place now known as the Bryant farm, one-half mile west of "Fox's Corners," where he lived until his death, which occurred in 1853 at the age of seventy-two years. At his request he was buried directly underneath the spot where the pulpit had stood in the old Asbury red meeting house, which had been burned a few years before and where he had preached so many times.

MOUNT, EVERT, who was born in New Jersey in 1758, was a soldier of the Revolution, participating in the battles of Trenton, Princeton and Monmouth, and coming to West Dryden in 1801, accompanied by his only son, Joseph. The latter was the father of William Dye Mount, and grandfather of the Mounts now living in Groton. Evert and his son built the first blacksmith shop at the corners, where they worked for a few years. They returned to New Jersey with the intention of bringing their families to their new homes, but while there hostilities between England and the United States broke out and Joseph Mount volunteered and was sent to the frontier. He was killed in the battle of Lundy's Lane, July 25, 1814. Evert Mount returned with his wife to West Dryden and resumed work at his trade, which he continued until the weight of years compelled him to relinquish it. He died at West Dryden in July, 1841, aged 88 years, and was buried in the "George" cemetery. His wife, Effie Dye Mount, survived him several years, living with her grand-daughter, Mrs. Wilson Hunt. They afterwards removed to Cattaraugus county, where Mrs. Mount died in 1849.

PRIMROSE, JACOB, came from Sussex county, New Jersey, in 1803, and settled on Lot 23, where he purchased one hundred and thirty acres of land. He was a weaver of coverlets and worked at that trade after he came here. His wife was Martha Dayton. They had three sons: Henry, who served in the War of 1812, and Lewis and Dayton. Of the four daughters, Ruth and Sarah married Silas and Benjamin Fulkerson, respectively. Sarah is still living at Clinton, Wisconsin, at the age of 88 years.

The farm has always remained in the family and is now owned by George Primrose, a son of Dayton.

SUTLIFF, DAVID, was an early West Dryden pioneer, coming from Hartford, Conn., to Genoa in 1804 and to Dryden in 1806, buying land on Lot 23 now owned by Geo. Fulkerson, and which remained in possession of the family nearly seventy-five years. He was the father of fourteen children, most of whom were born in Connecticut. The best known in Dryden were Uriah, Henry P., and Parintha, wife of Burnett C. Fulkerson, who was the last surviving member of that branch of the family. She died in 1892 in her 91st year.

WIRE, JARED, also came from Hartford county, Connecticut, and purchased a farm of fifty acres on Lot No. 12; but he removed to Pennsylvania, where he died at the home of his daughter, Mrs. Watson Sutliff, many years ago, leaving no descendants in this town.

HISTORY OF DRYDEN.

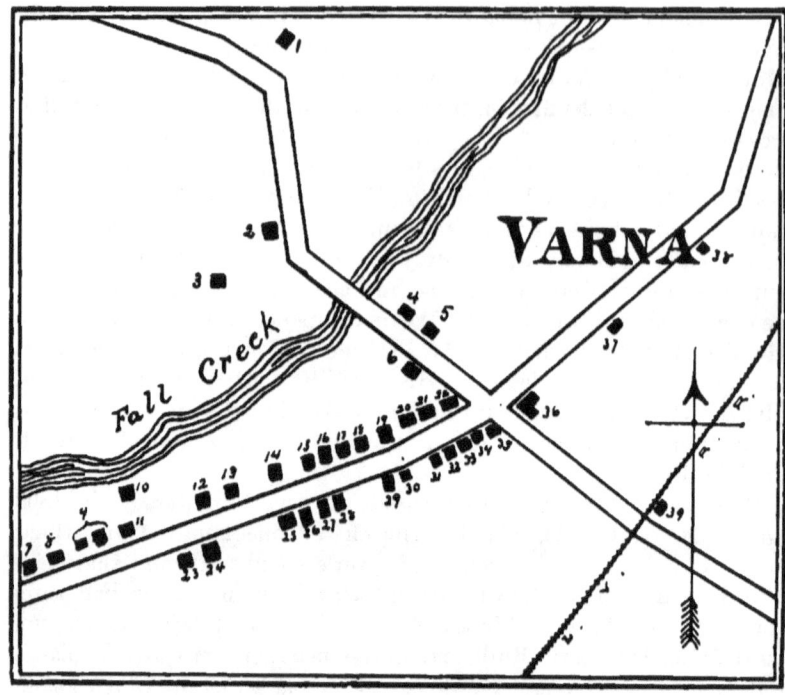

Key to the Map of Varna.

1. Geo. E. Underwood.
2. Ezra Ostrander.
3. Ezra Ostrander.
4. Mrs. Cooper.
5. Wm. J. Manning.
6. Wilson Baker.
7. Frank Powers.
8. Philip S. Snyder.
9. Mrs. Olive Crutts.
10. Grist Mill.
11. Wagon Shop.
12. Marenus Crutts.
13. Marenus Crutts.
14. Geo. Underwood.
15. Robert Smiley, Postoffice.
16. Ernest Snyder.
17. Milo Williams.
18. H. Brink, Store.
19. J. Whipple.
20. Blacksmith Shop.
21. Wagon Shop.
22. School House, No. 18.
23. Marenus Crutts.
24. W. C. Ellis.
25. J. Pierce.
26. Mrs. S. Grover.
27. O. T. Ellis.
28. Seaman & Snyder
29. M. E. Church.
30. M. E. Parsonage.
31. Wm. J. Manning.
32. Geo. Brown.
33. Mrs. Isaac Creamer.
34. Mrs. Sherwood.
35. Frank Ellis.
36. J. T. Morris.
37. Will Ross.
38. Frank Hazen.
39. Depot.

CHAPTER XXXII.

VARNA AND FALL CREEK.

The annals of the early settlement of Varna seem to be hopelessly lost. We cannot even obtain a hint as to the origin of the application of its name to this locality, the only other Varna of which we have any knowledge being a Bulgarian city of that name on the shore of the Black Sea. It, however, had an early history, and among its first settlers were men by the name of Dyer, Jarvis and Blue, followed by Ebenezer Brown, Erasmus T. Brown, Jonathan Knowles, James Bird, Gen. John Munson, Peter Talmadge, John Ewers, Dr. Call, James McElheny, Wm. H. Miller, Walter Dowe, Dr. Ide, Dr. Pomeroy, William Cobb, William Schutt and Isaac Creamer.

Both the first saw-mill and the first grist-mill are said to have been built by Gabriel Cain, in 1803, the former near the site of the Hart mill, where Amos Ogden, in later years, first instituted the custom of putting up flour in cotton sacks, for which paper has been substituted. The first tavern seems to have been built by a man by the name of Abner Chapin, near the site of the present hotel, in 1806, but the present hotel building was built by James McElheny in 1832, the first school house having been erected two years before on the opposite side of the street. On the site of the Crutts grist-mill there was constructed a saw-mill in 1818 by Gen. John Munson, and a sash factory was built in 1837 by Erasmus Brown, which was later occupied by Israel Brown as a distillery. Gen. Munson had a store in 1831 on the site now occupied by the Whipple blacksmith shop, the first blacksmith shop of which we have any record having been built by William Van Sickle in 1830. A tannery was built and operated by Z. Hartsough in 1840, followed by the building of the M. E. church in 1842 and the Presbyterian church in 1843.

The proximity of Varna to Ithaca has always interfered with its prosperity as a business center, but there was a time, near the middle of our Century Period, when it had quite a business of its own. In those days it was a great horse market, and many a drove of horses was started from there to New York in the old-fashioned way, some twenty-five horses more or less being attached with yokes to a long rope at the head of which was a leader on horseback, and a man with a cart or wagon attached to the other end of the line brought up the rear, while horses in pairs were attached to the rope all the way between. Such a troop of horses starting for the New York market in

VARNA, FROM THE RAILROAD STATION.

Photo by Silcox.

VARNA AND FALL CREEK.

this way would be a novel sight in these days of rapid transportation. Large droves of sheep and cattle driven along the highways of our town enroute for New York were a frequent sight fifty years ago, on all of our principal thoroughfares.

Not only was Varna in early times a great place for sending horses off to the cities, but it was noted as a home horse market where horses were sold and exchanged in great numbers, and where the running of horses as a test of speed was a common practice before the present custom of trotting horses came in vogue. At one time there were some parties there by the name of Sloan Bros. who for years made it their headquarters for peddling clocks of Eastern manufacture throughout the surrounding country.

The first M. E. church of Varna was organized at the school-house January 5, 1842, with the following as trustees: Hoffman Steenburg, William Cobb, Robert C. Hunt, Benjamin Davenport, George Emmons, John Munson and Isaac Seaman. Their church edifice was completed the next year at an original expense of fifteen hundred dollars, extensive repairs having since been made. The pastors of this church have been W. H. Miller, A. H. Hamilton, D. Lamkin, L. G. Weaver, J. W. Steele, Elias Hoxsie, David Davis, G. W. Smith, A. Ensign, Sylvester Minier, L. R. Grant, E. House, D. W. Sherman, L. T. Hawkins, E. A. Peck, R. L. Stilwell, N. M. Wheeler, F. M. Wheeler, W. M. Fisher, P. W. Mynard, E. D. Thurston, G. W. Reynolds, J. L. King, C. J. Pendleton, M. J. Owen, P. H. Reigal, J. E. Showers, F. H. Dickerson.

The Presbyterian church of Varna was discontinued over thirty years ago and their building was taken down and removed to Brookton.

It is not a little remarkable that a town which forms a part of the great watershed separating the St. Lawrence from the Chesapeake systems of water courses—the streams of Dryden being represented in each—should possess such valuable water power privileges as are afforded by Fall Creek and its tributaries. Rising in the town of Summerhill and flowing south through the eastern part of the town of Groton, Fall Creek enters Dryden near McLean and flows diagonally through our town in such a way as to afford an abundance of mill sites for water power. It is the central drainage artery of the township, receiving as tributaries Beaver, Mud and Virgil creeks on the south, and the West Dryden stream from the north, as well as other smaller additions. Although Fall Creek suffers considerable diminution in times of drouth, especially since the country through which it flows has been mostly deprived of the shade of the forests, it still has good lasting qualities even in the dry seasons of summer and autumn. The largest and most constant of these water powers are, of course, situated on the lower part of the stream, the last one in the town of Dryden running the present Crutts mill, which still does considerable business in flour and feed grinding. Peter Talmadge also had a mill near by but on the north side. Next above is the Hart mill, already spoken of, and next above in the order being the Wm. Allen site, the Wm. Bishop or Sherwood Mills, the George Robertson site, later sold to Jonathan Card and Ward Mallory, who there manufactured

MAIN STREET, VARNA.

chairs which are still in use, the Salmon Sharp site, the Rhodes site and the Wadsworth site, which brings us up to the Bartholomew mills in the vicinity of Etna.

All of these water powers were first employed in sawing the pine lumber, which was very abundant in and about Varna, the pine trees along the northerly side of Fall Creek being the largest to be found in this region, often five feet in diameter and each cutting twenty-five thousand clear shingles or five thousand feet of first class white pine lumber. If any one of our readers is inclined to doubt this statement or consider it exaggerated, we can call attention to the fact as corroborating our accuracy that an occasional pine stump in the fence of this neighborhood is still shown which, split in two in the middle, makes four rods in length of stump fence.

Of the pioneer families of Varna we can only speak of James McElheny, whose father, Thomas McElheny, came from New Jersey early in the century, first locating near Malloryville, where James married Betsey, a daughter of Judge Ellis. He was a justice of the peace of the town in 1830 at Ellis Hollow, afterwards a hotel keeper at Varna, and died in 1836 at the early age of thirty-five years. His father and the rest of the family had already removed to Allegany county, the children of James who remained here including John E. McElheny, of Dryden, and Thomas J. McElheny, of Ithaca.

Isaac Creamer, although not strictly speaking a pioneer, came to Varna with the clock peddlers whom he assisted, about 1835, and for a long time he remained a prominent character in that section of the town. Although a pronounced Democrat he served as justice of the peace and justice of sessions in 1864, and was a leader among the Democratic politicians of the county.

Esquire Wm. H. Miller, who was a justice of the peace of the town in 1833, came to Varna from Rensselaer county about seventy-five years ago, followed later by his father, Moses Miller; his sister, Mrs. Nancy Grant, now over ninety years of age and residing with her daughter, Mrs. C. D. Bouton, of Ithaca; and other sisters, Mrs. Samuel Rowland, afterwards residing at Willow Glen, where she died; Mrs. Angeline Brown, widow of Capt. Brown, now of Cortland; and Mrs. Charles LaBarr, now of Dryden village.

Peter Talmadge seems to have been a prominent figure in the early times of Varna, his stentorian voice being employed to advantage in driving his oxen and being heard throughout the whole settlement. Although illiterate and unpolished in his speech and manners, Father Talmadge, as he was called, possessed rugged virtues, and when others of his less independent Varna neighbors bashfully admitted to the out-of-town merchants with whom they traded, that they lived "just in the edge of Dryden," it is said that he patriotically affirmed in unmistakable terms that he was not ashamed to own that he resided "in the very bowels of Dryden."

136　　　HISTORY OF DRYDEN.

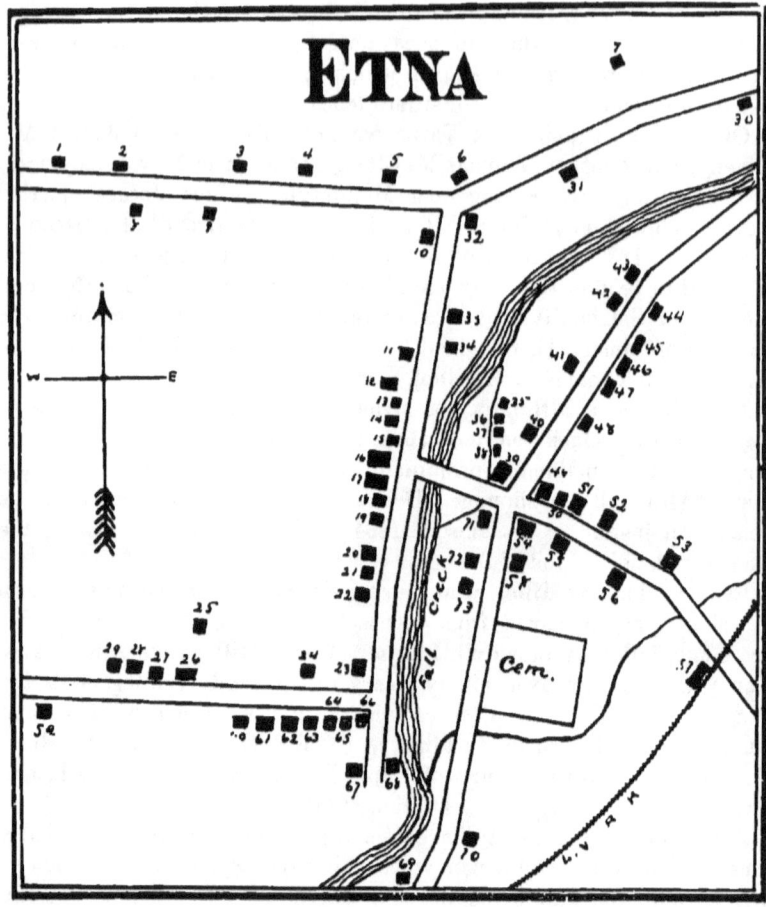

Key to the Map of Etna.

1. Mrs. C. Turner.
2. J. T. Primrose.
3. E. F. Weaver.
4. James Rawley.
5. Geo. Cowdrey.
6. L. Dusenberry.
7. Arthur Burr.
8. Mrs. H. Ralph.
9. Mrs. D. Weaver.
10. L. Freeman.
11. Wm. Smith.
12. School House, No. 11.
13. Shoe Shop.
14. David Brotherton.
15. Dr. G. L. Rood.
16. Baptist Church.
17. M. E. Church.
18. Wm. W. Sherwood.
19. Mrs. J. S. Weidman.
20. Dr. J. Beach.
21. Edward Gaston.
22. E. Snyder.

ETNA.   137

23. C. Bartholomew.
24. Mrs. Davenport.
25. E. Freeman.
26. L. Hemmingway, shop.
27. L. Hemmingway.
28. D. B. Conklin.
29. Mrs. John Reed.
30. Barbara Rulison.
31. Arthur Burr.
32. P. Brady.
33. Smith Stevens.
34. D. Brotherton.
35. Cabinet Shop.
36. Wagon Shop.
37. Blacksmith Shop.
38. Blacksmith Shop.
39. Houtz's Etna Roller Mills.
40. Store.
41. Ai Van Horn.
42. Ann Merchant.
43. Geo. L. Snyder.
44. Mrs. William Haskins.
45. Ladrew Sherwood.
46. Eli Conklin.
47. Wm. Tichenor.
48. Store.
49. Arthur Coggswell.
30. Meat Market.
51. H. A. Root, Hotel.
52. Geo. H. Houtz.
53. Mrs. C. Houtz.
54. Geo. H. Houtz.
55. W. Marsh.
56. Etna Hotel, C. Westervelt.
57. Depot, L. V. R. R.
58. Mrs. Mary H. Bartholomew.
59. T. Rhodes.
60. Freeman Bros.
61. J. Bartholomew.
62. S. Ralph Estate.
63. Milo Snyder.
64. Emma Snyder.
65. Mrs. Hurley.
66. Etna Creamery.
67. Blacksmith Shop.
68. Machine Shop.
69. Hannah Lee Estate.
70. Wm. H. Sherwood.
71. Geo. H. Houtz, Store.
72. Mary H. Bartholomew.
73. Mrs. G. B. Davis.

CHAPTER XXXIII.

ETNA.

We are not able to give the year when Rev. Wm. Miller and his brother Arthur, who was a blacksmith, commenced building in the wilderness of what is now known as the village of Etna, but was first called, after them, Miller's Settlement.

The first grist-mill there was on the same spot and in the same building lately occupied by Jesse Bartholomew as a planing mill. The date of the erection of this mill cannot now be accurately given, and it has been claimed that it ante-dated White's mill at Freeville, but so far as we can learn, without authority, and, as it seems to us, without reason, for Capt. Robertson would not have gone to mill at Ludlowville with his crops of 1799 and 1800 if there had been a mill so near to him as Etna.

The first date of Etna which we can give with any accuracy or certainty is that of the organization of the first religious society in the township, the first and we believe to this day, the only regular Baptist church of Dryden, which was organized February 29, 1804, at the home of William Miller. The meeting was opened with singing and prayer by Mr. Miller, Samuel Hemmingway being elected deacon, and John Wickham, clerk of the society. Among the original members are said to have been Francis Miller, Elijah Dimmick, Silas Brown, Ebenezer Brown, Nathaniel Luther, Job Carr, Ziba Randall, Timothy Owens, Jonathan Dunham, Joshua Jay, Abraham Woodcock, Nathan Dunham, Joel Whipple, Samuel Skillinger, Morris Bailey, Orpha Luther, Asher Wickham, Mehitable Carr, Betsey Brown, Abigail Dimmick, Mary Owens, Lucy Dunham and Katie Woodcock.

A saw-mill was built at about the same time as the grist-mill, upon the site lately occupied by the Houtz saw-mill, and afterwards a fulling mill owned by Joseph Newell and Stephen Bradley, on the ground now occupied by the blacksmith shop of Bert Conklin. Daniel Carr and John McArthur carried on the first store in the house formerly occupied by Wm. Miller and now owned by the Houtz family. The first blacksmith shop stood where is now the center of the road between Houtz's store and grist-mill. The first church building was of logs on the lands of Nathaniel Luther, but was replaced by a frame building on the same ground, which is where the Etna Creamery Co.'s building now stands, and the building is the same one which Caleb Bartholomew used as a pattern shop. At that time there was a bridge across Fall Creek at that point. The first school house stood on the site now occupied by the Houtz store and was the building afterwards used as the old cooper shop, which was finally taken away by high water a number of years ago.

About the year 1815 the place took quite a change. Wm. Miller sold out his property to the Houtz family and the new settlement from that time bore the name of Columbia until about the year 1820, when the postoffice was established under the name of Etna. In the meantime Bradley & Newell sold their fulling-mill to Rice Weed. Stephen Bradley owned and occupied the place now owned by Hiram Root, which afterwards became the property of Joseph Hemmingway. Here he built the hotel, and the original "Bradley House" of former years is a part of the present hotel.

The first shoemaker was Jacob Lumbard, whose descendants are well known in the town of Dryden. About the year 1818 a store was built on the ground where Ed Carbury now lives, just east of Root's Hotel. At the same time there was another store kept by H. B. Weaver in the building now known as Houtz's white shop. Henry Beach built a saw-mill which was burned on the island about where

ETNA, WEST SIDE.

Photo by Silcox

is now the center of the Houtz dam. Beach sold his interest in this property to J. H. Houtz, who rebuilt the mill, but later took it down to make room for a distillery. On that particular spot one saw-mill and two distilleries were burned and the last distillery was taken off by high water a few years ago, being remembered by the present generation as the old sash factory.

Another distillery stood on the island just back of Conklin's shop and was owned by John Dodge, who came from Maine.

Columbia had two bridges at that time, one of which has been mentioned, and the other extended across the creek nearly in front of where Dr. Rood now lives.

When Henry L. Beach sold his property to J. H. Houtz he moved to what was known as Lower Etna, where Truman Rhodes now lives in a house which was then built by Mr. Beach as a hotel, from which there was a road running south to the corner of the pine woods. At that time Lower Etna possessed a hotel, paper mill, blacksmith shop, store, wagon shop and several other buildings. The first tailor was John Weaver, who had a little family of children from which only nine attended shool at one time.

The First M. E. church of Etna was organized April 13, 1835, and their meetings were held in the village school house until 1837, when the present church edifice was erected at a cost of about two thousand dollars, seating two hundred persons. The first trustees were James Freeman, Alvah Carr, Michael Vanderhoef, Richard Bryant, Thomas J. Watkins, Oliver Baker and John H. Porter.

Fifty years ago Etna had a hard name, being then noted for its horse running and liquor distilling proclivities, there being no less than ten or twelve stills within two miles square of this section of the town. While the general business of the place has not increased in recent years the character of its inhabitants and industries has very much improved, and a stranger who now visits Etna finds it very pleasantly located upon the opposite banks of Fall Creek, which are here connected by a very substantial iron bridge, one of the largest and best in the township, and the dwellings and public buildings, including churches and schools, show abundant evidence of the thrift, good taste and enterprise of its inhabitants. The butter factory, recently incorporated, is one of the recent manufacturing enterprises which flourish, and for the past twenty-five years Etna has not been behind her neighboring villages in mercantile enterprise or in the educational advantages furnished by her excellent school.

The following pioneers of Etna have been brought to our notice :

BARTHOLOMEW, JESSE, SR., was born in Branford, Conn., in 1763, and about 1783, in Lee, Mass., married Mamra Bradley, who died in Dryden in July, 1823, after which he married Betsey Locke Updike in Dryden in 1831. He came in 1798 to Herkimer county, from which place, after living in Locke, Cayuga county, he moved to the town of Dryden in 1812 or 1813, and purchased and settled on the land now known as the Hanford farm, one-half mile east of Etna, from which he was subsequently driven off by a man who claimed a better title. While he yet lived on the corner where the Etna road joins the Bridle Road, and in the traditional cold season of 1816, he raised a field of corn, said to have been the only crop of that kind matured in the town of Dryden that year. He died in 1846 aged 83 years. He was a devoted Baptist and is said by his children to have been so even-tempered as never to have been seen in a passion. He was the father of fifteen children and the grandfather of over seventy. Among the former were Jesse Bradley, who carried on a distillery in Dryden village in the Pioneer Period and moved to Michigan, where he died leaving a large family; Lemi, who served in the War of 1812, having enlisted as the record says at Dryden, Cayuga county, N. Y., in August, 1814, in Col. Fleming's regiment, which rendezvoused at Cayuga Bridge, and was one of the volunteers who took part in the celebrated "sortie of Fort Erie." He died in Westfield, N. Y., in 1872. Daniel, Sr., was born in Locke in 1798, and in 1819 married Jerusha Griswold, whose children, Mary (Wheeler) and Daniel, Jr., are still well-known residents of Dryden. Caleb and Jesse, Jr., have for many years been prominent business men of Etna, where they both still reside, Caleb having been largely engaged in the manufacture and sale of scales and iron bridges, while Jesse has manufactured specialties, one of which was the first machine used in Etna which would do planing and matching of lumber at the same time.

CARR, JOHN, is said to have come to Etna from Pennsylvania as early as 1800, settling in the western part with his three sons, Job, Peleg and Caleb. His wife it is said used to call her sons in the morning, saying: "Come, boys, the birds are saying Job, Peleg and Caleb."

DUNHAM, JONATHAN, with his three sons, Henry, Louis and Nathan, coming from Pennsylvania, settled near Etna about the year 1800.

MCARTHUR, REV. DANIEL, from Scotland, arrived in New York May 29, 1811. He was originally a Presbyterian, but changed his religious views and went to Edinburgh, where he was baptised and united with the Baptist creed. Soon after he took passage for America in the hope that the change of climate would prove beneficial to his wife, who was in poor health but died upon the voyage and was buried on Staten Island. After spending some time with friends in America from his native land he met Mr. Quigg, of Ithaca, on the Hudson river and was influenced by him to come to Dryden, as he did, and died here in 1847, leaving many descendants.

HOUTZ, REV. ANTHONY, with his father, Philip Peter, migrated from Germany in 1768, when the former was only ten years of age, locating at Lancaster, Pa., where the son learned the trade of a tailor, and using this occupation as a means of support he studied theology and was licensed to preach by the German Reformed Church. The original family name was "Hauz"; but as they soon began to speak English they changed the spelling and pronunciation to Hautz and later to Houtz, which with the English spelling is the exact German pronunciation of "Hauz." During his pastorate in Pennsylvania, his first wife died and in 1803 he married Katrina Keller, who became the step-mother of his four children and in the year following the mother of his fifth child, John Heinrich Hauz, who was the old merchant and miller, John H. Houtz, so well known to the older residents of Etna, where now lives and toils at his roller mills his son, Col. George H. Houtz, the great-grandson of Philip Peter Hauz. In the years 1804 and 1805 Rev. Anthony Houtz preached at Canoga and Lansingville and as early as 1806 located at Etna, where he served the people not only as their preacher but also as a tailor, jeweler, or "time keeper," as they were called in those days, and as druggist and physician. His books, still preserved, show that the most universal diseases of the section at that time were the usual new country plagues, the ague and the itch. He was a very useful and much respected man in the new settlement, where he died in 1813 and was buried in the Etna cemetery.

THE RHODES FAMILY of the town of Dryden are of English descent, their ancestors having originally settled in Pennsylvania before the Revolutionary War and their great-great-grandfather was a cooper by trade who worked for Washington's Army and was killed by Indians in the massacre of Wyoming.

One of his sons, George Rhodes, came to Lansing from Northumberland county, Pa., in 1792, coming by the way of the Susquehanna river to Owego, from there to Ithaca through a forest road, and from there to Lansing, where they settled. They cut their way through the original forest, going east from Ithaca to a spot just east of Forest Home, where they crossed the creek and from there went north to the farm now occupied by John Conklin.

Of a numerous family, one son, Jacob Rhodes, left home in 1804,

ETNA, EAST SIDE.

Photo by Silver.

when he was twenty-one years old, to go for himself. Taking his rifle, ammunition and hatchet, he came to the present town of Dryden, sleeping the first night on the banks of a small stream a short distance southwest of the present site of the village of Etna. From there he went east to where Freeville, McLean and Dryden now are, camping the second night near the forks of the creek near Freeville. After prospecting for a number of days he came back to where he camped the first night and located, buying a claim owned by a Revolutionary soldier named Savage, from Rutland, Vt. His early life was the usual one of the early settlers. For years he kept house by himself and depended upon the forest and streams for provision. He was noted for his woodcraft and marksmanship. In fact, he was barred from taking part in shooting matches, for, with him, to shoot was to win, and at the present time spots can be pointed out where he killed deer, bear, etc.

He married Margaret, daughter of Christopher Snyder, and of a family of eight, four sons grew to an old age, the four daughters having died in childhood or youth. The sons were Wm. S., Geo. W., and Miles and Truman Rhodes. The old home of Jacob Rhodes was until recently owned by Miles Rhodes, and is now occupied by W. J. Davis.

Jacob Rhodes, by combining farming with a distillery, accumulated a large property, which is now owned by his grand-children, consisting of about one thousand acres of land, lying in nearly a solid body south and west of Etna.

CHAPTER XXXIV.

ISAIAH GILES AND GILESVILLE.

Early in the history of the country there came to New England from the mountains of Wales three sturdy brothers with their families, bearing the name of Giles or Gyles. They bore the characteristics that marked the sturdy and determined followers of Owen Glendower. Courageous, thrifty and resourceful, they regarded nothing better in man than honor and self-reliance. One of these families or their descendants came early into Eastern New York, and it is from this branch that sprang the family that forms the subject of the following sketch. Owing to a serious misfortune that befell the family early in the present century, mention of which will hereafter be made, many records of the history of the family were totally lost, so that much pertaining to such history, prior to that event, has been perpetuated more by tradition than otherwise. But in the preparation of this paper all the care that the time would permit has been taken to reject everything that did not seem to be well authenticated.

In the summer of 1801 Isaiah Giles came from Orange county to begin a home for himself and family in the town of Dryden upon lands that he had recently purchased on Lot 15. He began his little clearing about, and built his log cabin near, the spring that in later years has been known as the Cheese Factory spring, just northwest of Freeville. After building his cabin he extended his clearing sufficiently to put in a piece of corn the next spring. He then returned east and early the next year, in the month of March, he came back, bringing his wife and children. He did not have time when putting up his house to put on the roof, so that one of the first things to be done, when moving in, was to shovel out the snow, and then cut and put on basswood bark for a roof. Then with a blanket hung up at the doorway the home and castle of the Giles family in Dryden was complete, for the time. From that time until the opening of spring, he was engaged in splitting and smoothing up puncheons for a door and flooring, and in building bunks for sleeping. In all the toil and care incident to such a beginning he had an earnest and efficient helper in the person of his good wife, Sarah Lanterman, whom he had married some nine years before. Their family then consisted of seven children, including two pairs of twins. There were subsequently born to them two sons and a daughter. To these children we shall have occasion to refer farther on.

Isaiah Giles and his wife were earnest, thrifty, pushing people, and about them soon began to cluster the evidences of their industry and economy. In the fall of 1802 they harvested their first corn and potatoes. The winter brought many privations and discomforts, but they passed through it without serious sickness or mishap. In the summer of 1803 they harvested their first crop of wheat, and threshed it in the little log barn that they had built the year before. They winnowed away the chaff, and carried the first grist to the mill of Elder Daniel White, at Freeville, to be ground, and then had their first wheat bread in the town of Dryden. The clearings and improvements were extended each year by dint of hard labor and good management. But in spite of the energy and thrift of Mr. and Mrs. Giles a great misfortune was in store for them.

About 1806 there came a man by the name of Thompson who laid claim to the land which Isaiah had bought. Investigation showed that Thompson's title was good and that Giles had been defrauded in his purchase. Instances of this kind were not uncommon in the early history of Dryden. But the same spirit that had begun the first home in Dryden was ready to begin again. Gathering together his effects he went down upon Fall Creek at the point afterwards for years known as "Gilesville," and bought another tract of land and began anew. It was here that he, with his sons, built a saw-mill and a carding and fulling mill, and subsequently his sons built an extensive tannery.

Isaiah Giles was a man of considerable prominence in the affairs of the town, at one time serving as magistrate. In this connection a funny circumstance occurred. The writer repeats it as it was told him by Samuel Giles in 1870. Squire Giles, as he was then known, was an ardent Methodist withal, and one dark night a man by the name of Pipher, from the town of Groton, came with his wife to the Giles house and aroused the family, saying that they wanted to be baptised, and that the Lord's business was very urgent. They seemed to have the impression that the civil magistrate was the proper one to administer baptism. Esquire Giles explained the matter to them and directed them to Elder Daniel White, at Freeville, whom they aroused, and who administered the ordinance of baptism and sent them on their way rejoicing.

Although a strong Methodist and feeling the interests of the church of paramount importance, it is said Mr. Giles presented a resolution or motion at town meeting, "that the income from the gospel and school fund should thereafter be used wholly for school purposes." The resolution was carried through his influence, and that of some others.

Mr. Giles died when comparatively a young man, in 1822. His sickness was short and his death unexpected, but he died as he had lived, "diligent in business, fervent in spirit," and a firm believer in the tenets of the church of his choice. His wife survived him forty years, dying in 1862, a woman of great force of character, combined with very good judgment. These qualities were manifested in the manner in which she managed her household after the death of her husband.

Of the ten children of the family six lived to manhood and womanhood. Polly, the oldest of these, married John Van Nortwick, and died in 1823 at the age of twenty-six years. The other surviving daughter married Samuel Mead, and afterwards in 1857 moved to Iowa, where she died at the age of eighty years. It is of the sons that what follows will pertain more particularly.

Samuel and John Giles were twins born in Orange county in 1798. James Giles was born in the same county in 1800. These came with their parents to Dryden in 1802, and may be justly classed among the pioneers of the town. Samuel Giles learned the trade of cabinet making, and John served his time as a tanner and currier with Burnett Cook, late of Ulysses. It was here that he first saw her who was destined in after years to become his wife. She was then but a child in the cradle, and he a lad in his teens. Samuel and John, having finished their apprenticeships, worked as journeymen for some years. James in the meantime had staid at home with his mother and carried on the saw-mill and fulling mill, assisted by an adopted brother, George Van Horn, whose family was in after years well known in the town of Dryden.

About 1823 Samuel and James went west to seek their fortunes, going as far as Indianapolis, Ind. After prospecting for a time and working at intervals, they concluded that while the soil was wonderfully fertile and the country presented many inducements to young men, the "shakes," as they termed it, more than offset the advantages. So at the beginning of winter they started for Dryden on foot. It was on this journey that their knowledge of mechanics stood them in good stead. They had the opportunity of putting into operation for different parties several carding machines, and when they reached home each had more money than when they started.

It was just after this that Samuel and John decided to build the tannery at Gilesville. This business they carried on with considerable success until 1832, when they built the Tompkins House, a historic hotel in the city of Ithaca. John in the meantime had waited until the child whose cradle he had rocked when an apprentice boy had grown to young womanhood, and in 1828 he was married to her (then Miss Mary A. Cook.) The union was a happy one. Samuel was married in 1832 to Miss Susan Depew.

In 1843, tired of hotel-keeping, they bought the Eddy property on East Hill, at Ithaca, on which they afterward built them a home, which they occupied until their deaths. These twin brothers during all their lives after beginning the tannery business at Gilesville occupied the same house and did business in partnership. John died in August, 1862, and Samuel in July, 1871, and his wife in February, 1872. The widow of John is still living at Trumansburg, N. Y.

James Giles was married to Barbara Raymer and shortly after bought one hundred acres of land on Lot 34, of Dryden. By subsequent additions thereto he owned three hundred and twenty acres. He was a man of unusual force of character, and possessed rare mechanical ability. He was a thorough farmer and early turned his attention to dairying, and was among the first in the town to realize what was then known as fancy prices for butter. He early saw that machinery must play a prominent part in farming, and he began fitting his meadows for the mower, and it was upon his farm one of the first, if not the first, mowers was used in town. For many years he was actively engaged in selling mowers and reapers, and in buying and selling butter, of which article he was long known as being a competent judge. In his good wife he ever found an efficient helpmate and a wise counselor. They were the parents of eight children, one son and seven daughters. In 1867, feeling the weight of years bearing upon them, they arranged to give up the hard work of life, and passed the management of affairs to the son, Capt. J. J. Giles, of Freeville. Mrs. Giles died in November, 1887, and Mr. Giles in October, 1890, at the age of 90 years and 28 days. He had lived as long if not longer in the town of Dryden than any other person. Of the family of James Giles there are still living one son and four daughters.

Sarah Lanterman Giles, the wife of Isaiah Giles died in 1862 at the age of 91 years and 13 days.

In speaking of the misfortunes that befell the family of Isaiah Giles it may be mentioned that soon after moving to Fall Creek an event occurred that ever afterward cast a shadow over the life of James. It occurred during the time in the year when the latter was engaged in running the saw-mill. The little brother Weyburn, some four or five years old, had been down to the mill, and, as his brother supposed, had gone to the house, as he saw him go down the path and across the foot bridge spanning the race leading from the mill. But it seems that something in the race had attracted the child and he had either climbed down or fallen into the race, just as James hoisted the gate. The rush of the waters and the noise of the mill drowned his cries, but the brother caught a glimpse of his clothing as he was struggling in the water. To shut the gate was but the work of a moment and he rushed to his rescue, but it was too late; as he carried the dripping form to the house he found that life was extinct.

It was when the creek farm was nearly paid for, and at a time when Isaiah Giles had gone to Dryden to make the last payment, the family home was burned. Little or nothing was saved from the house. Then it was that the family records afore-mentioned were lost.

Ai W. Giles, born in 1810, was the youngest child. When he came to man's estate he worked for and with Samuel and John Giles until they left the Tompkins House. He then took charge of it and for some time conducted the business alone. He at one time had charge of the tannery at Gilesville for a short period. He was engaged in the shoe business for a short time at Ithaca, and at one time owned and occupied the property known as the Half Way House, on the Bridle Road. He was afterward connected with the milling business at Free Hollow, as it was then known, and kept a flour and feed store in Ithaca. He was married in 1846 to Miss Nancy Leach, of Chenango county, N. Y. He died childless in Ithaca in November, 1889. His wife survived him some three or four years.

In matters of politics the Giles brothers were Democrats until 1856, when they became Republicans and remained such until the end. They never took any active part in political matters and none of them ever held any public office save Samuel, who in 1835 was trustee of the village of Ithaca, and in 1845 was supervisor of the town of Ithaca. In 1854 Samuel Giles was named by the Legislature, with Stephen B. Cushing and Horace Mack, as a building committee in the act authorizing the building of the Court House at Ithaca. S. & J. Giles was a firm name known and honored among business men of Central New York. Unlike in temperament, yet they lived and worked together without friction. John died childless and Samuel lived to bury his last child, Miss Sarah Giles, in 1866.

The records of Tompkins county show that the first will proven in the county, September 6, 1817, was witnessed by Isaiah and Sarah Giles, being the will of John Morris, of Lansing, and presumably drawn by Isaiah Giles. The family name has now but one representative, and when Capt. J. J. Giles shall have been gathered to his fathers, a name for nearly one hundred years so well and favorably known in the town will be known only as a matter of history.

CHAPTER XXXV.

MALLORYVILLE AND McLEAN.

The larger part of McLean being outside of our territory in the adjoining town of Groton, we include in this chapter what we can claim of it as a part of Dryden. In the year 1820 Samuel Mallory, then 22 years of age, walked from his native place in Sharon, Conn., to Homer, N. Y., and five or six years later he purchased the mill site and water power at the point on Fall Creek, about one mile from McLean, which, from him, was named Malloryville. Here he built a saw-mill and added carding and cloth dressing machinery as well as a dyehouse, and finally established a chair factory, so that in these, their best days, the mills of Mr. Mallory gave employment to twenty-five or thirty men and one-third as many women in the different kinds of work. Some of the products of the chair factory are still in use to-day, indicating that the furniture of that time was much more substantial than most of that which we buy in these days. But in 1836 a great fire wiped out the flourishing industries of Mr. Mallory and he was so discouraged that he sold out and removed to a location in Wisconsin. Some years later, about 1845, barrels were manufactured at Malloryville by Wm. Trapp, who invented the first successful machinery for that kind of work. Still later the manufacture of tubs and firkins began to develop here under the firm of Howe & Watson, who later, in 1867, sold out to Rev. E. R. Wade, who conducted the business down to within a short time. Another fire in 1855 and still another in 1875 destroyed the manufacturing plant at Malloryville, but as often as it has been burned down it has been rebuilt, and in spite of the changes in the times the manufacturing industries at Malloryville still survive and have a promising future. The mercantile interests of Malloryville center at McLean, beyond our jurisdiction; but one hotel, the "Dryden House," of the management of which our town has not always had reason to be proud, the railroad depot,

SAMUEL MALLORY.

as well as the creamery of McLean, and one church, of the Roman Catholic denomination, come within our territory. The latter was erected in 1851 at a cost of one thousand dollars, the site and that of the Catholic cemetery near by having been donated by Michael O'Byrne. The society was formed in 1841 and among the first members were John Keenan, Patrick Corcoran, Matthew O'Byrne, James Walpole, Patrick Donnelly, Thomas and Patrick Kane.

Of the pioneers and leading men of Malloryville we will mention:

HOWE, SOLOMON L., who was born in Groton in the year 1824 and was educated at the old Groton Academy. Having relatives in Cattaraugus county he went there as a school teacher when he became of age and there married Miss Rispa Smith, of Yorkshire, in 1848. Returning to Tompkins county he settled at Malloryville in 1853, where he was employed by Howe & Watson, the senior member of the firm, Lemi Howe, being his cousin, in the manufacture of their wares on the contract system, making some practical improvements in the process of their manufacture. He was of a mechanical turn of mind and for many years, in addition to other duties, was the principal surveyor and civil engineer of the township. Among his other work in this line was the survey for the Dryden village water works and the laying out of the E., C. & N. R. R. through the town. He was at least twice elected commissioner of highways of the town and served two terms as school commissioner of the second district of Tompkins county. His death occurred July 25, 1895. His three sons are civil engineers in the West, his only daughter being the wife of F. J. Per Lee, of Groton. Wherever his duties called him Mr. Howe was always a faithful, upright man and an efficient officer.

MALLORY, SAMUEL, whose portrait is given at the beginning of this chapter and after whom Malloryville was named, was born in Sharon, Conn., April 18, 1798. He first married Nancy Hooper, of Homer, N. Y., who died in 1827. His second wife was Jane, daughter of Deacon Amos Hart, who, with four daughters, survives him. After leaving Malloryville he lived in McLean for a few years, but in 1844 moved to Elkhorn, Wis., where he engaged in hotel keeping in the early days of that country, serving two terms as treasurer of his county. He died in April, 1897, lacking only a few days of being 99 years of age. He was an exemplary man who in his long life made many friends, only a few of whom survive him.

WADE, REV. EDWIN R., was one of the Century Committee of Dryden's Centennial, and died since the writing of this History was commenced. He was a clergyman of the Christian denomination and, in addition to his clerical duties, in the year 1867 he engaged in the manufacturing business at Malloryville, which he continued there until near his death. His shop had at one time a capacity of turning out sixty thousand tubs and firkins annually, a large amount of the raw material required being, in later years, imported from other states. The changes in the demand for butter packages within the past few years have almost wiped out this industry, which was so flourishing at one time at Malloryville.

Elder Wade, as he was commonly called, came to Dryden from Cayuga county, where he had served as supervisor of the town of Niles, and in 1874 he was elected to the same office in our town. He was a man who united civil and religious virtues with a practical, honest, useful life. The writer has known him, at a funeral, to conduct the whole service alone, preaching, reading, praying, and finally singing the hymn without assistance or notes. He was everywhere recognized as a sincere Christian and an excellent citizen.

CHAPTER XXXVI.

THE VILLAGE OF FREEVILLE.

FREEVILLE GRIST-MILL.

Although it is the youngest, and hence the last to be considered among the villages and hamlets of the township, Freeville now stands foremost among them in the matter of railroad facilities, and only second in the number of its present inhabitants. As we have already seen, the grist-mill of Elder Daniel White on Fall Creek, the site of which was without the present village limits, was the first mill for grinding in the township, and we may now add that the present Freeville grist-mill, which replaced it on a site a short distance up-stream, was originally erected by John

White, a son of Daniel, in 1833, and is an old landmark of which we are able to give the accompanying view from a photograph taken some time ago.

Aside from these early grist-mills and some cloth dressing works which included a carding machine, and one or two accompanying saw-mills in the same locality, Freeville had no existence as a village or business center, not even containing a postoffice or church during the first half of our Century Period. The old Shaver Hotel, although improved to keep up with the times, is another old landmark, the oldest section of which was built about the year 1840 and was early kept by Erasmus Ballard. When the tannery building was removed from Gilesville a few years later the frame was brought here and used for an addition to the hotel, which is now kept by George I. Shaver, and appears as shown in the following view.

SHAVER'S HOTEL.

There was early built a nice log school house wholly of pine logs on the Shaver homestead, where Wm. J. Shaver now resides, then known as the Lafayette District, in which Henry H. Houpt, Esq., still living in Dryden, was the teacher in the winter of 1835-6. He taught four months of twenty-four school days in a month, for which he received forty dollars, which enabled him to still further continue his education. In speaking of his experience as a teacher there when he was twenty-one years of age, Mr. Houpt recalls the fact that one of the principal duties of the teacher in those days was to keep the pupils' pens in order, by preparing and sharpening them from goose quills, which were the only pens in use in those times.

The country in and about Freeville is remarkably level for this locality, Fall Creek, above the grist-mill, being now navigable for a mile and a half, as the stream crooks and winds, by a small pleasure steamboat kept for the use of pleasure parties in connection with Riverside Park. No such level stretch of water is found elsewhere on Fall Creek, which is noted for its frequent water-mill sites, which cannot exist upon level water.

The M. E. church of Freeville was erected in 1848, and it, together with the mills and hotel already referred to, formed what is now known as "Old Freeville," constituting the only signs of a village which existed here prior to the establishment of a railroad junction at a point about half a mile east, in the year 1872. Since that time the space between "Old Freeville" and the junction has been built up so as to form the main avenue of the present village; the church has been moved up nearer the center; Lyceum Hall, capable of comfortably seating five hundred people, has been constructed upon Liberal street; a new hotel known as the Junction House has been built near the railroad depot and several times enlarged into a structure of imposing proportions, as shown in the accompanying view of the railroad station; and Freeville has altogether taken upon herself the appearance and all of the essentials of an enterprising, modern village, somewhat resembling Western towns in her rapid development.

The following is a list of the ministers of the M. E. church who have served the Freeville charge since 1877, the pulpit having been supplied previous to that time by the ministers located at Dryden or Etna: Wm. M. Benger, A. F. Wheeler, Wm. F. Butman, R. L. Stilwell, S. W. Andrews, N. M. Wheeler, C. A. Wilson, James A. Roberts, T. C. Roskelly, Frederick E. Spence, J. Brownell Rogers.

About thirty years ago "Old Freeville" possessed a little old red-colored building called a school-house, the subject of repairing or rebuilding which then became the occasion of a school district quarrel and litigation, which continued for a number of years and involved the district and some of its inhabitants in expenses and judgments amounting in all to several thousand dollars. Since then a new and very respectable school-house has been built and an excellent school maintained.

Like many Western towns Freeville had a "boom," which arrived about the year 1880, when a great number of city lots were laid out and many of them sold and a manufacturing enterprise of great prom-

FREEVILLE JUNCTION.

ise was launched forth, first as a stove factory, and later as glass works. Since that time the community has been recovering from the stimulating effects of the unnatural excitement and the subsequent reaction, until it has now settled down upon a substantial basis of gradual growth and merited prosperity.

The village was incorporated July 2, 1887, to include in its limits a square mile of territory, being Lot No. 26 of the town, and now contains, according to the recent enumeration, three hundred and seventy-four inhabitants.

The following have been the principal officers:

PRESIDENTS.

W. H. Richardson,	-	1887-8	Orson Luther, -	- 1893
Fred E. Darling, -	-	1889	W. J. Shaver, -	1894
George DePuy,	-	1890	E. Blackman, -	- 1895-6
W. J. Shaver,	-	1891	W. H. Richardson, -	1897
N. H. Thompson,	-	1892	Dr. Homer Genung,	- 1898

CLERKS.

G. M. Watson,	-	1887	J. M. Carr, -	- 1891-2
E. F. George,	-	1888	Chas. W. Parker, -	- 1893
J. M. Carr, -	-	1889	W. J. Shaver, -	- 1894-5-6
Chas. W. Parker, -	-	1890	A. C. Stone, -	- 1897

No map of Freeville has heretofore been published, but it is believed that the one which accompanies this work will be found to be an accurate and complete topographical representation of the village as it now exists.

For so level a location Freeville is very fortunate in its water supply, many flowing wells having been developed in the village which furnish the purest of water in abundant quantities from a depth which prevents danger of contamination from surface drainage.

Riverside Park, on the bank of Fall Creek, although still a private enterprise belonging to Harris Roe, affords a commodious and attractive picnic and audience ground which is generously patronized in the summer and autumn months. During the past summer the Central New York Spiritual Association purchased ten acres of land in Freeville for a permanent camp ground, the location of which is also shown on the map.

KEY TO THE M

Mill Street.
2 Brewer & Son, grist-mill,
3 Chas. Shultz,
4 Sarah Lisdell,
5 Mrs. Mary Mineah,
6 M. D. Shaver,
7 Byron Brewer,
9 Mrs. A. Ellis,
11 George Seager.

Groton Avenue.
3 Seneca Smith,
5 David Robinson,
7 Frank Brotherton,
9 Burdette Heffron,
11 Edwin Smith.

Brooklyn Street.
2 J. L. Larkin,
4 John Sample,
6 John Brigden,
8 Brigden blacksmith shop,
10 W. R. Tripp.

Main Street.
1 Lewis Cole,
2 George Brewer,
3 Mrs. Rhoda Case,
4 Henry Brown,
5 F. Ray Willey,
6 Wm. Dolson,
7 N. B. Carl, store,
8 Chas. Monroe, carriages,
9 George Dolson,
10 Chas. Monroe,
11 H Pettibone,
12 Geo. I. Shaver, hotel,
13 J. Pierce,
14 H. A. Strong,
15 Albert Tripp,
16 William Monroe,
17 Luther Greenfield,
18 School-house,
19 M. E. Church,
20 D. M. Peck,
21 M. E. Parsonage,
22 J. M. Carr,
23 Wm. Fisher,
24 Sarah Bowers,
25 Will Cady,
26 Freeville Leader,
27 Wm. Skillman,
28 Mrs. C. Chapman,
29 N. J. Ogden,
30 Blacksmith shop,
31 Mrs. Kate Hanshaw,
32 Weaver blacksmith shop,
33 Wm. Dixon.

ise was launched forth, first as a stove factory, and later as glass works Since that time the community has been recovering from the stimulating effects of the unnatural excitement and the subsequent reaction, until it has now settled down upon a substantial basis of gradual growth and merited prosperity.

The village was incorporated July 2, 1887, to include in its limits a square mile of territory, being Lot No. 26 of the town, and now contains, according to the recent enumeration, three hundred and seventy-four inhabitants.

The following have been the principal officers:

PRESIDENTS.

W. H. Richardson,	- 1887-8	Orson Luther,	-	- 1893
Fred E. Darling,	- 1889	W. J. Shaver,	-	1894
George DePuy,	- 1890	E. Blackman,	-	- 1895-6
W. J. Shaver,	- 1891	W. H. Richardson,	-	1897
N. H. Thompson,	- 1892	Dr. Homer Genung,	-	1898

CLERKS.

G. M. Watson,	- 1887	J. M. Carr,	-	1891-2
E. F. George,	- 1888	Chas. W. Parker,	-	- 1893
J. M. Carr,	- 1889	W. J. Shaver,	-	- 1894 5-6
Chas. W. Parker,	- 1890	A. C. Stone,	-	- 1897

No map of Freeville has heretofore been published, but it is believed that the one which accompanies this work will be found to be an accurate and complete topographical representation of the village as it now exists.

For so level a location Freeville is very fortunate in its water supply, many flowing wells having been developed in the village which furnish the purest of water in abundant quantities from a depth which prevents danger of contamination from surface drainage.

Riverside Park, on the bank of Fall Creek, although still a private enterprise belonging to Harris Roe, affords a commodious and attractive picnic and audience ground which is generously patronized in the summer and autumn months. During the past summer the Central New York Spiritual Association purchased ten acres of land in Freeville for a permanent camp ground, the location of which is also shown on the map.

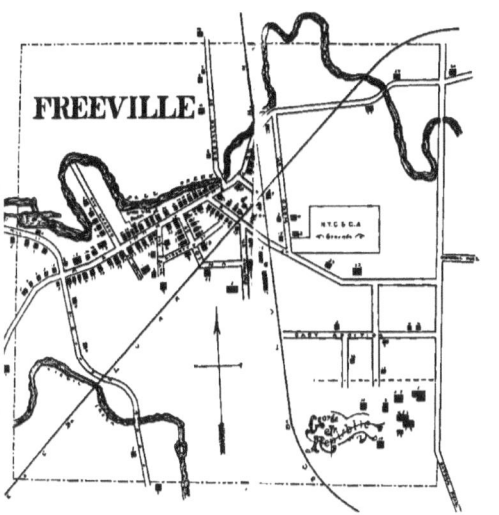

THE GEORGE JUNIOR REPUBLIC.

The George Junior Republic is a project which, for the past few years, has excited great interest throughout the whole extent of our country, and its influence as an educational force is rapidly becoming world-wide. In 1887 W. R. George, born near West Dryden, the son of John F. George and Eleanor Baker (George), went to New York city to engage in business. Being at heart a philanthropist, he spent many spare moments in forming friendships with the urchins on the streets of the East Side, and in striving to benefit them.

Their wretched surroundings so impressed him that, in the summer of 1890, aided by the Tribune Fresh Air Fund, he brought twenty-two children with him to spend his vacation of two weeks. These children were fed by kind neighbors and friends in the vicinity of

THE GEORGE JUNIOR REPUBLIC.

Freeville. For the next four years Mr. George brought out nearly two hundred and fifty children each summer for a stay of two weeks. During these years the plan of the Republic was slowly evolving. Mr. George saw that, while the two weeks of vacation gave the children a breath of fresh air and were helpful to them in many ways, the benefits could not be very permanent; the problems of pauperism and crime were still far from being solved. Brought up in homes of degradation and vice, having received most of their education from the slums, many of these children were accustomed to living "from hand to mouth." Many had been trained by their parents to depend on charitable societies for their subsistence, and their self-reliance was almost entirely lost. Others had come to consider it a glorious thing to be a "tough" and to be brought before police courts.

Mr. George tried experiments in making them work for their food and clothes and in having juries, composed of their peers, to judge them for their misdemeanors. These attempts showed him that the children were more self-reliant and more careful of their possessions when they paid their way; that, in trials by jury, these miniature men and women were more just in their decisions than were adults, because they could much better appreciate the situation; and that to be arrested, tried, convicted and imprisoned by citizens of their own size was a real punishment for the offenders. From these premises he argued that they might be trusted to make and enforce their own laws, to be entirely self-governing. Accordingly, in the summer of 1895, the Republic was formed.

It will, of course, be impossible to enter into details concerning the courts, the police department, the industrial classes, the school, the legislature, and all the varied activities of this little state. Much has been written concerning this enterprise in the best papers and magazines of the country.

The George Junior Republic is duly incorporated under the laws of the state and owns and occupies a farm of forty-eight acres, formerly a part of the Cady place, situated nearly one mile southeast of the Freeville postoffice, but within the corporate limits of the village. Other land, adjoining this farm, is rented and in the near future the Association will develop more fully the property which it owns. A view of their grounds is here given, and the location of their buildings as they now exist is shown on the map of Freeville.

The Republic has, at present, accommodations for about two hundred summer citizens and about fifty that stay throughout the entire year. It is achieving success and will undoubtedly attain to large proportions as the years pass by. But, better than all the material success which has been gained, are the mighty steps forward in the solution of that vast problem, the dealing with the poor in large cities.

The postoffice was established at Freeville during the War of the Rebellion, the Rev. I. Harris becoming the first postmaster. Mr. Harris was connected with the Sanitary Commission, which required a visit to Washington, upon which he presented a petition to the postoffice department and secured the location of the Freeville office with himself in charge of it.

After one or two unsuccessful efforts to maintain a newspaper at Freeville, The Leader, in charge of E. C. Smith, is now a lively weekly sheet which seems to be permanently established.

It should be remembered that as a business place Freeville is only about a quarter of a century old. Thirty years ago the locality of the railroad station was a lonely farm, then owned by George W. Tripp.

A stump fence even then lined a large part of what is now the main street of that village. After the establishment of the railroad junction in 1872 it was through the earnest and well-directed efforts of such men as Otis E. Wood, Albert C. Stone and John W. Webster that the destinies of Freeville as a village were cared for and properly shaped.

Freeville is too young to claim much connection with the pioneers of the township. Elder Daniel White, the first settler in this locality, has already been mentioned in connection with the building of the grist-mill and the settlement of the town itself, and we may also speak of the Shaver family, whose ancestor, John C. Shaver, originally from New Jersey, early in the century came to Ithaca, where he was actively engaged in building boats and boating on the waters of Cayuga Lake and through the Montezuma Marshes, Wood Creek, Mohawk and Hudson rivers to Albany, N. Y., which was the chief navigation from Ithaca to Albany and New York at that time. After leaving Ithaca he located with his family, May 6, 1823, on the farm where Wm. J. Shaver now resides.

Of his children, Ira C., the eldest, born in the year 1817, still resides at Freeville with his son Willard, one of the Centennial Committee; Julius M. and Wm. J. also reside in Freeville on the old homestead; Elizur W. lives in Portland, Oregon; Marcus D. also lives in Freeville; Ermana married Samuel Hanshaw, who is one of the most prominent farmers of the town of Ithaca; Mariah A. married Jacob Kline, also a wealthy and prominent farmer of the town of Ithaca. Mr. and Mrs. Kline are the parents of J. B. Kline, of Syracuse, N. Y., a foremost lawyer of that place and at present district attorney of Onondaga county.

CHAPTER XXXVII.

THE OCTAGONAL SCHOOL HOUSE.

Doubtless every old school house in the township has a record and a history, which, if properly reduced to writing, would be interesting and instructive reading. There is something especially fascinating connected with the education of children, and the story of the experiences of both the teacher and the pupil in their combined efforts to impart and develop, as well as to receive and apply, instruction is always interesting; but we cannot undertake here to write up the history of every school-house in Dryden, and what we shall say of this one, which has some especially interesting features about it and which is, in a general way, typical of the rest, must suffice for all.

If the plain and dingy walls of the brick building, a likeness of which is here given, commonly but inaccurately called the "Eight Square School House" could but tell their own story in such a way as to be fully understood, they would furnish an eloquent history which the writer of this chapter can but imperfectly imitate. They could truthfully say that within their inclosure were taught at least four school children who became supervisors of the town of Dryden, viz: Jeremiah Snyder, Smith Robertson, Hiram Snyder and Lemi Grover;

THE OCTAGONAL SCHOOL-HOUSE.

two, sheriffs of Tompkins county, viz: Thomas Robertson and Smith Robertson; two, school commissioners, viz: Smith Robertson and Alviras Snyder; one, a presiding elder, Wm. Newell Cobb; two, county superintendents of the poor, Jeremiah Snyder and Wm. W. Snyder; one, a millionaire, Orrin S. Wood; numerous others who became bank, telegraph and insurance managers as well as railroad superintendents, and last, but not least, one pupil of the gentler sex, Mary Ann Wood (Cornell), who in after years was destined to become the wife of a millionaire philanthropist and the mother of a distinguished governor of our Empire State.

THE OCTAGONAL SCHOOL HOUSE.

The age of this venerable but well preserved school-house is about seventy-five years. We think that some one had given us the exact date of its construction and the name of its chief builder, but if so the memorandum of it has unfortunately been mislaid. However, the precise date is not essential. From the year 1815 forward until it was built, a period of about ten years, upwards of one hundred pupils of school age were annually registered upon the records of the school district, (No. 5,) which, although occupying then, as now, a thinly settled agricultural section of the country, was remarkable in many respects, and doubtless afforded during the first half of our Century Period the best educational advantages to the largest number of appreciative school children to be found together in the township. At one time there were eight families residing in the district—coinciding in number with the eight sides of this unique form of a school building—which numbered among their members eighty-seven children, lacking only one in the aggregate of giving an average of eleven to each, and two single families at one time supplied the school with twenty-one pupils. Prior to about 1825 a small frame structure occupied the present site. Even then the greatest efforts were made to secure the very best of teachers for this school, some of them being obtained from Cortland and further east. During this time William Waterman taught the school six years, Almon Brown, one year, and David Reed, three years, Elmira (Bristol), the oldest daughter of Benjamin Wood, serving as assistant.

It was during Reed's administration as principal that it was decided that a new school-house must be built, the old building being so crowded with the swarms of pupils that some had to be sent out to play in order to give others a chance to recite. Accordingly the frame school-house was removed to a point about eighty rods north, where it served temporarily while the new brick building was being constructed, and afterwards it was sold and became a part of the Elijah Vanderhoef residence near the extreme northeast corner of the district.

We may well believe that the parents of these school children who were to be so successful in after life were not of the niggardly, narrow-minded class of citizens and did not begrudge the great effort under the circumstances required to construct a building which should be, as it was for half a century, the best of its kind in the township. The prime movers in the enterprise are said to have been Col. William Cobb, at the southeast, and Benjamin Wood, at the northeast corner of the district, and they were the first to have children who, after graduating from this school, sought higher institutions of learning; but the trustees who had charge of the work and who together conceived of and carried out the particular design were Capt. Geo. Robertson, Isaac Bishop and Henry Snyder, the nearest neighbors on either side, who employed as chief builder one Balcom from near McLean or Cortland. The brick was then made near by at the Grover-Hammond-Metzgar brickyard corners and the Jeremiah Snyder brickyard corners, last operated by Russel Sykes. Many of the less able residents contributed the other material and work, while the poorest families had their shares contributed by their more fortunate neighbors. Thus with the greatest harmony, as it is said, and entirely free from the jangles and controversies which too often in modern times distract and disgrace communities in such undertakings, the eight-sided brick school-house became an accomplished reality.

Reed as school-master was followed by Grinnell, Pelton and others in early days and later by such excellent local teachers as Ebenezer McArthur, Smith Robertson, Merritt L. Wood, Levi Snyder, Joseph Snyder, Alviras Snyder, Orrin S. Wood, William W. Snyder and Artemas L. Tyler.

While the Octagonal School House is still serviceable as an institution of learning we leave the reader to supply its present success and surroundings from other sources, our object being in this as in all other matters to emphasize and preserve that which is old and in danger of being lost to local history.

CHAPTER XXXVIII.

FURTHER HISTORY OF THE NORTH-WEST SECTION.

The pioneer families of this section of whom we have been able to gather sufficient data with which to make suitable mention are as follows:

BROWN, REUBEN, came from New Jersey to the town of Lansing about the year 1795.

In 1804 he removed to Dryden, locating on Lot 24. The most of the original purchase has remained in the family and is included in the farm of his grandson, S. N. Brown. In 1797, while living in Lansing, Reuben Brown was appointed leader of the first Methodist class at Asbury, being one of the very first in the county. He continued to lead this class for several years after his removal to Dryden, himself and wife often going on foot and carrying a child a distance of six miles through the then almost unbroken forest to attend church and lead his class. This continued until 1811, when a class was formed at West Dryden. The oldest and last surviving son, Freeman Brown, was born in Lansing in 1800 and died in 1889. Reuben Brown died in 1862, aged 86 years.

BUSH, CAPTAIN CALVIN, was born in Vermont in 1781, and at the age of twenty-one years came to Lansing and was employed by Samuel Baker, who owned a large tract of land near Teetertown. Soon after, he married Sarah Moore and removed to Dryden, locating first on Lot 34, on land now owned by W. H. Moore. His son Loren took this land and he purchased one hundred acres on Lot 3, now owned by Larkin Smith and Alvah Snyder. This was then a dense forest of heavy timber, which he cleared off, and here he lived until old age disqualified him from longer caring for the farm. Here the old people were cared for by their son-in-law, Freeman, and by their grandson, S. N. Brown, where Captain Bush died in 1864, aged 83 years. Before coming to Dryden he was at the head of a company of militia, and during the War of 1812 he led his company to the frontier.

GROVER, ANDREW, came in 1806 from New Jersey and first settled on the property since known as Woodlawn, which he afterwards lost from defective title. He then, about 1812, settled where his grandson, John S. Grover, now lives, and died in the year 1871. Of his children, Peter was the father of Major Grover, of the 76th Regiment, after whom Grover Post G. A. R., at Cortland, is named; Jacob is still living in Michigan, 90 years of age; Andrew P. was a justice of the peace of Dryden in 1849 and 1852, afterwards removing to Michigan. Others moved to Michigan and Steuben county, and a daughter, Parnelia Johnson, is still living in Dryden.

HANCE, THOMAS, SR., and sons, Thomas, Jr., and William, also two sons-in-law, Cornelius Conover and Benjamin Cook, came from New Jersey in 1800 and located one and one-half miles west of "Fox's Corners." Cook afterwards lived on Lot 5. Thomas, Sr., died in 1838, at the age of 97, and is buried at Asbury Church. The families were Quakers, among the first in town of that sect. Wm. moved to Ithaca in 1826, where he and his sons became prominent in business circles. William was known in his latter years as "Major Hance," from his prominence in the militia.

KNAPP, SAMUEL, was born in Belvidere, N. J., in December, 1759, and lived to the age of 91 years. He was a soldier in the Revolutionary War and was engaged in the battles of Trenton, Princeton, Stony Point and many others, and many were the stories told by him to his grandchildren of his trials and suffering. His wife, Charity Westfall, was born September 26, 1764, near Trenton, N. J.

About 1800 they started their journey into the interior, having all their possessions in a wagon drawn by a pair of horses. Thus they journeyed on, living in their wagon and by the aid of the gun and fishing rod, their only means of support, until they reached a place near where Varna is now located, from whence they cut their way through the woods to their destination and settled on Lot 14, where James Lumbard now lives, living in their wagon until a log house could be erected. Eight children were born to them, six girls and two boys, Mary, Catharine, Sarah, Betsey, Amy, Cable, Samuel, and Ann, who married Wm. Skillings.

McCUTCHEON, GEORGE, was about two years old when his parents, Andrew McCutcheon and wife, Jean Adair, came from Scotland in their own merchant sloop to this country. Finding acquaintances in the family of Robert Robertson in Saratoga township, N. Y., they were induced to remain there. When George was about sixteen years old he was pressed into the ranks of the Revolutionary Army and was in the first battle at Bemis Heights. He subsequently enlisted, in August, 1777, in Capt. Ball's company, Col. Shepard's Massachusetts Regiment, and served six years, being honorably discharged June 8, 1783, from Capt. Fuller's company, Col. Jackson's regiment. He was conspicuously brave in battle, in one of which he led his company in the capture of several Hessian regiments. He served in the battles of Monmouth, Valley Forge, at Saratoga during the surrender of Burgoyne, and many others. He returned home and after several years married Nancy Robertson, sister of Capt. Robertson, and they named their eldest son, born September 4, 1790, Robert, after her father, Robert Robertson. At the time Capt. Robertson moved to Dryden this son Robert desired to go with him and when about sixteen years old helped his uncle drive some cattle to his new farm.

Being greatly pleased with the new country he induced his father, George McCutcheon to move to Dryden. They left Saratoga on Feb. 26, 1807, performing the journey by land in ten days, camping by the way where night overtook them, sleeping on blankets on the ground, and arrived in Dryden, at Capt. Robertson's, on March 7, 1807.

They purchased a farm of Philip Robertson, now known as the Weaver farm, near Etna, bringing up their eleven children and living there until the mother's death and the father became too old and feeble to care for the farm. George McCutcheon died at the age of 85. Robert McCutcheon married Mary, daughter of Peter Snyder,

May 4th, 1812, after having volunteered on April 22, 1812, marching with his company in June to Buffalo, where he was in the command of Gen. Peterson at Buffalo, along Lake Erie, at Black Rock, and Niagara Falls, where they guarded the line. Most of the time he did scouting duty rarely being with his command, and with his company was honorably discharged May 22, 1813, and marched home, arriving in July of that year.

Peter Snyder had given to each of his sons one hundred acres and to each daughter as a dower fifty acres of land about one mile west of Etna and along Fall Creek. On the south side of this farm Robert built a log cabin of two rooms in July of the same year and in November the young couple went to housekeeping. The land was a heavy wilderness and Robert cut down the first trees and made the first clearing ever made on this land, putting in a crop of wheat about the cabin. In after years he added to this land 146 acres, put up good buildings on the north side of the same land, which is still in the family, being occupied and owned by his sons, Newton and Wm. McCutcheon.

Robert was active in educational affairs, helping to promote the building of the eight-square brick school-house and to form the library association for which it was noted, and especially active in naming the books to be purchased for the school library, which were so excellent in choice that he derived the benefit of almost a college education from them.

He and his wife were known as Uncle Robert and Aunt Polly to the whole neighborhood and his judgment was much sought after by the younger generation in all the affairs of life. They raised a family of fourteen children: Anna, Rensselaer, Parmeno, Betsey, Delilah (Emmons,) Jane (Fulkerson,) Marietta (Raub,) Miles, Arvilla (Emmons,) William, Catharine (Freeman,) Newton, Norman, Paulina (Peters,) of whom only five survive. Robert, after a long and useful life, seventy-three years of which was spent on the home farm, died in the ninety-fourth year of his age on February 2nd, 1884.

SKILLINGS, JOHN, was born in Ireland in 1756. In 1772, at the age of sixteen, he came to this country. He was a soldier in the Revolutionary War, having been captured by the Indians but afterwards making his escape. At the close of the war he married Miss Betsey Camel near Philadelphia, Pa., and about 1800 they came to Dryden and settled on the farm now owned by N. H. Mineah. They reared a family of six children, four girls and two boys, John, Jr., Margaret, Eleanor, Sally, Betsey, and William Skillings.

William Skillings married Miss Ann Knapp in the year 1827 and commenced keeping house on the farm now owned by N. H. Mineah. In 1836 he bought the farm now owned by James G. Sutfin, where he lived a few years and then moved on the farm now owned by S. M. Skillings, where they lived and died. Five children were born to them: John, who died in infancy; Eastman, who died at the age of 26; Betsey, who married Enos P. Moseley and now lives near the old homestead; Charity, who married Wm. J. Sutfin and lives across the way from the old homestead; Helen, who married James G. Sutfin, and now lives on the old Ward farm near by, and Samuel, who now owns and occupies the old homestead.

This briefly is the history of the Skillings family in Dryden. Children and grandchildren there have been, but among them all there is now but one left to hand the name of Skillings down, and that is Fay, the only son of Samuel Skillings.

SMITH. In the early years of the century five brothers, Benjamin, Isaac, Jacob, John and Henry Smith, with their widowed mother, left Stroudsburg, Pa., and came into the wilds of New York State. They selected land on Lot 11 in Dryden and began clearing off the timber. At the breaking out of the War of 1812 the four brothers first named volunteered and served throughout the war. Soon after returning Benjamin died. Isaac removed to Danby and later to Ohio. Jacob, John and Henry remained on the original purchase until their deaths. Their mother lived to the age of 104 years. The land is still held in the family, Ex-Sheriff William J. Smith and the heirs of James Smith, who were descendants of John Smith, being the present owners.

VAN NORTWICK, SIMEON, with his family, came from New Jersey early in the year 1804, settling on the extreme northeast corner of Lot No. 15, for which he traded property in Monmouth county, N. J., the transfer having been made in the year 1802. Among the witnesses to the deed as now appears upon the old document itself was Jacob Vanderbilt, the father of Cornelius Vanderbilt, who afterwards accumulated such a vast fortune, and whose descendants now wield such a powerful influence in the financial world. Upon their arrival in their new home it was found necessary to go four miles, nearly one mile west of West Dryden, to obtain a live coal to start their first fire. William Van Nortwick was six years old at this time, afterwards was a well known and prominent farmer until his death in 1866 at the age of 68 years. Sarah Van Nortwick still lives on the same farm where her grandfather settled ninety-eight years ago.

THE SOUTH-WEST SECTION.

CHAPTER XXXIX.

FURTHER HISTORY OF THE SOUTH-WEST SECTION.

This division includes all of the south-west quarter of the town except the Varna neighborhood, which has been treated separately, and also includes Lots 94 and 95 which are now a part of Caroline, but for historical purposes are still claimed as a part of Dryden.

The Free Will Baptist church on Snyder Hill, in this section, was organized April 3, 1824, with Elder Edward E. Dodge as pastor, and

CHURCH AT SNYDER HILL.

Wessels S. Middaugh and Daniel Reeves as deacons. The additional charter members were Salmon Hutchinson, Samuel Snyder, Benjamin Quick, Belden Meade and Chauncey Lee. The church building now in use was erected in 1856, but has lately been repaired and fitted up in modern style. The land upon which the church and school-house now stand was donated by Joseph M. Snyder, son of Jacob Snyder, the first permanent settler upon Snyder Hill.

The following are the names of the pastors of this church: Edward Dodge, Amos Daniels, Stephen Krum, H. H. Strickland, O. C. Hills, J. W. Hills, Oramel Bingham, J. M. Crandall, A. J. Wood, Evans, William Russell, L. D. Howe, S. W. Schoonover, Brown, D. D. Brown,

Woodruff, Cooley, F. D. Ellsworth, Charles Pease, Estus Van Marter, A. C. Babcock.

For a few years past a postoffice has been maintained at Ellis Hollow under the name of "Ellis," and in 1896 a new M. E. church was erected there, of which we are able to give the accompanying view. Until the erection of this building the class connected with it met in the school-house, the pastors being in 1896 Rev. J. E. Showers and since then Rev. Francis H. Dickerson.

ELLIS HOLLOW CHURCH.

Among the early inhabitants of this section of whom we are not able to give any family history are Israel Brown, Obadiah Brown, Zephaniah Brown, John Cornelius, Tobias Cornelius and Joseph Middaugh, a reference to Reuben Brown having been made in a preceding chapter. But we shall bring in the history of this section principally under the heads of its pioneer families, of whom we have records of the following:

BROWN, ZEPHANIAH. (See Chapter VI.)

BULL, AARON, and KRUM, MATTHEW, who were brothers-in-law, Mr. Bull having married Krum's sister, settled on one hundred acres in the southeast corner of Lot No. 95. They came from Marbletown, Ulster county, N. Y., now in Olive, of the same county. Mr. Krum's father, Henry W., was the owner, and the young men came to settle and clear it up in the year 1806, Krum in June and Bull in September. Bull had the south half and lived only a short distance from the south line of the Military Tract, then the south line of Cayuga county. He was a very bright, active, hard working man but of very little education, and it is said that he could not read or write until his wife taught him. He was originally from Bull's Bridge, on the Housatonic River, in Connecticut, and came thence to Ulster county, N. Y., where he married into the Krum family. Mr. Bull lived on the Dryden lot twelve years, when he bought the Cass Tavern, on the Turnpike (now the Henry S. Krum place), where he afterwards lived and died. He purchased of Nicholas Fish (father of Hamilton Fish) a large part of Lot 85 and adjacent lands in Dryden and engaged in lumbering, owning and managing, with his sons, a couple of canal boats. His family have always held an influential position.

Matthew Krum was of Holland Dutch descent and the ancestor of the most of the Krums of this county. He lived and died on the place now known as the Aaron B. Schutt farm. John Schutt, the father-in-law of Ruloff, also married a sister of Krum.

COBB, LYMAN, the author of Cobb's readers, spelling books, and other school books extensively used in early times in Central and Western New York and Pennsylvania, formerly lived in the white house near Snyder's Station, on the E., C. & N. railroad, a little east of Varna. He had his books published at Ithaca and the covers were made of thin boards covered with blue paper. He was born in Canaan, Connecticut (or, as some say, in Lenox, Massachusetts,) in the year 1800, and in his youth came with his father's family to Berkshire, Tioga county, N. Y., locating about a mile east of Speedsville. He afterwards taught school at Slaterville about three years and it was here that he compiled the first edition of his spelling book published by Mack & Andrus about the year 1819. He was afterwards a teacher in Ithaca. His wife was a daughter of Ephraim Chambers, who at one time resided on the Dan Rice farm in Ellis Hollow, and his sister was Mrs. Thomas Davis, who resided in Dryden from 1840 until her decease in 1860.

GENUNG, BENJAMIN, was a Revolutionary soldier, born May 10, 1758, and enlisted at Hanover, Morris county, N. J., in February, 1776, in Capt. Lyon's company of Col. (afterwards General) McDougall's regiment of the New York line for one year. He was in the battle of White Plains and in the retreat from New York after the battle of Long Island. In January of the year 1800 he bought of Rev. Asa Hilyer, of Morris county, N. J., a part of Lot No. 93 of Dryden, and in that spring he came to his new home with a yoke of oxen and wagon carrying all of his household goods and farming utensils, as well as his family, consisting of his wife and six children. They came by way of the celebrated "Beech Woods" in Pennsylvania to Owego and from there to Dryden, stopping with a man by the name of Iruna Peat on Lot 92 until he could locate his purchase, a part of Lot 93, where he settled on the land now owned by one of his grandsons, Benjamin Genung, Jr. Two of his sons, Barnabas and Aaron, were in the War of 1812, the latter, born December 25, 1787, being in the company of Major Ellis. His daughter Rachel married Wm. Pew, who came to Ithaca in 1803, and many of their descendants are now living in Ithaca and Dryden. His remaining children were Timothy, Pearon and Philo.

Joseph A. Genung, a son of Aaron, born in Dryden January 17, 1835, is an active member of the Centennial Executive Committee, his postoffice being Ithaca although residing in the town of Dryden.

In addition to Joseph A. Genung, Aaron had two other sons and three daughters. One son, Luther, married Phœbe Banfield and settled and died in the town of Danby, leaving a son, Amasa T., now residing in Ithaca. Another son, Jacob, married Angeline Pew and resides in the vicinity of Ellis Hollow. One daughter, Mary, married Jesse English and they resided on Snyder Hill. Another daughter, Rebecca, married John English and resided on Snyder Hill. Another daughter, Lockey, married James Hagadorn and they resided at Spencer, N. Y.

Joseph A. Genung married in 1859 Mary E. Cornelius and they had three daughters. Of these, Estella E. died in 1878, aged 17 years; Nellie M., born 1864, graduated at the Ithaca High School, married William Gillmer, a farmer; Mary Josephine, born 1876, prepared at the Ithaca High School, graduated at Cornell University 1897, married Leon Nelson Nichols, graduated at Cornell University 1892, a librarian.

Dr. Homer Genung, of Freeville, and Dr. Benjamin Genung, of Wyalusing, Pa., are sons of Benjamin Genung, son of Philo.

Dr. John A. Genung, of Ithaca, is a son of John, son of Philo.

The Genungs were nearly all of them prominent and respected farmers.

HAMMOND, THOMAS and ALICE (STONE). Shortly after the year 1800, presumably in 1803, there removed from Scituate, Providence county, Rhode Island, Thomas Hammond, in time of peace a seaman in the coast towns trade of New Bedford, Providence and New London, and attached to the vessels of war during the Revolution. He was born at or near that locality about 1730 and married Alice Stone, the daughter of Peter and Patience Stone, of that place. From them are descended one wing of the Benjamin Wood family, of Western Dryden, and of the Ezra Cornell family of Ithaca.

Thomas, grown too old to longer go before the mast and endure the rigor of the sea, still courted adventure in the haunts of the deer, bear, wolf and Indian, his earlier skirmishes with all of the last named having found more in him, in accord with his tastes, than even the sea fisheries or the comparative quiet of the war vessel. He therefore removed to the far frontier of Chenango Valley, N. Y., about 1803, taking with him his numerous family and several other friends (he being a man of push and leadership), together with all his earthly belongings.

This was not only a tedious but perilous journey, as it was performed with the proverbial ox team of that day, but on foot for all who could walk. The only entrance to his destination lay via Albany and the Hudson River crossing and the Mohawk and Chenango valleys to Oxford, N. Y. At this point the state was concentrating some interest by its highway cutting into the more westerly wilds, where the deer, bear, wolf and Indian had to be successfully routed, furnishing the excitement craved by Thomas, and an inducement for work to his grown and industrious children, and other kin of the party.

Of this party were his wife, Alice; his daughter, Amy, and her husband, Nathan Wood; his grandson, Benjamin Wood; his grandson-in-law, Orrin Squire; his son, Daniel Hammond, and his family, all of whom figure conspicuously as pioneers of Western Dryden, and who were clever artisans in brick making, cooperage and weaver's reed making, all essentials in opening new colonies.

Their first settlement was made at Oxford, next at Sherburne, next at Quaker Basin near DeRuyter; thence they came to Willow Glen a little later than 1815, and finally reached, about 1820, the south-west quarter of great lot No. 32, better known as Supervisor Lemi Grover's corner, and Woodlawn, next east. Here, after having buried the husband, Thomas, in Chenango Valley, the wife, Alice, lived and died, and is buried beside her daughter Amy (Wood) in the Captain George Robertson cemetery, a few of six generations following hers still clinging near there to-day.

William Wigton, the old hotel-keeper at Willow Glen, where now stands the Moses Rowland residence, became a conspicuous land owner in Western Dryden, with headquarters at this Hammond-Grover corner; and he was succeeded in the ownership of the Willow Glen hotel by Daniel Hammond, and also as landlord thereof.

A little later on Daniel also succeeded Major Wigton as owner of the Grover southeast corner of Lot 32 and Woodlawn. Upon this corner Daniel Hammond and his sons, assisted by Orrin Squire and Benjamin Wood, opened the first brickyard of Western Dryden; and from the material furnished, the "eight-square" brick school-house was largely built.

From the pioneer Alice, through her son Thomas, is descended the numerous Hammond family of Virgil; and through George and William and his wife, Polly Tanner, come the now well known law firm of Hammond & Hammond, of Seneca Falls, N. Y.

From pioneer Alice, through her daughter Amy and her husband, Nathan, and their son Benjamin Wood, and his wife, Mary Bonesteel, are descended the conspicuous Wood family, of Western Dryden; and through their daughter Mary Ann, whose husband was Hon. Ezra Cornell, of Cornell University fame, comes Ex-Governor Cornell, Chief Financier Frank C. Cornell, and Chief Civil Engineer O. H. Perry Cornell, nine children in all, only five of whom came to mature age and still survive; and they own the two-hundred-acre farm known as Woodlawn.

HARNED, WILLIAM, and Hanna Critisteen were married in New Jersey in the year 1794, and within a few years removed to Dryden. He built his first log-house on the north bank of Cascadilla Creek, a little east of the present bridge near the residence of Edwin Snyder. He was one of the highway commissioners elected at the first town meeting of Dryden held in 1803. Of a family of seven, one daughter, Mary, married Thomas George, Eliza married Dr. Harvey Harris, and Clarissa married Peter I. Rose, an early settler of the town. All are now deceased and S. M. George, of West Dryden, is believed to by the only descendant of Wm. Harned now residing in the town.

HARRIS, DR. HARVEY, an early physician of the town, registered at Ithaca in 1828, first practiced at West Dryden, afterwards at Etna for many years and finally moved to Illinois, where he died after 1860.

MIDDAUGH, JOSEPH, and his son WESSELS S. came to Dryden in 1807, from near the borders of Orange county, N. Y., where it joins the state of New Jersey. They were of Dutch descent and first settled in Dryden on one hundred acres of land near Ellis Hollow, to which they added by subsequent purchases and upon which they are both buried. For several years they kept a tavern.

Wessels S. was a supervisor of the town and raised a large family of sons, among whom were Orrin, the father of Fred and William Henry; Wessels, Jr., who now owns the Judge Ellis homestead at Ellis Hollow; and Harrison, who married a grand-daughter of both Judge and Major Ellis. One of his daughters married Edward Mulks, who succeeded to the Middaugh homestead and whose daughter, Mrs. C. L. Lull, now owns it.

THE SOUTH-WEST SECTION.

PALMERTON, ICHABOD, was the father of Marcus and Sylvanus Palmerton, and was one of several who followed Peleg Ellis from Royal Grant, in Herkimer county, to Ellis Hollow. He came in 1801, the year after Ellis arrived. From the same place soon after Asa Hurd came and settled on the present Gray farm, Van Allen on the Dan Rice farm, Joseph Smith on the Willey farm and Nathan Gosper on the E. J. Thomas farm.

ROBERTSON, PHILIP SCHUYLER, was born in Saratoga county, N. Y., May 4, 1774. His name was given him by Gen. Philip Schuyler, of Revolutionary fame, who gave with the name a life lease of fifty acres of land in Saratoga county.

His father, Robert, who was also the father of Capt. George Robertson, served during the Revolutionary war and died soon after its close, when Philip was but seven years of age. He lived with his uncle, George McCutcheon, for several years, and then commenced working with his brother, George, at the carpenter and mill-wright trade, making that his business for several years in Saratoga. In 1798 the two brothers, Philip and George, each driving a yoke of oxen and accompanied by two young men, said to have been Jared Benjamin and Walter Yeomans, (but others say one of them was Moses Snyder), started from Schuylerville, Saratoga county, for the West, coming by the way of the Mohawk Valley, Ithaca and Auburn, to the lot (No. 53) where M. J. Robertson now lives, arriving March 12, 1798. Philip lived with his brother George, until his marriage, July 25, 1802, to Elsie Sweezy from New Jersey. From that source there came seven children, George, Robert P., Mary, Peter, Allen, Anna (Snyder) and Oakley, of whom only the last two named survive.

Philip bought of his brother George the east part of the lot and locating upon that part now known as the Weaver farm, then all a perfect wilderness, he cleared thirty acres. As they had neither hay nor straw for their oxen they fed them upon browse from the trees as they cut them. During the work of clearing, Philip unfortunately had a tree fall upon him, breaking his thigh and crushing his left hand as it rested on his axe helve, besides injuring him internally and making him a cripple for the rest of his life.

That spring he planted among the logs four acres of corn, doing the work on crutches, and in the fall harvesting the crop of two hundred bushels of ears. Cutting and piling the logs that fall, they then sowed the land to wheat. On his way from his farm to the home of his brother George, where he boarded, the first season, he shot and killed seven deer without hunting an hour. He also shot a wildcat and coon; the latter, very fat, weighed sixty pounds and supplied grease for a barrel of soap.

For several years he lived upon and improved this place and then sold it to George McCutcheon and bought a place on the Bridle Road above Etna. Clearing about fifteen acres of this place he sold it and bought a farm above Varna on the same road, building a house and clearing a part of the land. This place he sold and moved to Brutus, Cayuga county, where he remained two years and then returned to Dryden, where he bought a quarter section of Lot No. 3, on the State Road, which was all wild land. He cleared this last place, where he died August 4, 1842, and the farm still remains in the family.

SNYDER, JACOB. In the spring of 1801 a family of emigrants set out from Essex county, N. J., traveling through the "Beech Woods" to Owego and thence to the present town of Ithaca. That family consisted of Jacob Snyder, his wife, three sons and one daughter, the youngest child being a year old and the oldest twelve. The father was a skilled workman in three trades, tailoring, carpentering and blacksmithing, as people now living can testify. Upon their arrival the family took up temporary quarters and waited for a time in order tha ttitles to the land might be investigated before purchasing, and thus avoid the spurious titles then so frequently met with. Mr. Snyder finally bought of James Glenny, of Virgil, (a grantee of a Revolutionary soldier, Lieutenant Wm. Glenny, to whom the lot had been awarded,) one hundred acres of land on Lot 82, for the consideration of $330. The deed, executed Sept. 14, 1802, was a relic on exhibition at the Centennial. He later purchased a part of Lot 92, which passed into the possession of his sons Daniel and Peter. Of the original purchase on Lot 82, a part afterwards belonged to his son Joseph M. Snyder and is now occupied by his sons Jacob and Harry. The daughter, Rebecca, who married Aaron, the son of Benjamin Genung, came into possession of the old homestead of the original purchase of 1802, which is now owned and occupied by their son, Joseph A. Genung. Upon this old homested there is still standing the same barn that was built by Jacob Snyder in 1806. He built his permanent dwelling in 1808, a substantial structure of hewn pine logs, which was occupied until 1872 and is still in a condition for use for many more years as a place of storage of farming utensils.

From this early settlement by Jacob Snyder the entire region grew to have the name of Snyder Hill, which it still bears.

THE NORTH-EAST SECTION. 175

CHAPTER XL.

FURTHER HISTORY OF THE NORTH-EAST SECTION.

Upon Lot No. 21 of Virgil, John Gee, a Revolutionary soldier who had drawn that lot, came and settled, according to Bouton's History, June 17, 1796, and some of his descendants still reside upon it. His nearest neighbor was four miles off at that time; but a few years later, probably in 1802, Joseph Schofield and his son Ananias settled on the adjoining Lot 20, of Dryden, and Joseph became one of the town officers when the first town meeting was held in 1803. In this extreme northeast corner of the township several mechanics, including the Mason, Hutchings and Bates families, early located; and on a branch of Beaver Creek, which still flows, but with diminished volume since the country has been cleared up, through the gully at the foot of Gulf Hill on the road to Cortland, and a short distance up-stream from this road, was established in the year 1809, according to Bouton's History, the Hutchings grist-mill, which accommodated the Virgil as well as the Dryden people in that section. This was more than twenty years before any grist-mill existed in Dryden village, but seven years after the White mill had been established at Freeville. It was here, near this pioneer grist-mill, in the town of Dryden, that the Hutchings apple had its origin. Not only was the grist-mill operated by them for a number of years, but a rake factory and other industries flourished, and it is claimed that the first successful power threshing machines were manufactured here. But these mechanics, or that portion of them who did not become farmers, afterwards drifted off to McLean and Malloryville, where the water power was more lasting and abundant and it is now a matter of surprise that a small branch of Beaver Creek near its source could ever have been considered capable of furnishing the water power necessary to run a grist-mill.

A thrifty and intelligent class of farmers have, however, always flourished in this section of the township, of a few only of whom are we able to give details, as follows:

ALLEN, WYATT, came to Dryden in 1805 from Aurora, Cayuga county, settling on the farm now occupied by John Mullen. In the year 1840 he removed to Dryden village, settling on South street where he died. Among his descendants is George W. Bradley of Dryden. Two of his brothers came later, married into the Foote and Clauson pioneer families of Willow Glen and moved with their families to the far West.

CARMER, ISAAC, and brother JACOB, came from near Essex Court

House, in New Jersey, about the year 1801, and settled on Lot No. 20 on one of the farms since owned by G. M. Lupton, where he died in January, 1853, within a few days of one hundred and two years of age. His children have long since died, but his grandchildren include Chester and Cleveland, children of his son John. The brother Jacob settled on the hill immediately south of Dryden village and his descendants are now believed to be non-residents.

GIVENS, SAMUEL, was an early settler in this part of the township, concerning whom we can give but few particulars. His descendants now residing or having died here are numerous, including Amos K., the father of our Darius Givens, of Dryden village; Col. Chas. Givens, an early town officer and the father of Edward and the late Wm. R. and Thomas; Lettie G., the mother of G. M. and Z. Lupton; Sarah, the wife of Abram Griswold; William, the father of Cortland Givens; and Jane, the wife of Zebulun Miller.

HILL, JOSEPH, and Sarah Bancroft were married at Flemington, N. J., November 30, 1809, and started for Dryden the same season. Two teams brought their goods. They drove two cows and made butter on the way by putting the milk in churns, the motion of the wagon bringing the butter. Mr. Hill had the choice of a section (six hundred and forty acres) of land in Seneca county or one in Dryden. He chose the latter on account of the pine timber. The land lay in Lot No. 6, upon which was already a small log cabin, but during their first night a heavy wind blew off the roof.

Mrs. Hill had been anxious to leave New Jersey, as it was the custom for farmers to keep slaves, and although her husband was homesick and wanted to move back she would not consent to go, as she did not like to live where they kept slaves. She wove woolen and linen cloth and in this way helped pay for clearing the land.

Joseph Hill died September 12, 1853, 71 years old. Sarah Bancroft Hill died April 8, 1874, 86 years old.

They had a family of eleven children: Mary, the oldest, married Hiram Graves, settled in Moravia and left a large family. Ambrose married Sarah Hart and finally settled on the old homestead. He left a family of four children. Isaac taught school in Dryden at one time in a school-house at or near the home of Chas. Perrigo. He married and moved to Dundee and again moved to Bay City, Mich., where he left a family of five children. Martha married James Van Etten and settled in Albany, N. Y., where Mr. Van Etten died. She afterward married Mr. Buck, of Chemung, and left three children. Elias B. did not marry and died young. Harris married and lived in Peruville, N.

Y., several years and afterward moved to Warren, Pa., where he left three children. Lucinda married S. C. Fulkerson and always lived in the town of Dryden. She left five children. Stacy B. married and moved to Canada. He left three children. Sarah married Ezra Beach, of Peruville. She left one child. Lorena married Edwin J. Hart, of McLean, who died April 16, 1895. In 1870 she married A. H. Vough, of McLean, and they live at present one-half mile west of McLean. Mrs. Vough is the only living child of Joseph and Sarah Hill. Thomas, the youngest son, did not marry.

Edwin Hill, a son of Ambrose, still lives on the original homestead.

LUPTON, NATHAN H. W., came to Dryden as a school teacher in 1815 or 1816, from Orange county. He was at one time a hotel keeper and in later years a thrifty and industrious farmer, among whose descendants now residing in the township are his sons, G. M. and Z. Lupton, and their children.

McKEE, JAMES and ROBERT, brothers, from Stewartstown, County Tyrone, Ireland, came to this country soon after the year 1800, James arriving first. Robert came in 1806, being six weeks and three days out of sight of land on the voyage. Coming up the Hudson river as far as Albany he there hired a teamster with a yoke of oxen and a lumber wagon to bring them through the forests to Dryden, where James was already located on what is now the Wm. B. Hubbard place, two miles north from Dryden village. Robert bought the adjoining Sickmon farm and built a log house near the line between the two farms. This habitation consisted of one room with a ground floor and bark roof, greased paper for windows and a blanket for a door, blocks of wood serving as chairs, and a pile of brush for a bed. They had brought with them two large chests well filled with clothing and bedding, and some provisions and tools with which to work.

The nearest postoffice was Milton (Lansing) and Mrs. McKee at one time went on horseback through the woods to Ludlowville, being guided by the marked trees, and paid out her last fifty cents in money to get a letter from her parents in Ireland.

The McKees were, however, thrifty and prosperous people and soon gained a foothold in their new home. Robert, in addition to farming, carried on a distillery and was at the same time a leading member of the Presbyterian church at Dryden village. By his first wife there were three children, viz: James R., Mrs. Leonard Hile and Mrs. Jane West. By his second wife there were twelve children, two boys and ten girls. Mrs. Mary McKee, who was the second wife of Robert, was a sister of Thomas Lormor, Sr., the old gentleman who was the ancestor of the greater part of the Lormor family in Dryden and died here about twenty-five years ago. In the earlier times Mrs. McKee spun and wove the clothing for the family, but in later years when her girls were grown up she bought calico for their dresses. At one time she went to Quigg's store, in Ithaca, and, after purchasing several dress patterns, the young clerk who was waiting upon her, desiring to be sociable, remarked that she must have quite a family of girls to require so much dress goods. "Yes," said she, "I have at home ten girls of my own and each of them has two brothers and a half." The clerk, who prided himself on his figures, computed in his head that it would make her the mother of thirty-five children, which, he said, was impossible, and offered to bet her a new dress that she was overstating it; but she insisted that her statement was true and accepting the wager agreed to leave it to the proprietor, who knew the facts and decided that she was entitled to the dress from the clerk. The two brothers were her own two sons, Robert and Thomas, and the half brother was James R., the son by the first wife. The ten daughters included Charlotte (Sickmon), the youngest and only one now living; Catharine (Out), the mother of Mrs. Geo. H. Hart, of Dryden village; Ellen, the wife of John Morgan; Sally, the first wife of Peter Mineah, and Mary, the wife of Thomas Mineah.

Robert McKee died in 1845 at the age of 77 years, while his wife survived until 1873, when she died at the age of 90. James McKee also left a large family of children, of whom one was John, the father of Samuel, William, and others, and another was Mrs. Alvin, the mother of the late James H. Cole.

MINEAH, JOHN, the ancestor of the family in Dryden having that name, not often met with elsewhere, came very early in the century from New Jersey with the McElhenys, the two families having been already connected by marriage. He located in the section of the township north and east from Freeville, where numbers of his descendants still reside. Of his daughters, Mary Ann was the first wife of Abel White, and Betsey married Charles Niver, who lived near Peruville. Of his sons, William was the father of George, John, James, and others; James was the father of John H., Nicholas, George, and others; Thomas was the father of Robert, while John, Jr., was the father of Edwin D., of Eagle Grove, Iowa. Two daughters of John, Jr., Albina and Anna, were formerly school teachers in different districts of the township and are now proprietors of a ladies' select school in Chicago. The daughters also included Mrs. Luther Griswold, of Dryden, and Mrs. D. C. Avery, of Baltimore, Md.

SEAGER or SAGER, (spelled both ways.) This family consisted of a number of brothers and a sister who came from Orange county to Dryden early in the century. Jacob came first in 1808, John in the fall of 1809, Philip, who was born in 1799, and his sister Katie, a little later. Jacob and Katie afterwards moved to Bath, Steuben county, but John first settled on Lot 39 near where Elliott Fortner now resides, afterwards removed to Lot 40, where he lived until his death at the age of 94. He came in a covered emigrant wagon by way of Owego, and from there up the Turnpike to Ithaca and then to Lot 39 in Dryden, where he and his family arrived in January, 1810. It was very cold and the snow was deep. They were obliged to live for three days in the wagon until they built a log house, which for a long time had neither door, window nor fireplace. They used a blanket for a door, and built the fire on the ground. There they lived in this way all winter with five small children, viz: Abram, Henry, Betsey, Joanna and John. That winter John, Sr., cut and prepared for burning eight acres of heavy timber, in place of which he planted corn the next summer. Three children were born to them in Dryden, viz: Robert, Samuel and Katie Ann. John Seager and his children altogether cut and cleared about one hundred fifty acres of land in Dryden.

John and Abigail, his wife, were exemplary citizens, loved and respected by all who knew them. Robert, one of the younger children, who lived and died upon the old homestead, was throughout his long and useful life one of the first to find out and relieve distress, and his works for good in and out of the M. E. church, of which he was an active member, will long be remembered.

Philip came to the town of Dryden in early manhoood, first stopping with people who lived on Lot No. 20 and in 1827 he married Anna, daughter of Capt. John Gardner, a wagon master of the Continental army, who assisted Washington in crossing the Delaware. Gardner came from New Jersey, locating on the farm still owned by his son, Robert B. Gardner. In the year 1830, Philip Seager purchased the farm on Fall Creek now owned by his son George. There was on it, even at that time, a small frame house, which is still standing in a fair state of preservation as a relic of the old dwelling, but the log barn, which was also there when Philip Seager purchased the farm, disappeared a few years ago.

After many years of toil and privations, such as were known only to the early settlers, and after accumulating a comfortable fortune, Mr. Seager passed away at the advanced age of 85 years. In his declining years he enjoyed relating how he and his good wife managed to get along, raising a large family and many times not having fifty cents ahead. He drew all of his grain in these early days to Cayuga Lake with an ox team, himself going barefoot. His wife spun and dyed wool for the clothing of the family in winter and flax for summer use. Philip Seager was a man of excellent judgment, determined stability and good common sense.

SCHOFIELD, JOSEPH, already referred to in the beginning of this chapter, came from Stamford, Conn., and settled on Lot No. 20 in the year 1802, being the earliest pioneer in that part of the township. Ananias, the oldest son, accompanied him, as well as David, who was then an infant, and afterward the father of our Henry Schofield. Solomon, a son of the pioneer Joseph, was a clergyman and wrote a book describing the scenes and incidents of the pioneer journey of his parents to Dryden. Theodosia (Bacon), a daughter of Joseph, was the mother of Mrs. Harriet Carpenter, now an old lady of Dryden village, who is therefore a grand-daughter of pioneer Joseph.

SHERWOOD, ANDREW, a soldier of the Revolution, accompanied by his son Thomas, came from Poughkeepsie, of this state, in 1802, and located on Lot No. 9. He died at the age of ninety-nine years. Thomas, the son, took part in the War of 1812, was a miller by trade and a worthy citizen. His eleven children, all of whom are now deceased, are the ancestors of many present residents of Dryden.

SUTFIN, the pioneer of the Sutfin family in Dryden, who is supposed to be the Derick Sutfin who is recorded as a justice of the peace of the town in 1803 and a town clerk and one of the charter members of the Presbyterian church society in Dryden village in 1808, came from New Jersey in 1801 and settled on Fall Creek on what is now the Duryea farm. In 1803 tradition says that he built a frame barn, one of the first, if not the first, in the township, and to do the raising of the frame he was required to call upon his neighbors from three towns, the inhabitants were then so few and far between.

CHAPTER XLI.

FURTHER HISTORY OF THE SOUTH-EAST SECTION.

This corner of the township includes Dryden Lake, of which a view has already been given at page 3 of this volume. It is located in a good farming locality near the summit which divides the streams which flow southerly into the Susquehanna from those which flow northerly into the St. Lawrence system of watercourses.

THE SOUTH-EAST SECTION.

James Lacy, the youngest one of the five brothers who came to Dryden from New Jersey in 1801, was the first to settle near its shores, and he soon built a dam at the outlet, thereby enlarging its natural capacity and furnishing power for a saw-mill which he soon constructed for the purpose of manufacturing lumber from the abundance of pine which was there found. At one time five saw-mills were operated upon the outlet flowing from the Lake before Dryden village was reached and at least one saw-mill existed at the head of the Lake upon its inlet.

Some species of fish were found naturally existing in the waters of the Lake when first discovered, but others, including pickerel and perch, were afterward introduced and have multiplied, furnishing excellent fishing for an inland town, which is appreciated by the inhabitants for many miles around. A number of flat-bottom boats are kept and rented by the proprietors of the Lake for fishing purposes and are in great demand annually from the fifteenth of May, when the fishing season begins. For some years past the saw-mill at the outlet has been allowed to run down for the want of raw material and the only use made of the Lake except for fishing and pleasure parties has been the ice harvesting industry, which has developed within a few years into an extensive business in its season. A large storage ice-house has been erected on the bank near the railroad by the Philadelphia Milk Supply Company, and at the proper season large quantities of ice are harvested and stored or shipped at this point, which combines the advantages of a high altitude, pure lake water, principally derived from springs in the neighborhood, and convenient transportation.

In this connection we are obliged to chronicle an event which happened in this locality December 18, 1887, the murder of Paul Layton. He was a farmer who had formerly lived on Long Island, near New York, and had lived in Dryden quite a number of years, owning and occupying a large farm to the northeast of the Lake. Of a somewhat miserly disposition, employing only cheap help with whom he lived, and having no family of his own, Mr. Layton had acquired considerable property and was frequently known to carry a good deal of money about his person. At the time of his death in the winter time he had no one living with him and he was chiefly employed in caring for his stock, which required his attention about the barn, situated in a secluded location some little distance from the highway. Here, on the morning of December 18, 1887, he was found with his skull broken, evidently from the effect of blows upon the head, but with no evidence as to who had committed the crime. His pocketbook, in which he carried his money, was gone and it was concluded that money was the incentive which influenced the villain to commit the deed, but although great efforts were made to investigate the matter, no satisfactory proof as to who committed the act was ever obtained, and it seems likely ever to remain an unsolved mystery.

Of the pioneer families of this section we can only mention:

BAILEY, JESSE, who, with his son Morris, bought thirty acres of land on Lot 56, upon which they were living as early as 1804, being a part of the farm now owned and occupied by Cyrus Tyler. Morris Bailey is named among the original members of the Baptist church of Etna in 1804 and he was the father of the Bailey brothers for so long a time residents of Dryden village but only two of whom, Wm. and Amasa, now survive.

CARPENTER, ABNER, whose deed of about three hundred acres of land on Lot No. 70, near the head of Dryden Lake, bears date March 17, 1804, was among the very earliest settlers in that part of the town, where some of his descendants still reside. There seems to have been a controversy between him and Jacob Hiles at the foot of the Lake as to some rights connected therewith and among his papers we find the bond of Jacob Hiles, executed December 3, 1814, according to which they agree to submit to John Ellis, Jesse Stout and Joseph Hart all of the matters in controversy.

Of the children of Abner Carpenter, Laura married Wm. Tillotson; John moved to Cortland; Harry moved to Illinois; Barney remained in Dryden, where he died in 1892; Daniel moved to Groton; Polly married Henry Saltsman and went West, and Candace married Jarvis Sweetland.

DEUEL, REUBEN, was a Quaker and an early settler on Lot No. 76, in what is now known as the Dusenberry neighborhood. He was a shoemaker and came to Dryden from Orange county, N. Y., about 1806. We have already referred to him as one of the traveling shoemakers who in those days went about from house to house among the farmers making up their home-made leather into boots and shoes.

He was the ancestor of the Deuel families of Dryden and Caroline, which have intermarried with many other families, and T. S. Deuel, of Dryden village, is his grandson. His children included Morgan, Lyman and David Deuel, and Mrs. Thos. Freeman, of Etna.

HEMMINGWAY, DEACON SAMUEL, about the year 1810, bought and cleared up the farm now owned by Cyrus Knapp on Lot 65. He has already been mentioned in connection with Etna as one of the founders of the Baptist church there in 1804.

HOLLISTER, KINNER, a few years later, about 1813 or 1814, settled on Lot No. 85, clearing up the farm now in possession of his grandson, Frank Hollister.

HILES, JACOB, with his sons John and George, came from New Jersey early in the century, purchasing the Lake mill property of James Lacy before 1814. John succeeded to this property, upon which he resided for many years and finally died, leaving a large family and considerable property. The widow of Jacob became the second wife of Judge Ellis. George Hiles married Percy West and was the father of Harrison and John W.

POWERS, ELIJAH, settled on Lot 86, where Chauncey L. Scott lived years ago. He was there as early as 1807 and in 1808 he built a sawmill called the Bottom Mill, which passed into the possession of the Van Pelts many years later. This was the first saw-mill built on Upper Six Mile Creek and antedated others at Slaterville.

RUMMER, GABRIEL, came to Dryden and located in this section in the year of the total eclipse (1806) and left children which included Anne (Stevens), Levi, Polly (Purvis), Eli, Lydia (Ballard), and Phœbe F. (Joyner). Peter Rummer, who owned the farm now known as the Rummer farm in Dryden village, and his son Cyrus were of another family.

SIMONS, BENJAMIN, was born January 29, 1766, and came to Dryden from Orange county, settling upon South Hill in 1808 with five children and his wife, Isabelle McWilliams, who was a native of Scotland. Of the children, John and James went later to Allegany county; Andrew to Pennsylvania; Jane married the Rev. Reuben Hurd, an early minister of the Presbyterian church in Dryden village, and they afterwards moved west; Sarah married Edwin Cole. Benjamin, Jr., the old gentleman who recently died here, had remained in Orange county until after his marriage, and Adam was born after his parents came to Dryden, the former being the father of our Andrew Simons and his sisters and the latter of Nancy, Luther, Henry and William. Benjamin, Sr., was a devoted pioneer in the Presbyterian church of Dryden and went on foot to Orange county about 1820 to secure aid for the completion of its building.

SMITH, WM. R., came to Caroline in 1816 and cut a road from Norwood's Corner to the Pumpelly lot, No. 100. He cleared sixty-five acres, upon which he built a log house in 1820. His father had served in the War of 1812 from Massachusetts, and he was the oldest of a family of seven children, all of whom came to this section of country. He had married in 1818 Polly Vickery, and to them were born thirteen children, which include Cynthia O'Cain, who lives in Iowa; Betsey Amy and Hannah Eastman, who have died; Mary Ann Schutt; Adelia Whitman; Clara Quick; Sarah Hulslander; Frances Oak; and Ellen Cinderella. Two boys, William R. Smith, Jr., who recently died, and Gilbert, who is living, have children who reside upon and near the old homestead in the extreme south-east corner of the township. The old gentleman died September 30, 1881, 83 years of age.

CHAPTER XLII.

THE DRYDEN AGRICULTURAL SOCIETY.

This institution, of which the whole town of Dryden is justly proud, was organized in the month of July, 1856, under the Act of 1855 for the formation of Agricultural Societies. The project was first agitated by H. D. Rumsey in his publication called "Rumsey's Companion," being the first newspaper published in the town, the first number of which was issued in the spring of that year. The society's first exhibition was held on the small grounds which the society leased of Col. Lewis Barton, opposite to the present permanent location, and the principal attractions were all shown under a large tent procured from Ithaca, for the use of which a rental of seventy dollars was paid. The date was October 8 and 9, 1856, the total receipts being $525.63, $140 of which was borrowed money and should be deducted to ascertain the actual proceeds of the first fair, and the expenditures were $475.33, as shown by the report of the treasurer. It was considered a great success at the start, although, as seen from the foregoing figures, the first exhibition did not pay expenses and the receipts were not one tenth part of the receipts of the last exhibition of the society. The temporary grounds contained about four acres, not one-fifth of the present grounds, which are found none too large to accommodate the recent fairs.

The first officers of the society were Elias W. Cady, president; Jeremy Snyder, vice-president; Otis E. Wood, secretary, and David P. Goodhue, treasurer. The directors were Charles Givens, Luther Griswold, Zina B. Sperry, Freeman Stebbins, Caleb Bartholomew and James H. George. Encouraged by the success of their first exhibition, which then seemed great, the citizens of the town united their efforts to make the society permanent. At the first annual meeting, held at Blodgett's hotel in January, 1857, Smith Robertson was elected president and John Mineah, vice-president, the other officers being

DRYDEN FAIR, MAIN BUILDING.

substantially re-elected. It was by this board of officers, under the intelligent and wise guidance of their leader, that the foundations of the future success of the society were laid. Permanent grounds and buildings were decided to be essential and in order to secure them a considerable amount of money was required. In order that the ownership of the property might rest with the people of the whole town, scrip was issued in shares of ten dollars each and taken by leading citizens in all parts of the township, so that the title and interest in the success of the enterprise might be distributed as widely as possible. This scrip, which is carefully worded to favor the society as to the terms of payment, and is still held by the people of the town, who have never received any payment of principal and but a very few years, interest on these contributions to the capital stock of the society, reads as follows:

"DRYDEN, N. Y., October 15, 1857.

"The Dryden Agricultural Society, in consideration of a loan, agrees to pay to ...., or bearer, Ten Dollars, payable as soon as the funds of the society will admit, with interest annually from date. For which payments the property of the society is hereby pledged to the holder.

"S. ROBERTSON, President."
"ALVIRAS SNYDER, Secretary."

Of this scrip 223 shares were taken, furnishing, with $781 which was borrowed on a note of John Southworth, about three thousand dollars, with which the permanent grounds were to be provided. The original purchase of eight acres was made of John Southworth at $125 per acre, and the main Fair house, a duodecagon in form, was built by Daniel Bartholomew as contractor, upon a plan somewhat original, at a cost of about one thousand dollars. This building is a model in its way, for the purpose for which it was designed, having been imitated by numerous agricultural societies in the West, and no one ever claims to have seen a building so completely adapted to the requirements of a country fair. A track was then constructed under the supervision of Amos Lewis, as large as the grounds would admit, one hundred and twelve rods in length, surrounding in its circuit all of the principal buildings. The construction of the tight board fence and other smaller buildings exhausted the funds and with these accommodations the succeeding exhibitions of the society continued to be annually held. In the last year of the war (1864) the receipts of one day of the exhibition were given for the benefit of the Ladies'

Sanitary and Christian Commission under the local management of Mrs. A. McDougall, and about fifteen hundred dollars was thus realized in aid of the comfort and care of the disabled soldiers at the seat of war. Upon this date Hon. Daniel S. Dickinson, of Binghamton, then a man of national celebrity, addressed the multitude in a manner which is still rememberd by many who listened to him upon that occasion. Since then Governor David B. Hill, Hon. Frank Hiscock and Hon. Warner Miller have delivered addresses at these annual exhibitions, which have been uniformly well attended. The finances of the society have not always been successfully managed, and in two or three instances unfavorable weather has materially diminished the receipts. At one time a law-suit, brought against the society for damages growing out of a collision on the track, threatened serious trouble and imposed considerable unusual expenses from which the society suffered some embarrassment, but as a general rule the weather has been favorable and the results very creditable to the managers.

About eighteen years ago the grounds were enlarged by renting for a term of years of the Southworth estate about ten acres in the rear, upon which a half-mile track was extended wholly north of the main building, which adds much to the safety and convenience of the ground; and, within the past year, an additional purchase of three acres, was made widening the grounds in front. During the past ten years under the energetic and able assistance given to the management of the affairs of the society by its efficient secretary, J. B. Wilson, as well as others, the exhibitions have become exceedingly successful and popular, and many improvements have been inaugurated and new features added by means of increased receipts and state aid, which has been received for two years past, without increasing the small indebtedness which has usually existed. Within the last few years a large grand stand, capable of seating one thousand people, has been constructed facing the track, and very commodious sheds and covered pens have been constructed, for the accommodation of horses and stock. The front fence of a fair ground inclosure is usually a weather beaten, rickety affair, covered with rough boards, liberally plastered over with unsightly advertisements in a helter-skelter fashion, making it anything but attractive in appearance. As an example of what our officers have originated and done for the society within a recent date, the old fence in front was torn down and a new one built of the best material, finished in panels of planed pine boards painted white, which were sold as space for advertising purposes, in which the purchasers were required to have painted attractive and tasty advertisements, some of which are really artistic in their novelty and design; and in this way the present fence more than paid for itself and has become a source of revenue instead of expense to the society. This feature, due to the practical enterprise and forethought of our Dryden officers, has since been followed in other places.

All the buildings inside of the grounds have recently been painted white, and, with the tents scattered about, give one the impression of a white city when entering the grounds. A marked improvement has also been made in the management of the exhibitions, effectually excluding from the grounds all gambling devices and the sale of intoxicating beverages, as well as preserving good order in spite of the large attendance. It may be safely said that the affairs of the society were never in as prosperous condition as they are now, the present management, with good reason, predicts that, with as good a fair as it had last season, exceeding in its receipts all previous exhibitions, it will be able to turn over to its successors the society entirely out of debt, with all of the present substantial improvements fully paid for. At some periods of its history the horse-racing element has seemed to predominate and to run the society into unnecessary expenditures; but within the past few years this feature of the exhibitions has been made to subserve rather than dominate the management of its affairs, and increasing prosperity and popularity of the Dryden Fair has been the result. Still, due regard has been had to the claims of the horsemen, and upwards of a thousand dollars has been expended upon the construction and improvement of the present track, which has a record of 2:20¼, is ditched and fenced throughout, and is so well constructed and graded as to be adapted to all kinds of weather.

Among the features developed in later years, is the public dancing, none too well accommodated in a building originally built for an eating hall, where the young men and maidens from all the country round meet and publicly dance to good music in a manner freed from many of the objectionable features which attend all-night public dances at poor country hotels.

At the last fair the exhibition included over four hundred head of stock; the awarded premiums, which have always been paid in full, exceeded two thousand dollars; and the total receipts, as shown by the report of the treasurer, were more than four thousand six hundred dollars, the attendance probably exceeding ten thousand people, at least more than double the number of the whole population of the township.

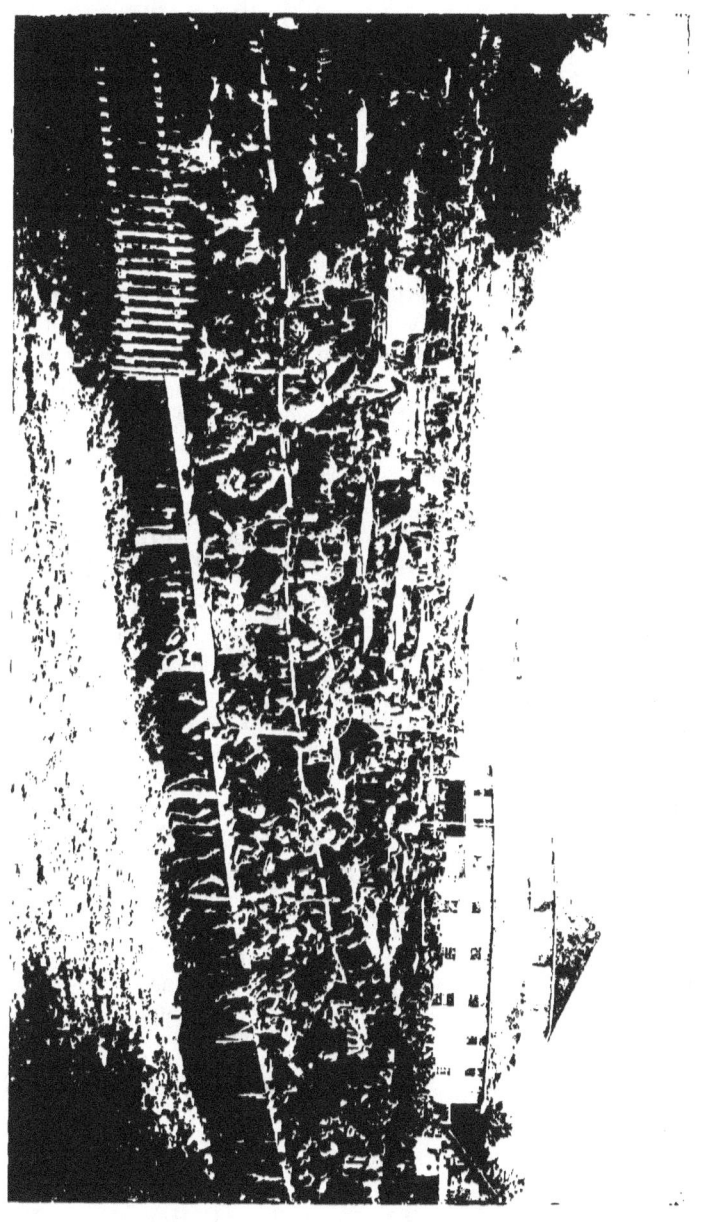

SCENE AT DRYDEN FAIR.

As illustrating the popularity of the Dryden Fair in our neighboring towns and villages, a traveling agent came into town on the train from Cortland in the afternoon of the last day of the last year's exhibition with a discomforted look on his countenance. When asked what the matter was, he said he had started out that morning in Cortland to sell some goods to the merchants. In the first store at which he called he was told that the proprietor was attending the fair at Dryden and would not return until evening. Having a similar experience at the second and third stores he visited in the usual course of his business, he concluded it was a poor day in which to find Cortland merchants, and he started for the livery barn, intending to drive to some of the neighboring villages, such as Truxton, Solon, etc., which were included in his route; but when he reached the livery office he was informed that the proprietor had let every conveyance which he could rig up to go to the Dryden Fair and had gone himself to take the last load. Completely discouraged, he returned to his hotel inquiring when there was a train for Dryden, declaring that he too was going to the Dryden Fair where all of his customers had gone before him.

The principal officers of the society from its organization to the present time are as follows:

PRESIDENTS.

Elias W. Cady,	1856	Lemi Grover,	-	- 1872-3
Smith Robertson, -	- 1857	R. W. Barnum,	-	1874
John P. Hart, -	1858-9	O. W. Wheeler,	-	- 1875
Alviras Snyder, -	1860	G. M. Lupton,		1876-82
Peter V. Snyder,	1861	Martin E. Tripp, -		- 1883
Charles Givens, -	- 1862-3	G. M. Lupton,		1884
Jacob Albright,	1864	G. M. Rockwell, -		- 1885
Nathan Bouton, -	- 1865-6	John H. Kennedy, -		1886
C. Bartholomew,	1867	Theron Johnson, -		- 1887
Luther Griswold, -	- 1868	Benjamin Sheldon,	-	1888-9
Robert Purvis,	1869	Chester D. Burch,		- 1890-4
A. B. Lamont,	- 1870	Seward G. Lupton,	-	1895-8
Chas. Cady, -	1871			

SECRETARIES.

Otis E. Wood,	1826-7	Alpheus F. Houpt,	-	1862-3
Alviras Snyder, -	- 1858-9	Simeon Snyder, -		- 1864
Luther Griswold,	1860	W. S. Moffat, -		1865
M. Van Valkenburgh,	- 1861	Henry H. Houpt, -		- 1866

THE ELLIS FAMILY. 191

C. D. Bouton,	-	1867	W. E. Osmun,	-	- 1874 6
Alviras Snyder,	-	- 1868-9	Wm. H. Goodwin,	-	1877-82
John H. Kennedy,	-	1870	Geo. E. Monroe,	-	- 1883-4
Geo. E. Monroe,	-	- 1871-2	A. M. Clark,	-	1885
Alviras Snyder,	-	1873	Jesse B. Wilson,	-	1886-98

TREASURERS.

D. P. Goodhue,	-	1856-7	Isaac P. Ferguson,	-	1873 6
Thomas J. McElheny,		1858-60	Wm. I. Baucus,	-	1877-82
Eli A. Spear,	-	1861-3	J. B. Fulkerson,	-	1883-4
D. P. Goodhue,	-	- 1864	David E. Bower,	-	- 1885-7
Eli A. Spear,	-	1865-71	DeWitt T. Wheeler,	-	1888-98
Walker Marsh,	-	- 1872			

CHAPTER XLIII.

THE ELLIS FAMILY IN DRYDEN.

From the prominence of the Ellis pioneers in the early history of Dryden, and the fact that many of the present inhabitants trace their ancestry back to that family, a special chapter is here devoted to its early history.

From an old family record we find that Gideon Ellis and Elizabeth (Manchester,) his third wife, lived, before and during the War of the Revolution, at West Greenwich, Rhode Island, where they became the parents of seven children, of whom three were destined afterwards to become the ancestors of many Dryden people. One of these was Oliver, born July 2, 1769; another, John, born May 22, 1771; and the youngest, Peleg, born May 9, 1775. An older half-brother, Gideon, Jr., was a pioneer of Cayuga county, and some of his descendants are now living at Aurora and Ithaca. The three brothers mentioned emigrated to Fairfield, Herkimer county, N. Y., before the year 1800, where Oliver met an accidental death, never having come to Dryden, but his widow, Hannah (Reynolds,) afterwards settled with some of her children near Malloryville in Dryden, and two of her daughters became successively the wives of Andrew K. Fortner, the son of an early pioneer of Dryden, and another, Susan, the wife of Charles Grinnell, both soldiers and afterwards pensioners of the War of 1812; and another, Lovina, was the old lady, Mrs. Grant, who recently died in Dryden village. There are many descendants of Oliver now living in other places and some descendants of the children named still reside in Dryden.

John Ellis before leaving Rhode Island had married Rhoda Rathburn. There had recently died at Royal Grant, Herkimer county, Dr. Samuel Cook, a Revolutionary surgeon of the 5th N. Y. Regiment, to whom had been assigned four lots of the Military Tract, a surgeon's bounty. In March, 1768, John purchased of the Cook estate Lot 23 of Virgil, upon which he settled in the same year. After remaining there about three years he sold that lot to Moses and Isaac Olmstead and came to Dryden, first settling near Malloryville in 1801, whence he removed to Ellis Hollow a few years later. His first wife having died, he afterwards married the widow of Jacob Hiles, the ancestor of the Hiles family in Dryden, and took up his residence on the farm now owned by Wesley Hiles, where he died in 1844. His prominence in the political history of the town is unrivalled, he having held the position of school superintendent, commissioner of highways, and other offices, in addition to having been supervisor twenty-seven years, fourteen of which were consecutive, member of assembly twice, and judge of the Court of Common Pleas of both Cayuga and Tompkins counties. In our times a politician who holds the office of supervisor of his town for a few years subjects himself to sufficient criticism and envy to blast his future political ambition, if he has any; but it was not so with Judge Ellis, whose record as an office-holder of the town of Dryden will doubtless always remain unequalled. He was a large land-owner and acted as the agent of a few non-resident holders of Dryden real estate, notably the McKay and Howland estates. At one time he was connected in land speculations with Daniel J. Shaw, who was then a Dryden village merchant.

MAJOR PELEG ELLIS.
From an old picture in the possession of the family.

Of his children, Charlotte married Charles Hart; Betsey, James McElheny; Amelia, Mahar Wigton; Nancy, John Southworth; and Lydia, her cousin, Warren D. Ellis, of Varna. His sons were James, Ira, Willett, John, and Peleg second. To those who are familiar with the present inhabitants of Dryden these names will suggest many of the descendants of Judge Ellis, "King of Dryden."

Peleg Ellis, the pioneer of Ellis Hollow, as we have seen, exchanged his real estate in Herkimer county with the same Cook estate for Lot 84 of Dryden, to which he came, as has already been described in a former chapter, in 1799. Here, on the headwaters of Cascadilla Creek, he built his log house, to which the next year, on July 12, 1800, he brought his wife, Ruth (Dawley,) and two daughters, Mary, aged about four, who afterwards married Silas Hutchinson and died about five years ago aged 96 years, and a second daughter about two years of age, who died in childhood. Ten children were born to them at the Ellis Hollow home, viz: Delilah, born Jan. 30, 1801, who married David Mulks, of Slaterville; Olive, who married James Mulks, of Ithaca; Lydia, who married Benjamin Ames; Mahala, who married Peter Worden, of Dryden; Warren D.; Ruth, who married John H. Kimball, of Berkshire; Huldah, who married her cousin, John C. Ellis, of Rhode Island; Sally, who married Marcnus Ellis, late of Freeville; John J. Ellis, and Ann H., the widow of John M. Smith, late of Ellis Hollow. Of these, four daughters are still living, viz: Ruth, Huldah, Sally, and Ann H.

Peleg died May 9, 1859, aged 84 years upon that day. His wife survived him until 1870, when she died in her ninety-third year.

Major Ellis was not, like his brother John, a politician, but in early life turned his attention to military affairs. When the War of 1812 broke out, being captain of the early state militia in Dryden, he volunteered with his whole company, instead of waiting as others did to be drafted; and instead of refusing to cross the Niagara River when the battle of Queenston was about to be fought, as did so many of the New York militia at that time, he followed across the frontier under the leadership of Winfield Scott, with his whole company, under Col. Bloom, of Lansing, and at the conclusion of the battle, together with about forty of the Dryden men, was among the prisoners of war; but they were immediately paroled and sent home. Like some others, Major Ellis acquired in his army experience the habit of the intemperate use of intoxicating drink and in after years when he indulged too freely his martial spirit manifested itself and he would go through the manual of arms, in imagination commanding his company as of yore, with all the preciseness and dignity of actual military service. As his years grew upon him, however, he came to realize that his intemperate habits, first acquired in the army, were a detriment to him, and with a resolution stronger than many men of our times can muster, he suddenly broke himself of the growing habit, and his last few years were characterized by his strict sobriety and a religious life.

John and Peleg Ellis were men deservedly popular and influential with their associates, both being selected as leaders of their fellow citizens, one in political and the other in military affairs. Both performed their duties faithfully and well, and both were so constituted as to become ornaments of the generation in which they lived and worthy of the honor and gratitude of their posterity and of the subsequent generations of the township which they served as leaders in their respective capacities.

For a portrait of Judge Ellis see frontispiece of this volume.

CHAPTER XLIV.

THE SNYDER FAMILY IN DRYDEN.

We here treat of that branch of the Snyder family which descended from the pioneers Peter and Christopher Snyder, now constituting a multitude, and who have cherished and preserved their family history since leaving their old home at Oxford, N. J. The details of their pioneer journey and early settlement in Dryden are so carefully and minutely given, affording some new facts regarding pioneer life and manners, that we are pleased to insert in full the annals of the family as prepared and revised under their family organization, which has an annual meeting in our town called the "Snyder Picnic." Another branch of the family, descending from the pioneer Jacob Snyder, who came to Dryden from near the same locality and at about the same time, probably more or less nearly related to a common origin, settled near and gave its name to "Snyder Hill," and is treated of briefly among the pioneer families of the South-west Section.

The following is the history of the Snyder family of the town of Dryden which was read by Alviras Snyder at the first annual picnic of that family, Friday, September 18, 1874, and lately revised by him:

In the latter part of the winter of 1746-7, a colony of about one hundred Germans emigrated from near Tinnen and near the Ems River, n the extreme western part of Germany, and near the Holland line, and settled in the northwestern part of New Jersey. Among this number was Cristoffer Schneider (meaning a tailor) and his wife, Katrina, who settled in what was then Sussex but now Warren county, near Oxford and Oxford Furnace on what was known as Scotch Mountain. It is about five miles from the village of Belvidere, in a southwesterly direction, and two to three miles from the Delaware River. Trenton was their nearest market, being about sixty-five miles distant, and Greenwich, since changed to Montana, was their postoffice.

There were born to them five sons and one daughter. The sons' names were Christopher, George, Peter, William, and Henry, and their only daughter was Anna, who married John Shults. The youngest son, Henry, remained on the old homestead, and the son William and the daughter settled near by. The son George settled in Genoa, Cayuga county, N. Y. The four older sons were in that part of the Continental Army of the Revolutionary War which was stationed in New Jersey. The musket that Peter carried in the service and brought home with him was very short, having a flint lock, and was sold after his death, at his vendue, to some person residing in the eastern part of the town of Dryden.

Peter Snyder was born in Oxford township December 26, 1752, and died July 23, 1832. He was both a wagon-maker and a blacksmith by trade and at the marriage of each of his children presented them with a wagon, chains, and other utensils necessary for farming. He kept the teams shod until he became infirm. His shop was located just north of the four corners near Bradford Snyder's, and where the creek now runs. In 1776 he married Mary Shaver, also a German, who was born in the township of Oxford, June 25th, 1753, and died October 20, 1839.

There were born to them eleven children, viz: Elizabeth (Nail), born October 25, 1777, and died September 22, 1802; George, born May 11, 1779, died May 9, 1843; Henry, born May 2, 1781, died August 29, 1870; Catharine (Grover), born June 28, 1783, died January 18, 1860; Peter, born April 15, 1782, died June 25, 1875; William, born April 9, 1787, died December 4, 1878; John, born February 12, 1789, died February 26, 1861; Anna (Whipple), born February 1, 1791, died February 26, 1811; Abraham, born November 23, 1792, died October 4, 1857; Mary (McCutcheon), born July 17, 1796, died March 7, 1865, and Jeremiah, born October 25, 1799, died May 7th, 1857.

Early in April, 1801, Peter Snyder and his brother Christopher came to the township of Dryden, then Cayuga county, and selected

Lot No. 43, which they intended to purchase. They thoughtlessly and incautiously revealed their choice to one William Goodwin, who immediately proceeded to Albany and purchased the lot, consisting of six hundred and forty acres, from the state. Shortly thereafter the two brothers, on arriving at Albany, learned of the purchase by Goodwin, but they subsequently bought the entire six hundred and forty acres of him for three dollars per acre. Immediately on their return to New Jersey the two brothers and Henry, son of Peter, and George Dart, son-in-law of Christopher, came to Dryden and chopped the trees from six acres of land on their newly acquired farm on the west side of what is now Bradford and Delilah Snyder's farm, and on the northwest bank of Fall Creek, after which they returned home. In August following the two brothers and George Snyder and George Dart returned, logged and burned over the six acres that had been chopped the previous spring. They purchased wheat of one John Ozmun, in the town of Lansing, for three shillings per bushel, sowed their fallow and returned home.

On the first day of June, 1802, Peter Snyder and his entire family, together with his son-in-law, Henry Nail, and wife and child, consisting of sixteen persons, together with all their worldly goods packed in three lumber wagons covered with white canvas, started for their future home in the Far West. One of these wagons was drawn by two span of horses, one by two yoke of oxen, and the other by a span of horses. The three sons, William, John, and Abraham, barefooted, drove eight cows the entire distance through the woods.

They were accompanied by Christopher Snyder and family, Jacob Crutts, son-in-law of Christopher, and family, and George Dart and family. There were in all thirty-two persons, ten teams, and six wagons. They crossed the Delaware river at Belvidere, came through what was known as the Beech Woods in Pennsylvania to Great Bend, and thence to Owego. From Owego there was a track cut through the woods as far as Pewtown, one mile east of Ithaca, along which they came. They were obliged to cut their own road from Pewtown to Judd's Falls, whence they came up the Bridle Road and arrived at the inn of George Robertson on the evening of the eighteenth day of June, having been eighteen days on their journey and having traveled a distance of one hundred and sixty-five miles. Their slow progress, only nine miles a day, is accounted for in part by the bad condition of the roads, but mostly by the fact that the horses and cattle had to be fed in the morning before starting, which was done by browsing; that is, by cutting down basswood, maple, and beech trees, and letting the animals eat the tender leaves and small twigs or branches, and the same was repeated at night, but in time so that all the animals could be properly tethered after their supper, otherwise they would wander astray.

Before starting they cooked a large quantity of provision for the journey and made tea night and morning in a kettle which they carried for that purpose, either building a fire where they encamped or getting permission to "boil the tea kettle" over the old fashioned fireplace. Their principal subsistence was mush and milk and samp and milk and journey-cake, now johnny-cake, and these constituted their main subsistence until after the harvest of their wheat. At night they slept in inns when it was convenient, the remainder of the time in their covered wagons. They obtained fire by striking a flint stone with a piece of steel made for that purpose and so held that a spark therefrom would come in contact with a piece of punk wood, which was easily ignited. On arriving at Charley Hill, the upper half of the east hill at Varna was found to be impassable, so that they were compelled to cut a new road around and to the south further than where it now is, and then back again.

On arriving here, the two brothers threw up a chip, "Wet or dry." By chance Peter won the choice and chose the western half, each retaining a half interest in the wheat that was on this half. The wheat was harvested, not with a binder, but was cut with sickles administered by eight sturdy hands, and threshed, not with a Groton thresher and cleaner, but with flails, upon the ground, which had been smoothed off for that purpose. It was cleaned in true Egyptian style, by pouring it from an eminence, while the wind was blowing, and the wheat was thus separated from the chaff. This wheat was carried to Ludlowville on horseback, where it was ground.

The next day after their arrival, June 19th, all the working force commenced work on Peter Snyder's log house, which was located opposite the present residence of B. Snyder. It was 20 x 24 feet, and was completed in a few days, with green hewn basswood floors, and the roof was covered with basswood bark. They had just moved into this house when the children came down with the measles, which they had contracted at the Water tavern in Pennsylvania. Gerchen Nail, the only child of Henry and Elizabeth Nail, died on July 2nd from this disease, which was the first death in the town, and she was followed on Sept. 22nd by her mother from consumption, which was the first adult death in the town. Peter Snyder chiseled these names and deaths on a brown quarry stone which still stands at their graves in the Robertson cemetery. Up to the time of the completion of this house, the families staid at George Robertson's, which was about a mile distant, and the men while at work found their way back and forth through the woods by means of marked trees.

Immediately on the completion of this first house, one was built by Christopher, where Catharine Rhodes now lives.

After having been here about two weeks, the horses, allowed to run at large, took "French leave" one night and started for their former home. They took a straight course for Owego, instead of the circuitous one they had taken when they came, but were recognized by the settlers and were subsequently recovered at Owego.

These houses were further improved in the summer by building a stone fireplace about seven feet high, the upper portion of the chimney being composed of sticks and clay. The crevices between the logs were filled with clay, an opening about two feet square was left in the west end for a window and a split and hewn basswood floor was completed for the chamber, which was reached by a ladder, and the roof was covered with shaved shingles. Up to the time the chimney was completed the cooking was done out of doors by means of a pole placed upon crotched sticks, from which the cooking utensils were suspended, and this department was now transferred to the fireplace. It was now done by means of a green pole placed across the chimney some six feet high, called a "lug pole," from which trammels and trammel-hooks were suspended so that the cooking utensils could be raised or lowered at pleasure. At this time it was not an uncommon occurrence for this pole to get on fire and break, and down would come the dinner. It was then a common expression to say of a person of a weak mind, or rather below mediocrity, that he had been "hit on the head by the lug pole." The doors were hung on wooden hinges, rudely constructed, with a wooden latch, and a "latch string" extending through a small hole in the door above the latch and running to the outside. The fireplace was afterwards improved by means of iron cranes and still later by andirons.

There being no friction matches at this time, the settlers were often compelled "to borrow fire" of one of the neighbors in the morning, when their own had gone out.

After the families became settled, George Snyder returned to New Jersey, where he remained with his family until February, 1805.

Peter Snyder subsequently purchased all of Lot No. 42 of a Mr. Constable for $2.75 per acre, but shortly thereafter sold one hundred and twenty acres of this to a Mr. Skillinger, so that he was enabled to give each of his sons one hundred and six acres of land and each of his

THE McGRAW FAMILY. 199

daughters fifty-three acres in one contiguous body. Thus it is seen that our ancestors followed, to a certain extent, the old English rule of giving the sons more than the daughters. He afterwards purchased fifty-eight acres of land on Lot No. 90, Ulysses, now Ithaca, which came into possession of his daughter Anna (Whipple.)

The descendants of Peter Snyder, commencing at the time of their marriage in 1776, and including all who intermarried therein, were, on Sept. 15th, 1874, 668; deaths in that time, 128; males in the family, 325; deaths therefrom, 66; females, 343; deaths, 62; then living, 540; males, 259; females, 281. As far as a census at the present time could be taken there have been in the family 1068 persons; males, 517; deaths, 138; females, 551; deaths, 143; now living, 887.

This family instituted an annual picnic in 1874 and the family has had an annual reunion every year since.

Christopher Snyder died the next year after his settlement in Dryden, in 1803, leaving eight children, viz: Katrina (Crutts,) William, Mary (Brown,) ——— (Dart,) Christopher, Sarah (Sovocool,) David, and Margaret (Rhodes.) The Rhodes and Crutts families of Dryden are descended from this branch.

CHAPTER XLV.

THE MC'GRAW FAMILY IN DRYDEN.

Some time about the year 1827, two sturdy lads, tall and well proportioned but clad in homespun clothing and barefooted, came to "Dryden Corners" from the South Hill neighborhood, driving an ox team and bringing to market a wagon load of pine shingles which they had shaved by hand. They drove up to the store kept by Phillips & Brown near the spot where the M. E. church now stands, and, after exchanging their cargo of shingles for such store goods as they needed and could afford to buy, returned to their home in the Irish Settlement. These young men were Joseph, Jr., and John McGraw, who afterwards became men of prominence and influence in the business and social affairs of their native town of Dryden, afterwards becoming residents of Ithaca, where both resided when they died.

Their father, Joseph McGraw, Sr., had emigrated in the year 1806 from Armagh, in the north of Ireland, a locality inhabited by a race of Scotch people who came there from Scotland at or before the time of Cromwell. The maiden name of their mother was Nelson, and the McGraws, Nelsons, and Teers brothers, as well as Hugh Thompson and others of this Scotch-Irish descent, temporarily settled in Orange county, N. Y., where Thomas, the oldest son of the McGraws, was born in the year 1808. After another sojourn of two years in Delaware county, they moved to Dryden, where they founded the "Irish Settlement" in 1811.

It seems, at first thought, surprising that the early settlers should many of them have sought their homes in the most inaccessible and least productive portions of the township, but we must remember that the qualities of the soil in the different localities were not known then as they are now, and the higher hilly lands were then considered more healthful than the low lands of the valleys, which, in early times, while the swamps were being drained and subdued by their first cultivation, were subject to epidemic fevers, which in those days prevailed with malignant severity and caused the premature death of many of the inhabitants.

As pioneers, Isaac Teers made his home on what is now the Cole place, and John upon what is now known as the Miller farm, while the McGraw family lived on the Hammond place, in the old log house then standing about four rods north-east from where the frame house on that farm is now located. In this log house Joseph, Jr., was born in the year 1812 and John in 1815, their only sister, Nancy (Clement), being older than either. There was still another son, Henry, a bright, promising boy, who died under twenty years of age.

As already stated, the father was a weaver by trade, a man of fair education for those times, a great reader and a good talker, being able to quote from a good memory much of what he had read. The mother was a woman of intelligence, possessed of a quiet and amiable dis-

JOHN MC'GRAW.

position, and very much loved and respected by her friends and neighbors. Both lived to old age, residing in the fifties a half-mile north of "Dryden Corners," and later at Willow Glen, where they both died. Their oldest son, Thomas, who, as we have seen, was born in 1808, died before he was thirty years of age. He is spoken of by those who knew him in terms of the highest admiration and is described as a compact, well built, handsome fellow, with good features and a face beaming with intelligence, naturally easy, graceful and attractive in his manners, and large-hearted and generous in his disposition. His early business enterprises as a merchant at "Dryden Corners" were successful and, had he lived to full maturity, his prospects seemed equal to if not greater than those of his younger brother, John, who became a millionaire. His early death was greatly lamented at the time. He left a young wife, Sarah Ann (Southworth), who afterwards married Henry Beach and after his death Dr. D. C. White, all of whom she survived and is still living in New York city.

Joseph McGraw, Jr., also became a Dryden merchant and, in 1840, built the brick store now kown as the Hardware block on the southeast of the Dryden four corners. He afterwards went into mercantile business with George W. Phillips in the brick store on the opposite corner, thus forming a partnership which resulted in a long and expensive as well as an unprofitable litigation for both parties. Joseph afterwards turned his attention to farming, bringing into the country improved breeds of farm stock, and finally retiring to Ithaca, where he resided when he died, in the year 1892. His first wife was Sarah Clement, by whom he had two children, Sarah Jane (Simpson) and John, both of whom were survived by their father, but both of whom left surviving issue. By his second wife, Sarah A. Sears, he had five children, all of whom are now living, viz: Thomas H., at Poughkeepsie, N. Y.; Lettie (Gauntlett), in Ithaca, N. Y.; Georgie (Curtiss), and Joseph W., at Portsmouth, Mich.; and Frank S., at Buffalo, N. Y.

With the exception of a son of Nancy Clement, the children and grandchildren of Joseph McGraw, Jr., are the only descendants of the original McGraw family of Dryden which now survive.

John McGraw, the youngest and most noted of the children who reached maturity, was in some respects different from the other members of the family. The others, like their father, were sociable and loquacious, while John was reserved and sedate, but all were possessed of a gentle dignity which was characteristic of all of these brothers. The florid complexion, with light or sandy hair, which prevailed in the family, found an exception in John, whose hair was black.

We are told that his father obtained for him a position as a clerk with Daniel J. Shaw, who was then a Dryden merchant, at a salary of eight dollars per month, one-half of which was given to his mother. In after years he said that one of the happiest moments of his life was when, after working for his employer for the first few weeks, he ventured to ask him one evening after the store was closed if he was satisfied with his services, and received the reply, "More than satisfied." Upon the death of his older brother, Thomas, John succeeded to his business, in partnership with their common father-in-law, John Southworth. Soon after this, in September, 1840, his only child, Jennie McGraw-Fiske, was born in the house since owned by Erastus Lord, nearly opposite to the Southworth homestead, and in 1847 his wife, Rhoda (Southworth,) died of consumption.

While a Dryden merchant, Mr. McGraw became interested in lumber speculations in a small way, which prepared him for his future success upon a large scale in that line of business, first in Allegany county, and afterwards in Michigan, where he operated near Bay City one of the largest lumber mills in the country. He at one time resided in New Jersey and again in Westchester county, N. Y., after taking for his second wife, Nancy Amelia Southworth, who died in 1857. He afterwards retired to Ithaca, where he married Jane P. (Turner,) widow of Samuel B. Bates, who survived him, he having died in the year 1877, possessed of a fortune of over two millions.

Of John McGraw, the late Henry W. Sage, at one time his partner in business, said: "He was upright, prompt, true, and sensitive to the nicest shade of honor. His active, practical life was a living exponent of that within, which abounded with faith, hope, courage, and fidelity —the qualities which make up and stamp the noble man." He was the donor of the McGraw building to Cornell University and in his latter years was president of the First National Bank of Ithaca.

Of his only child, Jennie McGraw-Fiske, who survived him, we have spoken more fully in the chapter devoted to the Southworth Library, of which she was the founder.

CHAPTER XLVI.

THE BENJAMIN WOOD FAMILY.

Benjamin Wood was born in 1789, at Scituate, Providence county, R. I., and died at his well-known home in Dryden, on Lot 32, Woodlawn. He was directly descended from the Rhode Island off-shoot of the Judge Elijah Wood family, of aristocratic English or Welsh extraction, which settled Gorham, Mass., in the seventeenth century, and in that day flourished its coat-of-arms. Of this Rhode Island branch, came Benjamin Wood, Sr., of Revolutionary fame, born about 1740, who was everywhere and widely known as "Captain" Benjamin Wood, having been a captain of "Minute Men" of Providence county, R. I., who did good service in the Revolutionary War. He kept the "Way-Farers' Inn" at Nitmug Hill, near a famous quarry of that celebrated stone in Scituate. The entertainer of that day of no books and no newspapers, or almost none, was the general and local news headquarters of a locality. Captain Benjamin was a man of great influence, often the arbiter of local disputes, and one who shaped public opinion upon the general or local questions of interest, so that his fine physique and affable manners at his popular hostelry quickly indicated him as a leader against Indian or British encroachments. His military title was easily won in that way. He is said to have worn it well. He died at great age at the above place. Of his numerous but unfortunate family of twelve children, two came to their deaths by accident and only one lived to mature age, Nathan, born at the place above-named, about 1764, who died at Albion, Mich., in 1846. At the breaking out of the Revolutionary War, he became, at twelve years of age, the body servant of his father in his campaigning tent life. Growing up in the easy habits of camp life, Nathan became a man of no force of character and never better than a second man on his job. As such he married Amy, the daughter, of pioneers Thomas and Alice Stone Hammond, who have already been referred to in Chapter 39, and with them removed to the wilderness of Chenango Valley in 1803. He worked as a brick-maker in the different brick works of his brother-in-law, Daniel Hammond, through his pioneer pilgrimages in Chenango Valley, Willow Glen, and lastly on Lot 32 of Dryden, the Lemi Grover brickworks corner.

From Nathan Wood and Amy (Hammond) were born Lydia, Benjamin, Nathan Jr., Polly, and Martin B. Wood. Lydia married Orrin Squire, who also assisted in the above-mentioned brick works, and later established those on West Hill, Ithaca. They built the log house in the first clearing at Woodlawn about 1820. This was located forty rods west of Woodlawn cemetery, where the clearing had been made before Maher Wigton's time, by Andrew Grover, Sr., but his title had proven false, and he had to abandon it. From them is descended, with a few others, Mary Squire, wife of David B. Howard, auditor of the Wabash Railway System, St. Louis, Mo.

Polly Wood became the wife of John Robertson, the first miller at the first grist-mill in West Dryden, built by Capt. George Robertson on the north side of Fall Creek, between his house and the house of the late Casper Miller. They have left a very few descendants near Albion, Mich.

Martin B. married Phebe, sister of Hon. Ezra Cornell, and became a banker of considerable means, but died suddenly, leaving a very few descendants at Albion, Mich.

Some peculiarities of the life of Benjamin Wood may well be scanned to see if they do not furnish the "cause and cure for hard times," of which our later nineteenth century citizen delights to complain. He was, in all respects, the opposite of his father, Nathan, taking the make-up of Captain Benjamin, for whom he was named. Born to the hard crusts of rocky Rhode Island, his push made him, at an early age, a good mechanic in cooperage, brick making, and the use of edge tools; and he was a model farmer, always alternately plying the vocation which promised the best returns. Two rules of his life grew out of this condition: "Never risk your eggs all in one basket" and "Every trade is worth one hundred dollars to its owner, to fall back upon." Coming to Chenango Valley, N. Y., in 1803, with his grandparents' party (Thomas and our pioneer, Alice Stone Hammond, and their son Daniel's family) and working in every trade through Oxford, Sherburne, and farther up that valley, he met, wooed, and won in 1807, a beautiful, strong, healthy girl, Miss Mary Bonesteel, of German parentage, who, with ancestral thrift, was working her way from her birthplace, Warren's Bush, near the line of Montgomery and Herkimer counties, down through this valley, doing work at the best price for every one who could raise money enough to pay for it; which, in those days, even outwitted the gold basis of to-day, to find. He was eighteen years and she seventeen years old and their entire capital on both sides was good health and the Yankee grit for work; he had a corn meal sieve, and she a good feather bed; each had a few cents only in money, and clothes for simple decency, both homespun and homemade, and that was all, she being a beautiful girl and he a brave, ambitious young man. We have heard of but one Dryden man who started married life with less capital than this, and made a nice success of it—Nathan Dunham, of Etna, whose wife, Millie, owned three ducks, and he had to borrow a dollar to pay the parson's fee.

From the marriage of Benjamin and Mary Wood, sprang eleven children: Elmira (Bristol), Mary Ann (Cornell), Lydia, Orrin S., Merritt L., Emily (Dunham), Harriet (Dunham), Caroline, Norman B.,

Otis E., and Cordelia M. (Chase), all of whom, excepting Lydia and Caroline, who died single, lived to full age, married, and reared children.

After the birth of their second child, Mary Ann, in 1811, they found that the constantly growing scarcity of money made it impossible to sell for money a day's labor, or one article of produce, in the newly developed territory of Chenango Valley or westward. Just then the incipient factory system of Southeastern New England, struggling for its very existence, had received a stimulus, not so much from National betterment as from the coldness of foreign relations, placing a check upon imports, and presenting a prospect of a speedy second war with England, and only the factories were paying ready money for wages. The next three years, to 1814, by reason of the war, were prosperous ones, and having gone there in 1812 to enjoy them, they had saved some ready money, but the reactionary collapse came, the factories were all crushed, and all work and money pay stopped. During their stay there Benjamin's skill with edge tools as a worker of wood had introduced himself into the repair and improvement of reeds used by the factories for weaving. His pretty good natural foresight satisfied him that for the next few years, at least, clothes, which must be had, must be raised upon the frontier farms and made of wool and flax, at home, with such exchanges of these products for cotton cloths as might be made with such factories as might run. Chenango Valley, N. Y., which, many years later, became quite famous in cotton industries, had just taken a taste of them when their collapse came, but Benjamin believed that the rapidly settling sections of Western New York might foster this factory work, and it proved so.

When the Rhode Island stoppage came he immediately took his family, then consisting of himself, wife, three children, his parents, and youngest brother, Martin B., all of whom were dependent upon him, and putting upon one ox-team, all, except such as could walk, started with all their earthly goods, upon an early winter trip for Chenango Valley and farther Western New York. Reaching Albany, after considerable suffering, they found the ice too thick for the ferry and too thin to cross with teams and goods. After a day or two of delay, the ice thickening, they, with the stretch of all the chain, rope, and other possible ties, between the oxen and the vehicle, and scattering out the party to the utmost, crossed in safety, wended their way this time to Sherburne, in Chenango Valley, and a little later, soon after 1818, to their few years' home in fertile Quaker Basin, just east of DeRuyter. Here grew the acquaintance of Ezra Cornell, a lad of nine, from Crumb

Hill, and Mary Ann Wood, the child of five years, which in 1831 ripened into matrimony.

Benjamin had, through these years, kept up a small trade in weaver's reeds and reed repairs, and in their exchange for cotton cloths sold by him to frontier farmers and small dealers; but he also realized that he had not reached out far enough in Western New York for the location of his weaver's reed manufacturing industry, because the chief customers must be the occupants of frontier farms who needed to use his reeds in the manufacture of their wool and flax product for clothes. Accordingly, in 1819, he located near Willow Glen, Dryden, N. Y., led there by his uncle, Daniel Hammond, and lived for two years in the house first east from the Chas. Cady residence of later years, still continuing large gardening operations, of which he was very proud and from which he always derived a living. In 1821 he followed this Uncle Hammond to the Supervisor Grover corner of Lot 32, Western Dryden, taking the first fifty acres east of said corner, now Woodlawn, and at this location first established a regularly located weaver's reed manufactory, in connection with labor in the uncle's brickyard, and with felling the huge pine forests to bring forward his new fertile farm, which he thus increased to two hundred acres.

The success of Benjamin and Mary Wood lay in the management of family and business. The first duty of every one of their eleven children, and of other motherless ones left to their care, numbering fifteen in all, was to be every moment in school. Out of school-hours every child was made to scrupulously pursue, both boys and girls, such home labors as were allotted, according to age and strength, so that every one became a source of profit at ten years of age, and nearly all of them at seven years. No playing was done by old or young, in the place where work belonged. The weaver's reed shop furnished work for all, at leisure farm seasons, for nearly thirty years, and was then sold out and abandoned. The farm-house work was always systematically divided, so that the family, usually consisting of twenty members, were all profitably employed. To Mary Ann, until her marriage to Ezra Cornell in 1831, fell the duty of spinning and weaving every yard of cloth, both flax and wool, worn by the entire twenty persons. Nothing was bought which could be raised from the farm, whether of food or clothing. Whole grain was rarely fed or sold, but the coarse parts were used as food for animals, and hay, straw, or other fodder was never sold, being required for animal food or bedding, and to absorb the liquid fertilizers to make the farm lands better. Smoking, drinking, and profanity were strictly forbidden, and not a member left the family with these habits. A most exemplary farmer, his fences and buildings were neatly kept; and his lands, well tilled, constantly gained in fertility, so that he became, along with Colonel Brewer, William Carman, and such men, one of the first presidents of Tompkins County Agricultural Society. The same rigid money habits were recognized on the farm, and on public days a son was allowed twenty-five cents pocket money for himself, for dinner, and, to meritorious members, if allowed a horse, twenty-five cents more for its dinner. In these times on all public days most young men of all grades, sons or hired help, will present a five-dollar bill to be changed for their railway fares.

Sylvester Snyder, whose unequaled habits of thrift were formed on this farm, in fifteen years of labor upon it, mostly at twelve dollars per month, $144 dollars per year, put away regularly nineteen dollars for boots, clothes, hats and expense moneys for an entire year, and $125 dollars was "salted down" and was used to pay for sixty acres of the best land in Lansing when he began to farm for himself. There is a pattern for boys who earn farms.

Benjamin Wood had an executive ability which was his fotrune. He was a true American "boss;" he took the charge of his work, in personal brain work; he did his regular day's hard hand labor with every hired person, asking no one to do more than he. At the same time he always shrank from public office honors; never would accept any office but overseer of highways; always wanted and always had that honor, and his highway was so well kept that in his later life it was the only one in town which became infested with horse racing, and hence was a source of chagrin to him. Although Woodlawn was naturally a cold, wet farm, it became a model one, and the water was so well kept going from it, and from the highway, that the neighbors below declared it to be a genuine misfortune to live below so wet a farm as his.

Benjamin Wood and his friend Col. William Cobb, of the opposite end of his school district, were the first clamorers for the Eight-Square Brick School-house, and were the first persons to furnish graduating scholars from it, to higher schools, from that school district. Under his advice, Mr. Smith Robertson, one of his most efficient employees, accepted two and one-half years of school there, as teacher, at thirteen dollars per month, the same price he had there received as farm hand, and which led to his preparation just after at Homer Academy, and his graduation from Union College in 1843.

Of the eleven children of Benjamin and Mary, Elmira became a teacher, married John S. Bristol, and died in 1847. Her husband,

and their two sons, M. Channing and Charles H., became successively Superintendents of Construction of the Western Union Telegraph Co., a most responsible and lucrative place; in charge at Chicago of all their vast work west of the Alleghanies, through the Middle, Western, and Northwestern states and territories to the Pacific coast, and all along that coast. Mary Ann became the wife of Ezra Cornell, of University fame, and from them were descended Ex-Governor Alonzo B. Cornell, Franklin C. Cornell, chief financial officer of Ithaca Savings Bank and Ithaca Trust Co., and other children, mostly of Ithaca. Lydia, born in Rhode Island, died single. Orrin S. and Otis E. Wood will be mentioned in Chapter LII of this volume. Merritt L. married successively, Caroline B. Sage, and Adelia M. Irish; no children. His business has been successively superintendent of telegraphs and superintendent of railways, and he is now an orange grower in Florida. He was instrumental in bonding Ithaca for the original one hundred thousand dollars for the building of the railway now known as the Elmira & Cortland Branch of the Lehigh Valley System. Emily married Jonathan Dunham, whose family of three children, married, live in the North-west. Harriet married Jonathan Dunham, and died soon after, without children. Caroline died unmarried. Norman B. married H. Anna Spencer, and is simply missing in the North-west. Cordelia M. married Alonzo Chase and has three daughters, all living at Redfield, South Dakota.

CHAPTER XLVII.

JOHN SOUTHWORTH.

The subject of this chapter impressed those who personally knew him as a man of no ordinary ability. His long life, extending throughout a large portion of our Century Period, during which he accumulated a princely fortune, had a marked influence in the town of Dryden. He was born at Salisbury, Herkimer county, N. Y., September 26, 1796, and died in Dryden, December 2, 1877. His ancestors were from Massachusetts, and his father, Thomas, in August, 1806, came to Dryden with his family, which included John, then a lad ten years of age.

Thomas, who was a tanner and currier by trade, and a man of moderate means but of exemplary character and habits, first located in Dryden upon a farm of eighty acres which he purchased at Willow Glen. Afterwards he lived with his son at Dryden village, where he died in July, 1863, 91 years of age.

JOHN SOUTHWORTH.

Soon after coming to Willow Glen, young John was sent off some distance with his father's team, which he took the liberty of trading for another. The exchange, like most of his dealings in after life, proved a fortunate one, but his father was greatly displeased that his son should have taken such unauthorized liberties with his property, and reproved him severely, predicting certain disaster as the result of such precocious tendencies. When John was twenty years of age, he married Nancy, a daughter of Judge Ellis, and purchased fifty acres of land adjoining the farm of his father. He was then obliged to borrow the money in order to pay for a pair of steers with which to do the team work on his farm. After a few years he sold out his first purchase of land and bought the farm in Dryden village which afterwards became his homestead. In these early years he developed a remarkably quick and accurate judgment as to the value of property, which followed him through life and enabled him to acquire a fortune, while others, with the same surroundings and with more toil, barely made a living.

JOHN SOUTHWORTH.

In a dozen years from the time of his start in business for himself, he was worth as many thousands of dollars.

His first wife died March 16, 1830, while he was living in the house where Will Mespell now resides, on East Main street in Dryden village. By her he had five children, viz: Rhoda Charlotte, who died December 14, 1847, having become the first wife of John McGraw and the mother of Jennie McGraw-Fiske; Sarah Ann, who became successively the widow of Thomas McGraw; Henry Beach, and Dr. D. C. White, and who is still living at an advanced age in New York city; John Ellis, who became a successful man in business, but who died in early manhood in New York city without issue; Nancy Amelia, the second wife of John McGraw; and Thomas G., who married Malvina Freeland and still lives at Rochelle, Ill. John Willis and his children are the only descendants of Thomas G., and the only living descendants of John Southworth by his first wife.

In 1831 he married Betsey Jagger, by whom he had five children, viz: Betsey Fidelia, who died in youth; Rowena, who became the wife of Hiram W. Sears, and the mother of John G. Sears, formerly district attorney of Tioga county, N. Y., now a lawyer of Denver, Colorado, and died October 9, 1866; Charles G., who died unmarried in 1872; William H. Harrison, who married Ella Ward and died in 1885, leaving a family of three children; and Albert, who married Diantha Bissell, and died in 1886, leaving a family of three children.

In November, 1833, Mr. Southworth engaged in the mercantile business with Thomas McGraw, afterwards his son-in-law. In 1836 he built the original brick store on the corner of South and West Main streets and in the same year his brick house on North street. He early experienced some business misfortunes, but his dealings were on the whole very successful. The purchase of a large tract of pine lands in Allegany county in partnership with his son Ellis and his son-in-law, John McGraw, was one of his most successful investments. The bulk of his wealth, however, was not made in large transactions, but in the careful, constant, shrewd management of small affairs, out of which his genius derived profits when others would have failed.

To the writer, who had some personal intercourse with him in his declining years, John Southworth was a very interesting character. Having no business education except that acquired from common experience and observation, and no schooling except of the most rudimentary kind, he would express himself clearly in unpolished but forcible and terse language, and would write out with his own hand a contract which, for precision and completeness, few lawyers could equal. Of a genial and social nature, he could tell a good story as well as make a good bargain. He was kind hearted as well as penurious and one of the anecdotes of his career so fully and correctly illustrates the combination of these somewhat conflicting qualities that we feel impelled to insert it here, as follows: In his dealings with a shiftless, unfortunate man who lived in the South Hill neighborhood, he took a mortgage on the poor man's only cow to secure the payment of what was due him, which was about equal to the value of the animal. Receiving no payments, he came to the conclusion that the only way in which he could collect what was justly due him was to take the cow on the mortgage. Convinced of this, he started out one morning with a boy to assist in bringing home his property. Arriving where the man lived and finding the cow in the door-yard, he directed the boy to let her out into the road while he went into the house and made known his business. The man did not appear, but his wife came to the door with her little children following and clinging around her. She said to Mr. Southworth that her husband was away and that the cow was all that she had left with which to feed her little ones. Bursting into tears she continued, saying that if the cow was to be taken from her she should die in despair. Mr. Southworth stood at the door listening to her statement, while the children cried in sympathy with their mother, until he, too, commenced to weep. The boy, who was driving out the cow as directed, seeing the situation, hesitated, suspecting that feelings of sympathy would overcome Mr. Southworth's first intentions; but he was mistaken, for, observing the delay in carrying out his instructions, Mr. Southworth dashed the tears from his eyes and, calling to the boy in a severe tone, he said: "Why in h—l don't you drive along that cow?" The firm determination to have what belonged to him overcame his sympathetic impulses, which were also strong. The cow was legally and equitably his property and, as he considered it, he paid in large taxes his full share towards the support of the poor.

While Mr. Southworth never held any public office, his time being fully taken up in his many business interests, to all of which he gave his own personal attention, he was not insensible to his public duties as a private citizen. When volunteers were being called for during the dark hours of the War of the Rebellion, he contributed at one of the war meetings five hundred dollars for the aid of the families of those who should go to the front. When the question of building a railroad, which resulted in securing to Dryden the Southern Central branch of the Lehigh Valley, was being agitated, and other more narrow-minded property holders refused their aid, he was a liberal contributor to its stock, which was then of very doubtful value and afterwards of none at all.

While he was not known as a religious man, and, in his forcible use of language, was often quite profane, the church people of the village did not always apply in vain for his assistance in their financial affairs. He was at one time pursuaded to attend one of the meetings of the M. E. church society, the object of which was to raise funds with which to enlarge and repair their church edifice. Bishop Peck, who, in his youth, was one of the first M. E. clergymen located at Dryden, and with whom Mr. Southworth had thus formed an old friendship, was present at this special meeting to raise funds for the church. After Mr. Southworth had consented to subscribe one hundred dollars, the bishop, minister, and church members endeavored to obtain smaller contributions from those of less ability. In this effort Mr. Southworth readily joined, finally offering to contribute fifty dollars more if John Perrigo and another man would sign for twenty-five dollars each, which would thus add another one hundred dollars to the fund. When the others hesitated, Mr. Southworth, in his earnestness to carry out the scheme and unmindful of the company he was in, said : "Why, d—mn it to h—l, Perrigo, you can do that much." It is needless to say that the bishop and church members who surrounded him did not severely rebuke him for his strong language upon that occasion.

While Mr. Southworth was a man of a strong will, which would bear no contradiction, he was not altogether heartless or unreasonable, and he always manifested a disposition to help those who were inclined to strive to help themselves. Unmerciful to those who were unfaithful to their agreements with him, there was no limit to the confidence which he placed in those by whom he thought confidence was merited. While extremely simple and economical in his personal habits, his hospitality was unbounded. His faults were for the most part on the surface, and of his better qualities he made no display. Notwithstanding the rapid decline in the value of his real estate shortly before his death, his accumulated property inventoried nearly a million.

CHAPTER XLVIII.

MILO GOODRICH.

The subject of this chapter was born at East Homer, N. Y., January 3, 1814. His parents, who had recently emigrated from the East, were natives of Sharon, Conn., and were in humble but respectable circumstances, his mother, Almira (Swift,) being a woman of great industry and ambition, while his father, Philander, was a mason by trade, serving at one time as a captain of the state militia, and noted as a man of high character and genial disposition. When Milo was about two years of age, his parents moved and located upon a small farm near the Marl Ponds in Cortlandville, where the childhood of our subject was spent. He early manifested a great fondness for books, and when he was sixteen years of age he commenced teaching the same district school at South Cortland where, up to that time, he had re-

ceived his education. Thereafter he pursued his studies by means of the money which he could save in teaching, being a student of the old Cortland Academy at Homer, and afterwards at Oberlin Institute, in Ohio, which had then recently been established to aid students who were obliged to pay their own way. In the meantime he taught district schools in Groton, Peruville, and Berkshire, N. Y., as well as in Mahoning, Pa., and Brooklyn and Weymouth, Ohio. In the year 1838 he commenced the study of law in the office of Judge Barton, at Worcester, Mass., where he was admitted to practice in 1840. He then went West, to the territory, as it was then, of Wisconsin, where he practiced law in the new country at Beloit. After two years of this experience he returned to New York, and in 1844 he married Eunice A. Eastman, of the town of Groton, and soon afterwards removed to the adjoining town of Dryden, which was his home for the next thirty years.

Here he commenced his practice of law in a very humble way, renting only rooms in which to commence housekeeping, possessing no means, and not yet being admitted to practice in the higher courts of this state. There was, however, in those days, much litigation in justice's court, which served as a school in which his great natural ability rapidly developed, and he was thus enabled to rise from the lowest to the highest grade of his profession. In 1849 he was appointed postmaster at Dryden village and at about the same time he served as superintendent of schools for the township.

In 1848 his parents moved to Dryden, building with him the home on South street where they lived together until their death.

In 1867 Mr. Goodrich was elected a delegate to the state constitutional convention of that year, and subsequently was a member of Congress from his district. In the former capacity, as a member of the judiciary committee and among men of the highest rank in the state, he alone submitted a minority report in favor of an elective judiciary with a term of fourteen years for its judges, instead of changing back to a judiciary appointed for life; and his report, substantially as submitted by him and subsequently adopted by the convention and finally by the people of the state, embraces the system which has ever since prevailed.

In the year 1875 his increasing practice in the U. S. courts and the higher courts of his own state influenced him to remove to Auburn, where he continued to be engaged in a business of great activity and success until about two weeks before his death, which occurred April 15, 1881. His remains were brought to Dryden, where they rest with those of his parents and of several of his children, who had died before him. During the past year, his wife, Eunice A. Goodrich, who was a woman of domestic habits but possessed of a strong character, and was a devoted wife and a noble mother of his children, was buried beside him.

Of their eight children three only survive, viz: George E., who occupies the homestead and continues the practice of law in Dryden; Frank, who is now a member of the faculty of Williams College; and Fanny G. Schweinfurth, of San Francisco, Cal.

It will be impossible to convey to the reader who did not know him an adequate conception of the magnetic power of Milo Goodrich as a speaker, especially when engaged in the trial of cases before a jury. When he was attending court in Ithaca and Cortland there were but few important trials in which he was not engaged. He devoted himself almost exclusively to his chosen profession, which he pursued for the success which awaited his efforts in it, rather than for the pecuniary compensation. Many of the expressions in his arguments were so impressive that they are still remembered and cherished by those who listened to them. He was endowed by nature with a strong physical constitution, which rendered him capable of incessant work, and he possessed great mental power, which, when fully developed, impressed all who came in contact with him. Not alone distinguished as a lawyer, he developed rare literary taste and culture, and some of his poetry upon local subjects exhibited his abilities in that direction. Upon public occasions he frequently delivered addresses, and in all political campaigns of his time he was one of the foremost local speakers.

He was a Republican in politics until the Greeley campaign, which caused him to separate himself from the party to which he had, up to that time, given his earnest and conscientious support. Of a generous and public-spirited disposition, he liberally supported all public enterprises, and, when the Southern Central railroad was contemplated, he united his efforts with others in securing its accomplishment, without seeking its emoluments. His magnetic influence as a speaker and his high character as a man will always be remembered by those who personally knew him, but he cannot be fully appreciated and understood from any description which can be given.

CHAPTER XLIX.

JEREMIAH WILBUR DWIGHT.

Jeremiah Wilbur Dwight was born at Cincinnatus, Cortland county, New York, April 17th, 1819. He was the oldest son of Elijah and Olive Standish Dwight, and a direct descendant of John Dwight, who came from England in 1635 and settled in Massachusetts. John Dwight founded a family which has produced, perhaps, as great a number of talented men who have distinguished themselves on progressive lines, as any family in this country.

Through his mother, Mr. Jeremiah Wilbur Dwight was a lineal descendant of Captain Miles Standish, who came over in the Mayflower in 1620. In 1830 Mr. Dwight's parents moved from Cincinnatus into Caroline, Tompkins county, and six years later, into that part of the town of Dryden known as South Hill. His parents were poor and unable to give him an education except that afforded by the common schools. His necessities aroused his ambition. In 1838 he came to Dryden village and, for forty-nine years, was identified with her interests and history. He entered the store of A. Benjamin, to learn the mercantile business, and an incident connected with this real starting point in his life shows the strong characteristics which ever marked his subsequent career. He was a stranger, but, feeling the responsibility of aiding his father's family, he determined to secure a foothold. Six dollars, his savings from farm work, constituted his entire capital. The coveted clerkship was already filled, but the clerk who served was willing to sell his position to young Dwight for his six dollars. Dwight risked his all, confident that he could make himself so useful that he would become a necessity to his employers. He succeeded, as he remained constantly with the firm until the business was sold to A. L. Bushnell. Meantime, he had taken advantage of instruction at odd times at the Burhans school, and, when the new mercantile firm was formed, he went with it and a few years later was taken into partnership.

Their store was located at the south-east corner of Main and South streets. After remaining there a few years, a new firm was organized by J. W. Dwight and I. P. Ferguson and they occupied a small store on the north side of Main street. In 1852 Mr. Dwight was able to build the stone store building, in which he continued the mercantile business under the firm name of J. W. Dwight & Company. Probably no store in this section of the country at that time transacted a larger or more prosperous business. As a merchant, Mr. Dwight was a success. By early and late application to business, strictest economy, truthfulness, honesty, and exemplary habits, Mr. Dwight made hosts of friends and won the confidence and respect of the people.

As he became more prosperous, he invested in real estate. His first venture was the purchase of the Goddard farm. In this new enterprise he showed his innate business sagacity, did well for himself, and, at the same time, helped to develop Dryden village. He laid out "The Square," by cutting Pleasant and James streets through the farm, platted the farm into building lots, and reserved for himself that portion which is now known as the Dwight homestead. From the remainder developed Union street, nearly all of the east side of South street, and more, as the farm ran south to Virgil Creek and east to the Tucker farm, including what is now the school lot. Later, in partnership with Dr. Montgomery, he purchased part of the Tucker farm, which ran further east, and also partially laid that out into streets and building lots.

Since his investments proved successful, he invested again with others in the Dryden Woolen Mill, the Stone Flour Mill, and the Dryden Lake property. In the management of all these enterprises he demonstrated his able judgment, his correct estimates of values, and his comprehensive grasp of financial problems. At this time, as his acquaintance broadened and opportunities presented themselves, he made investments elsewhere. First, in New Jersey, later on, in pine lands in Wisconsin. Later, in 1880, he organized the Dwight Farm and Land Company, of North Dakota, which purchased there sixty thousand acres of land. The present town of Dwight, located in North Dakota in a part of the holdings, bears his name. His business transactions, so successful that any man might be proud of them, were the legitimate outgrowth of investments made in real estate and developed by courage and the strictest application.

As a citizen he early took an interest in all public improvements, and was always in the front ranks, bearing his full share in the work of village incorporation, school improvements, church repairs, and organization of the Agricultural Society and of a Cemetery Association worthy of the town and the times. He was a prime mover in the organization and building of the Southern Central railway, feeling that the time had come when Dryden should be connected with the outside world by other means than that of the stage coach. Into this project he threw his characteristic zeal to make the undertaking a success. He was for a long time director and vice-president and gave generously both his time and money to the work. Though absorbed in his own business affairs, he was frequently called upon to administer estates for others, and was selected by Jennie McGraw-Fiske as one of the trustees of the Southworth Library bequest. All trusts he fulfilled conscientiously, and according to the dictates of his best judgment. He was always the friend of the unfortunate and those struggling against adverse circumstances.

Believing that the policy of the Republican party would best insure the safety and development of his country, which he loved, he was an ardent Republican. For many years Dryden was known as the banner Republican town of the county and the credit was due as much to Mr. Dwight's devoted efforts as to any other cause. He never failed to attend every caucus and election or to brave severe storms in order to go to surrounding school-houses to speak when duty called. In 1857 and 1858 he was elected supervisor of the town of Dryden and during both terms was chairman of the county board.

In 1859 he was elected Member of Assembly and was re-elected in 1860. In the early years of the war he was appointed by Governor Morgan as a member of the war committee for his own senatorial district and he served until the committee disbanded. In 1868 he was sent as delegate to the National Republican Convention at Chicago, where he supported General Grant for President. He was a member of Congress for six years, representing the twenty-eighth New York Congressional District, at that time composed of Tompkins, Broome, Schuyler and Tioga counties. He was first elected, in 1876, to the forty-fifth Congress and then re-elected to the forty-sixth and forty-seventh Congresses. In 1884 he was a delegate to the Republican National Convention, at Chicago, where he supported James G. Blaine for President. In politics he was noted for his fertility of resources, fidelity to party, loyalty to friends, and, though he was in the political maelstrom, his high moral character protected his name from the taint of corruption.

In 1845 he married Rebecca Ann Cady, daughter of Hon. Elias W. Cady. Their descendants are: Mary M. Dwight, who married Sanders E. Rockwell and has one son, James Dwight Rockwell; Olive Adelia Dwight; Julia R. Dwight; Annie A. Dwight, who married Richard S. Tyler; and John W. Dwight, who married Emma S. Childs.

Mr. Dwight died November 26th, 1885, at the age of sixty-six. He rests in Green Hills cemetery.

CHAPTER L.

JOHN C. LACY.

The Lacy (or Lacey) family is of ancient English origin, being known as DeLacey when they came with William the Conqueror from Normandy to England. Richard, the grandfather of John C. Lacy, was born in England. Benjamin, his father, was born in Mansfield, Morris county, New Jersey, October 1, 1768, and died in Dryden October 1, 1820. He came to this township, as a pioneer, in the fall of 1801, with his wife, who was a daughter of Captain Cornelius Carhart, of English and German descent, who commanded a company of sixty men in the battle of Monmouth, June 18, 1778. She was a woman of sound mental qualities, as well as of industrious, frugal habits. She survived her husband thirteen years, keeping her family of six children together on their farm in what is now Dryden village, until her decease.

Benjamin was a farmer, a man of sturdy character and one of the most enterprising and public-spirited pioneers of Dryden. He did much for the cause of education, which was then in its infancy in the new community, Daniel Lacey, the son of his brother Richard, as we have seen, having been the first school teacher in Dryden in 1804. In 1819 he erected the first clothing works in Dryden, almost on the present site of the Dryden Woolen Mill, and, in the next year, which was the last of his life, he and two of his brothers developed the Dryden Mineral Springs, where the Sanitarium is now located. They had discovered the value of these springs while prospecting for salt. If, in their search for salt, they had possessed the modern means for boring deeper, their search would doubtless have been successful, since extensive beds of this mineral are now found in the adjoining towns of Ithaca and Lansing and in other places in the county where great depths have been reached.

John C. Lacy was born on his father's farm in Dryden near the location of the present stone grist-mill, October 21, 1808, and was, consequently, only twelve years of age at the time of his father's death. His means of education were very limited and two years later he commenced, with his older brother Garret as his partner, to carry on the farm and to pay off the incumbrance which existed upon it. Their efforts were successful and enabled them to eventually buy out the interest of the other children. The partnership of the two brothers continued until 1857, when Garret decided to remove further west, selling

JOHN C. LACY.

out his interest here to the subject of this chapter, who was thus the only representative of the Lacy pioneers of 1801 to remain in Dryden. About that time, or soon after, he married Maria A., daughter of the late Asa M. White, of Candor, N. Y., whose ancestry is also worthy of special notice. She was in the direct line of descent from Peregrine White, who was the first child born in New England of English parentage, being born on board the Mayflower in the harbor of Cape Cod about December 10, 1520.

Mr. Lacy died October 4, 1893, and his wife, July 18, 1895. Their only child, Ada Belle, is the wife of D. F. Van Vleet, of Ithaca, one of the leaders of the Tompkins County bar. Their son, De Forest Lacey Van Vleet, is the only grand-child of Mr. and Mrs. John C. Lacy.

While Mr. Lacy was a man of conservative judgment and thoughtful, prudent disposition, he was always one of the substantial and reliable men of the community in which he resided. The reminiscences which he wrote on his eightieth birthday, from which we quote on page 74 of this volume, illustrate the thoughtfulness of the man, and preserve for our benefit the knowledge of events which would otherwise be lost. His literary taste, for one brought up as he was without educational advantages, was also very commendable, and the writer remembers from childhood with what skill and enthusiasm Mr. Lacy used to take part in the debates at the old school-house, forty years ago, with J. W. Dwight, T. J. McElheny, Dr. Montgomery, and others. In 1862 he served as president of Dryden village, and was chosen at other times as assessor and as highway commissioner of the town. He belonged to the first temperance organization in Dryden and, in 1861, he joined the First M. E. church of this village, of which he was always, from that time, a stable and constant member, contributing largely of his time and means to its management and support. While others were more headstrong and impetuous in the pursuit of their undertakings, Mr. Lacy was always deliberate and judicious. He was a man who would have commanded success in any sphere of business to which he might have been called, a thorough and persistent reader and thinker, and possessed an accurate estimate of men and things. His natural kindness of heart and his benevolence endeared him to the community in which he lived, and his pure integrity and honesty of purpose in whatever he did has never been questioned.

Mrs. Van Vleet has recently given a beautiful tribute to the memory of her father and mother by placing in the tower of the Southworth Library building a clock, which has already been mentioned. The accuracy and precision of Mr. Lacy, in all of his course of life in the past, is well symbolized by this time-piece, which is so located as to guide and regulate in Dryden village the affairs of men in the future. Mrs. Van Vleet is also devoting some of her thoughts and leisure time to the improvement of the little farm in Dryden village, upon which her father was born ninety years ago, planting it with nut-bearing trees and orchards, and grading and laying out avenues and walks in such a manner as to stimulate and develop the taste for the beautiful, which she is thus disposed to cultivate in connection with the memory of her parents.

CHAPTER LI.

ANDREW ALBRIGHT.

The biography of the subject of this chapter affords a typical instance of the young man, born and reared in the country, who is destined, in the eternal fitness of things, to become a prominent factor in the business life and interests of the great cities of our country. As in all ages the masses of people, congregated together to form the great centers of commerce and manufacture, draw their sustenance from the sparsely settled rural districts, so the great aggregations of people which form our metropolitan cities are continually drawing their most enterprising leaders in commerce, manufacture, and government, from the sons of the humble but industrious farmers of the country towns.

The parents of Andrew, Elisha and Elizabeth B. (Smith) Albright, were natives of New Jersey, and were married there about the year 1818. Elisha had, a year or two before, been to Dryden, where he worked as a lad for his older brother-in-law, John Hiles, in the sawmill which the latter then operated at the foot of Dryden Lake. Their oldest son, Jacob, was born at Belvidere, N. J., September 4, 1819, and, when he was four months old, they came to seek their fortunes in the new country of Western New York. They brought themselves and all their possessions—which then consisted of a few house-keeping articles and sixty dollars in specie—not upon the traditional ox-sled of other pioneers, but in a one-horse wagon, in which they drove all the way from Belvidere to Dryden. They first took up their abode in a log house then located upon the now vacant knoll nearly opposite the Dryden Woolen Mill, on Main street in Dryden village, and afterwards lived in a plank house which Elisha built on a farm now owned by S. C. Fulkerson, in the north part of the town, where Aaron was born January 7, 1823. Again moving, they settled at one time on Fall

Creek near the Oliver Cady farm, and at another, near the residence of Elliott E. Fortner, where Andrew was born, June 23, 1831; until finally in 1832, having accumulated some property in spite of his frequent changes of location, he purchased of Selden Marvin his homestead farm three fourths of a mile north from "Dryden Four Corners." Here he reared his family of eleven children and developed from what was almost a wilderness one of the best farms in Tompkins county. The writer recalls the fact of seeing, in his childhood, about the year 1850, Elisha, then a tall, muscular man, surrounded by his sturdy sons, going out to the fields like a small army of giants to do the haying with scythes and hand rakes in the old-fashioned way. The time of his prosperity had then come and his productions were not confined to the bare necessities of life. His farm was noted for the fruit as well as the grain and butter which it produced. A strain of the Winter Steele apple grown to perfection in his orchards in great abundance had a local reputation. Although "stronghanded," in his latter years by the aid of his sons, labor saving devices were not disregarded and a home-developed water power was ingeniously made use of on the farm to do the threshing.

Being among the younger children, Andrew had the advantage of a fair common school education and remained upon the farm until he was of age. He then began to develop tendencies looking beyond the drudgery of a farmer's life. His inventive turn of mind was first directed to a patent wagon brake, which came to naught. One day, while driving, the thought of the use of hard rubber for harness trimmings, for which only leather had been used up to that time, occurred to him and he resolved to apply himself to the development of that subject. He was told by experts in the use of rubber that his idea was impracticable and that it was impossible to make use of rubber in that way, but, like all true inventors, he was not to be easily discouraged, and, concentrating all the energies of his resolute nature upon that subject, he finally demonstrated his success in achieving the desired result.

It is a well known fact that most true inventors lack the ability to reap the rewards of their own inventions, but here is where Albright differed from the generality of his class. As soon as his invention was made known, such experts as had ridiculed his designs as visionary were now ready to contest his title to the discovery. Suits had to be commenced and maintained in the U. S. courts, to sustain and protect his patent, or it would have availed him nothing. Mr. Albright was without pecuniary means at his disposal, while his rivals were connected with wealthy corporations. But here was the opportunity of his life. As Shakespeare puts it,—

> "There is a tide in the affairs of men
> Which, taken at the flood, leads on to fortune."

In this emergency Mr. Albright called upon his father for help to sustain him. The old gentleman, who had acquired what little he possessed in the most laborious manner, and who had some doubt as to the final success of his son's enterprise, at first hesitated, but the necessity of this aid was so imperatively presented by the son, whose whole future depended upon it, that the father and older brothers at length lent their aid. The suits were decided in Albright's favor and the crisis of his life was successfully passed. Let not visionary young men be encouraged by this to embark their means in hazardous adventures. As the result has proved, Mr. Albright, when he applied for the aid of his family, was not about to try an experiment, but he was demonstrating a practical certainty. His success, from that time on, from a business point of view, has been without material interruption and he is now numbered among the most wealthy and successful manufacturers of the cities which cluster around the "Greater New York."

The merits of his invention, which was not a mere accident, but the result of thorough study combined with native genius of high order, are fully attested by one of the Goodyear brothers, who first discovered the process of vulcanizing rubber, and who wrote of Mr. Albright that he deserved "more credit than any licensee that has ever taken up any branch of the hard rubber business."

After his business success had become an accomplished fact, Mr. Albright was allured into politics and not only was he nominated for Congress, when, against great odds, he failed by only a small majority, but he was, several times afterwards, prominently brought forward as a candidate for governor of his state, and, had he consented to use the means commonly adopted in New Jersey, as well as in too many other places, to secure the election, his nomination, as well as election, would have been assured.

But the same resolute characteristics which carried him to success in his business career, firmly opposed all inducements to secure the nomination by any but honorable means, and the prize therefore fell to those who were less scrupulous in this regard. Like Henry Clay, who would "rather be right than be president," he preferred to forsake political ambition rather than be governor with the loss of his integrity as a man. Since that time he has occupied a position in politics above party lines, taking broad views of his own which have controlled his actions.

Unlike many men of fortune, since his days of prosperity have come to him, Mr. Albright has made liberal use of his means for his own comfort and for the public good. When the people of Dryden village were about determining to put in a system of water-works, he donated to them a beautiful fountain to adorn the common in his native town as a memorial for his father and mother. When the new log cabin was recently suggested as a feature of the Dryden Centennial Celebration, he sent in without solicitation, his check for thirteen dollars, to represent the thirteen members of his father's family in that enterprise.

Some of the marked traits of character of Mr. Albright are those which distinguish most self-made men of note. A strong and rugged constitution, developed by work on the farm, and life-long habits of temperance and regularity have enabled him to give untiring, personal attention to his business. His contact with men in all walks of life, and his custom of finding out all about every point involved, have given him an unusual knowledge of human nature, which has been of great value in the numerous negotiations and contracts in which he has been engaged, and has kept him from making many bad bargains. Although not trained as a mechanic, he has fine mechanical instinct, and quickly appreciates and understands machinery; and he has suggested a large number of improvements in the machines and processes of his factories.

His extensive litigation in the United States Circuit and Supreme courts, both as complainant and defendant, has given him a much better knowledge of the leading principles of the patent laws, evidence, and equity than one usually finds among laymen; and his less experienced friends among manufacturers often consult him on questions relating to the construction and extent of patent claims. His own experience of an inventor's troubles in perfecting an invention, getting his patent, and then sustaining it against infringers, has made him a close sympathizer with other inventors; and he has many times furnished lawyers' services and other substantial aid in developing their inventions and protecting their rights. Nothing in his life affords him more pleasure than the recollection that he has given such help to many deserving inventors.

While always ready to stand up for his rights, he is willing to give consideration to the wisdom and expediency of compromise where there appear to be conflicting rights. Gifted with persuasive speech, he has exceptional facility in conducting a negotiation. Swift in judgment and action, he does not waste time in over-consideration or needless delay. To many his manner, at times, is bluff, and, like all strong men, he is apt to appear too down-right and positive. But his employees, many of whom have been with him over twenty years, know that his heart is in the right place, and have a warm regard for him. He has never had a "strike," and he has never closed his factory, even when the recent hard times entailed loss by keeping it open. He preferred to suffer loss rather than to distress his faithful working men by shutting down.

These are some of the traits of character which have enabled the farmer boy of Dryden to become one of the truly useful leading men of his day, giving employment for many years to hundreds of men, and have made him one of the foremost citizens and widest known manufacturers of Newark, the Birmingham of America. In the eyes of practical men, one such citizen is worth more to the country than a hundred brilliant politicians. The inventor and manufacturer, he who produces in field or factory, is the citizen who chiefly adds to the wealth, prosperity, and happiness of the community in which he lives.

In October, 1878, Mr. Albright married, at Dryden village, Mrs. Almira D. Strong, widow of P. B. Strong, a soldier in the War of the Rebellion who died in the service. Two children, a son and a daughter, both now married, are the result of this union and both reside near their parents at Newark, N. J. A fine picture of the beautiful home of Andrew Albright has recently been presented to and now hangs in the Southworth Library at Dryden.

CHAPTER LII.

OTHER DRYDEN MEN OF NOTE.

In this chapter, which was not contemplated in the original conception of this work, we seek to give short biographical sketches of a dozen men whose lives are to some extent connected with the town of Dryden, which has at some time claimed all of them as her citizens, but who in the main have made their fortunes elsewhere. All have, in one way or another, become worthy of notice here, and our regret is that we have not the time to extend the list to one hundred instead of a dozen, for the larger number mentioned could easily be selected from those citizens who have gone out from Dryden and made themselves somewhat distinguished for their achievements. We consider ourselves fortunate in being able to head the list with the likeness of one of the sons of Capt. George Robertson, the so-called "Father of the Town."

SMITH ROBERTSON.

SMITH ROBERTSON was born at the old homestead on the Bridle Road May 1st, 1814, and is therefore now upwards of eighty-four years of age. He was a pupil and afterwards a teacher in the Octagonal School-house District, besides being a student at Ithaca, where he lived with his older brother, Thomas, when the latter was sheriff of the county, in 1828-'31, and afterwards at Cortland Academy. In 1843 he graduated from Union College, and in the fall of that year he became superintendent of schools of this county, in the performance of the duties of which office he traveled from district to district, almost always on foot, throughout his territory. Having afterwards settled down to farm life with his brother, Mott J., on the old farm, he was made the first marshall and the second president of the Dryden Agricultural Society, organized in 1856, and under his management and direction the foundations of the future prosperity of the society were laid. Through his instigation the first temporary grounds were given up, the present site was purchased and the main building, somewhat typical in form of the Octagonal School-house of his home district, was constructed. In 1858 he was elected sheriff of Tompkins county, and in 1860 it was he who conveyed his prisoner, the notorious Ruloff, to Auburn, to evade the threats of an angry mob of citizens, who were determined to lynch him. This act, which was very severely criticised at the time, commends itself to the sober second-thoughts of all, and doubtless saved the county from a disgraceful exhibition of lawlessness and barbarity. In 1864, under the appointment of an old school-mate, Orrin S. Wood, he superintended the construction and reconstruction of the Northwestern Telegraph lines in Wisconsin, Minnesota, and the upper peninsula of Michigan, after which he was appointed land agent of Cornell University, at Eau Claire, Wis., a position which he still holds.

Mr. Robertson is justified in making a hobby of physical culture, and is fully able to illustrate in his own life the reality and value of the theories to which he holds upon this subject. Although an octogenarian, he prides himself upon being as active and spry as a boy, and, with his straight figure and erect form, his appearance is that of a man not over sixty years of age. He attributes his health and apparent youth to temperate habits, regular and abundant exercise and a buoyant disposition, which often avail much in successfully combatting the effects of the infirmities of age. He was one of the leading personalities at our Centennial celebration, an account of which follows this chapter.

WILLIAM MARVIN was born at Fairfield, Herkimer county, N. Y., April 14, 1808. In the first year of his infancy his parents removed to Dryden, as already mentioned in Chapter XXIII. He and his older brother, Richard, were therefore brought up as Dryden boys, on the farm afterwards and still owned by the Albright family, north of the village. Both worked on the farm and attended the Dryden village district school, and William, who now lives at Skaneateles, ninety years of age, is one of the oldest, if not the very oldest, of Dryden boys now living. As we have seen, his father moved to Chautauqua county in 1832, where he and his second wife and an older son died in the same year, leaving a number of small children. It devolved upon William to look after these smaller children, which he did with paternal care and mature judgment. He had already commenced the study of law by himself, and in 1833 was admitted to practice and immediately opened an office at Phelps, Ontario county, where

WILLIAM MARVIN.

his abilities were soon manifested. In 1835 professional business called him to the territory of Florida. Here he made the acquaintance of some persons, upon whose recommendation he was appointed, by President Andrew Jackson, U. S. district attorney for the southern district of Florida. Very few, if any, other men are living to-day who were appointed to office by Andrew Jackson, over sixty years ago. He then removed to Key West. He was a member of the first constitutional convention of Florida in 1839 and in the same year he was appointed by President Van Buren judge of the Superior Court of the district. In 1847 he became U. S. district judge, an office which he held until 1863, when his health, impaired by the long residence in a hot climate, influenced his return to the North. He had, although a staunch Democrat, strenuously opposed the secession movement and continued to hold his court at Key West in the trying times of the War of the Rebellion, when the duties of his office were very arduous.

WILLIAM MARVIN.

At the close of the war he was appointed, by President Andrew Johnson, Provisional Governor of the state of Florida, and, as such, took part in the reconstruction of the state government. He was elected to the United States Senate by the new State Legislature, but, being a Democrat in principle as well as in name, he, as well as his state, could not at once accept negro suffrage, and his credentials as United States Senator were, therefore, never accepted. Unlike the notorious carpet-baggers of those times, who were willing to do anything to secure and retain office, his political career, but not his stable consistence as a man, came to an end.

Governor Marvin has been twice married, first to Harriet Newell Foote, at Cooperstown, N. Y., by whom he has an only child, a daughter, wife of Marshall I. Luddington, Quartermaster General, United States Army. His second wife was Mrs. Elizabeth Jewett, of Skaneateles, N. Y., whom he married in 1867, since which time he has made Skaneateles his home.

He has always been a great reader and has published several books, one being a law book treating of the law of wreck and salvage, a subject which came before him frequently when district judge, and which he treated in such a way that his publication has become a work of standard authority upon that subject. He has also, in later years, written a work upon the authenticity of the Four Gospels, in answer to an infidel work attacking the evidence of their commonly accepted origin, which seems to be so fairly and logically written as to be unanswerable.

Mr. Marvin still takes great interest in public affairs and in the local concerns of his present home village, having been president of the library association of Skaneateles for upwards of fifteen years, and, a few years ago, president of the village. In politics he has been a lifelong Democrat; in religion an Episcopalian. The valuable aid which he has given the writer in the compilation of this work is acknowledged in the Preface.

RICHARD PRATT MARVIN was born at Fairfield, Herkimer county, N. Y., Dec. 23, 1803. He was therefore about six years of age when his parents removed with him to Dryden, where he was brought up and lived on the Albright farm until he was nineteen years of age. By teaching district schools, he enabled himself to study law and was admitted to practice in 1829, when he settled in Jamestown, Chautauqua county, which was afterwards his home. Mr. Marvin's ability as a lawyer soon developed and, in 1836, he was elected a member of Congress from his district and was re-elected, holding that office for four years. In 1847 he was made judge of the Supreme Court, a position which he held for twenty-five years consecutively, administering its duties with marked ability. At one time in sentencing a man convicted of murder he urged him to prepare for death, using the following language: "I greatly fear, sir, that you have not always prayed. Although I have never made any profession of peculiar piety, I have ever believed—since I have grown to man's estate and reflected upon the nature of mind and reason—in the great efficacy of prayer. If a mother teaches her child to repeat the beautiful prayers of infancy, and if the child continues this habit of appealing to God for guidance in this vale of tears, it will have a sacred influence, and if he should pass on to riper years it will make him a wiser and better man." When we consider that these words were spoken by a son of Selden Marvin, whose prayers in the pioneer Methodist meetings in the school-house could be heard throughout half the extent of the village, as we have seen in Chapter XXXIII, we must concede that, in this instance at least, the religious habits of the father were not lost in their effects upon his children.

RICHARD PRATT MARVIN.

In 1834 Richard Marvin married Isabella Newland, of Albany, by whom he had eight children. She died in 1872 and he, after crowning his career of active life with a season of travel in Europe, died at Jamestown, in 1892, at the ripe age of eighty-nine years.

His children who still survive him include General Selden E. Marvin, of Albany, N. Y.; Robert N. Marvin, of Jamestown, N. Y.; Richard P. Marvin, of Akron, Ohio; Sarah Jane Hall, of Jamestown, N. Y., and Mary M. Goodrich, of Cambridge, Massachusetts.

THOMAS J. MCELHENY, of Ithaca, is one of our former townsmen, whose accompanying likeness, it is needless to say, will be quickly recognized by our readers. He was born in Dryden, June 5, 1824, being the second of the seven children of James McElheny, one of the pioneers of Dryden, from New Jersey, who was an early justice of the peace and an inn-keeper of the town. From his exemplary habits and high moral and religious character as a man, one would hardly suspect that, at one time, Thomas served as bartender at the Varna Hotel. He also taught school and served as school superintendent, after which he was engaged in mercantile business in Dryden village prior to 1861. He then, as a member of the war committee of the town, gave his time and energies almost exclusively to the work of supplying soldiers from the town of Dryden, and of caring for them and their families during the dark hours of the Rebellion. We have said something

THOMAS J. MC'ELHENY.

in the preceding pages of his performance of these arduous duties, and much more might truthfully and properly be said upon this subject. In the year 1865 he was elected from Dryden to the office of county clerk and, in 1868, was re-elected to the same position from Ithaca, being the first to be elected to that office for a second term. His natural taste for neatness and order in all matters committed to his charge made him especially qualified to manage and improve the details of the county clerk's office, where his services are still appreciated in his capacity as deputy to our present popular county clerk, L. H. Van Kirk.

Although a pronounced partisan in politics, Mr. McElheny is everywhere recognized as an exemplary, consistent, public-spirited man, whose sympathies and judgment are always found upon the side of justice and humanity. His happy faculty of relating anecdotes makes his company always enjoyable, and it has always seemed to the writer that Mr. McElheny should, before his decease, write an account of the experiences of his lifetime, which, if written with the ability which he displays in narrating them, would always be interesting.

Mr. McElheny has been twice married, first at Dryden, in 1853, to Ada Taber, who died in 1871. By her he had three children, two of whom, Mrs. Mary Young, of Wellsboro, Pa., and Mrs. Edna Goodwin, of Trumansburg, now survive. In 1875 he married, for his present wife, Mrs. Drake, a daughter of the Rev. V. M. Coryell, of Waverly, N. Y.

ORRIN S. WOOD, born December 14, 1817, at Sherburne, N. Y., now a resident of Rosebank, Staten Island, though eighty years of age, is still hale and hearty. The fourth of the eleven children of Benjamin and Mary (Bonesteel) Wood, he was the oldest brother of the late Mrs. Ezra Cornell. Being a few years his senior, she, a girl of much personal charm and force of character, was almost his self-appointed guardian through all his early years. Retiring, peace-loving, and thoughtful, he early became the victim of the cruel jokes of his brother next younger, who was exactly his opposite. This circumstance, as much as any other, fitted him to battle with the difficulties which he had to meet on his road to worldly success. He is believed to have accumulated, perhaps, the greatest wealth of any person raised in Dryden. After living with his parents a short time at Sherburne and elsewhere, he came with them, early in 1819, to become a resident of Dryden, at the small, old house, recently demolished, east of the Cady homestead, on the Bridle Road; and, two years later, in the then wilderness, now known as Woodlawn, two miles west from Etna.

He and Smith Robertson pursued their education together, at the "Eight-Square Brick School-House," and at the Ithaca and Homer Academies, and thus formed a lifelong friendship. Quitting school early on account of the call by the State for his practical knowledge of advanced mathematics, Mr. Wood began work in the new Canal System, and as a civil engineer aided many years in its construction. When that work ceased, in the early forties, he engaged with Hon. Ezra Cornell in the opening of the first line of telegraph, between Washington and Baltimore, built by the congressional appropriation for the Morse system.

ORRIN S. WOOD.

He is the lucky owner of the certificate from Prof. S. F. B. Morse, to the effect that he was the first operator taught by Morse to operate his telegraph, and opened his first telegraph office at Washington; thus he was the first telegraph operator in the world. Pushing northward and westward, with the opening of that system, he was appointed to complete and open the New York, Albany and Buffalo Division. When the two terminal offices were opened, he acted as superintendent for a short time and then resigned in favor of Hon. Ezra Cornell. Livingston & Wells were then the sole owners of what later became, and now is, the American Express Company. They had appointed Mr. Wood to build, develop, and superintend the great Canadian telegraph system, at such a liberal salary that, with his thrift, he was enabled to save three-quarters of it; this became the foundation of his present great fortune. The longest and best portions of his life were spent in this service. Cautious investments in the profitable holdings of this system made possible his great wealth.

Persistently loyal to his belief in the right, he found himself, at the breaking out of the War of the Rebellion, a contributor of five hundred dollars, as the foundation of the war bounty fund of his home town of Dryden, and the few brave fellows that are left of the first company sent out by the town of Dryden will remember his money as the first to be devoted to that purpose. Mr. Wood married Miss Julia A. Forbes, who became the mother of his two children now surviving. She was the sister of the wife of Minister of Finance Holton. Disgusted with the hostile Canadian sentiment towards our country during the war, he sold out all his Canadian property at advantageous prices and returned to the States for a residence.

Just at this time, he, with a friend or two, was enabled to invest his already large wealth in the purchase of the entire Morse Telegraph System of Wisconsin and Minnesota, which, though widespread, was at that time weak. His friend Smith Robertson was placed in charge of the system, which, a very few years later, rebuilt, greatly extended, and improved, was sold to the Western Union Telegraph company at many times its cost, thereby greatly increasing his wealth. Shortly afterwards the development of the Staten Island ferries and the Rapid Transit Railway made an opening for most of his large fortune; and this was just before that enterprise was required as a New York terminal of the Baltimore and Ohio Railway, from which he realized a greatly increased fortune.

Having removed to New York city when he made great investments there, he located at Rosebank, adjacent to Fort Wadsworth, on Staten Island, on the shore of the lower bay, in the beautiful home which he still occupies. Kind and indulgent to the needy, he numbers among his benefactions an endowment of fifty thousand dollars to Smith Infirmary, situated near his home. He is now president of the board of managers of the institution.

Though still entirely competent to transact a regular business, he has passed it over to his only son, H. Holton Wood, of Brookline, Massachusetts, who was recently a member of the Connecticut Legislature, and to his only daughter, Mrs. Mary Wood Sutherland, who is the wife of a prominent young physician of Montreal. Mr. Wood is thus spending the evening twilight of a useful, successful life in quiet retirement.

OTIS E. WOOD, a Dryden lad reared on a farm, was born at Woodlawn, near Etna, N. Y., the son of Benjamin and Mary (Bonesteel)

Wood, who were also the parents of Orrin S. Wood and Mrs. Ezra Cornell. After a good school training, mainly at the "Eight-Square Brick School-House," under the immediate direction of Smith Robertson, the first college graduate and first school superintendent of Dryden birth, he, then fourteen years old, went out with Mr. Ezra Cornell, in 1846, to assist in building the new Morse telegraph system. At the very opening of the first line from New York he was attached to the Buffalo office. Shortly afterwards, he was promoted to New York, and not long after that was placed in charge at the Buffalo office—at that

OTIS E. WOOD.

time, though only fifty years ago, farther west than any other telegraph office in the country. The most notable feature of his connection with that wonderful service consists in his having been identified with perhaps the greatest change in its working since its inception and popular adoption; namely, the discovery of a way of reading by sound. Late in 1846 George B. Prescott, Esq., the first Western Union Electrician, in the first book devoted to the history and science of telegraphy, speaks of his accomplishment in these words: "The first time we saw any one read in this manner, was in the winter of 1846-7, in New York, by Mr. Otis E. Wood, at Harlem Bridge. No trick of legerdemain has ever been able to excite so much interest in our mind as this." Being obliged to give up this position on account of illness, he, after partially recovering, resumed the early purpose of his life, the completion of a college course. He studied in the academies at Ithaca and Aurora, and at the latter he taught for two years the lower Latin and Greek classics. Driven from this purpose by ill health, he resumed work under the telegraph system and was appointed superintendent of the New York, Albany and Buffalo line, so much before he became of age that, according to The Telegraph Age, he still holds the world's record of having been the youngest superintendent ever appointed to the service. His charge included over five hundred miles of the most important line then in operation.

The year after the opening of the direct railway from Syracuse to Rochester, he, while building its first telegraph line, was again compelled to flee to country life by his great enemy, ill health. During this interval he married Miss Olive A., the oldest sister of Col. George H. Houtz, of Etna, with whose family he carried on, for a long time, the business of merchandise and milling at that place.

We cannot in the brief space afforded us undertake to detail Mr. Wood's connection with the construction of the old Ithaca & Cortland Railroad, accomplished through his assistance, under great difficulties, and resulting in the present efficient Elmira & Cortland Branch of the Lehigh Valley, affording to the town of Dryden excellent railway facilities. The village of Freeville is also specially indebted to the devoted and efficient efforts of Mr. Wood in laying the foundation for its present prosperity. He is now the secretary and practical originator as well as business manager of the Coöperative Fire Insurance Co., whose principal office is at Ithaca, but whose business extends into ten counties and comprehends in its risks and basis of its revenue ten millions of property.

He is identified with every attempt at local improvement. He was the earliest investigator of electric power and light for Ithaca, and was the organizer and first president of the Ithaca Street Railway Company. He was also the first secretary of the Dryden Agricultural Society. He also built the line of telegraph between Dryden and Etna, in order to accept the management of the north and south line through Dryden township; and it was under his superintendency that all of the scattered highway lines through Dryden and Groton townships were rebuilt along the railways of Dryden township, and are now a part of the telegraph system of the Lehigh Valley Railway.

Abhorrent of office holding, Mr. Wood is retiring, even socially, always busy with progressive problems of business. While not an inventor, he is an organizer. Lacking in selfishness, he has never yet made his fortune; but his busy life will "round up" with such relations to business enterprises, of many of which he has been the pioneer, as will make him richer in spirit than most men who amass great fortunes.

JOHN MILLER is another Dryden man whom we shall mention, whose parents, Archibald Miller and his wife, Isabel (McKellar), emigrated, in the year 1836, from Tighnabruich, Argylshire, Scotland, locating in what is known as the South Hill neighborhood of the town of Dryden. The passage was then an experience of six weeks on the ocean instead of being made, as it is now, in as many days. They were of the Scotch Presbyterian orthodox stock, noted for their industry and integrity, and died in Dryden in the years 1890 and 1877 respectively. Their children include Miss Jeannette Miller, Mrs. David Chatfield, and Mrs. Geo. Cole, of Dryden; Archibald Miller, Jr., of Eagle Grove, Ia.; and John Miller, ex-governor of North Dakota, now of Duluth, Minn., who deserves from us special mention in this chapter, and whose portrait is here given. He was born in Dryden, October 29, 1843, and received a common school and academic education, completed at the old Dryden Seminary.

JOHN MILLER.

In 1861 he commenced business as a clerk for J. W. Dwight & Co., with whom he became a co-partner in 1864. A few years afterwards, with David E. Bower, he purchased the entire interest of J. W. Dwight & Co., forming the firm of Bower & Miller, which continued business at Dryden until 1891. He was one of the originators and first stockholders of the Dwight Farm & Land Co., which was organized in 1879, and he went to Dakota soon after to assist in the construction of the first buildings upon the lands of the company.

In the year 1882, he was made the general superintendent of the company, a position which he held until his resignation in 1896, when he organized The John Miller Co., at Duluth, Minn., for the purpose of engaging in the grain-commission business at that point, of which latter company he is now the president and general manager.

In 1888 he was elected, as a Republican, to the Territorial Council of the territory of Dakota, and, upon the admission of the state of North Dakota, he was nominated and elected as its first Governor, for the term ending July 1, 1891, declining to be a candidate for re-election.

Much important legislation of necessity was passed upon by the governor during this beginning of the state government. A scheme of transplanting the Louisiana Lottery system to North Dakota, which had then found some favor, was effectually opposed and shut out by Gov. Miller, whose ancestry and training were not of the character suited to tolerate gambling in any of its forms. The state prohibition law of Dakota was also enacted during his term. An offer by his friends to support him for United States Senator was declined, during this time, the acceptance of which would have created a vacancy in the office of governor, and this he did not feel at liberty to do.

In 1882 he married Miss Addie Tucker, of Dryden, and their present residence is at Duluth, Minnesota.

SAMUEL D. HALLIDAY was born in the town of Dryden, near the Ithaca line, January 7, 1847, and although, since maturity, his home has usually been in Ithaca, where he now has an elegant residence half way up the East Hill, he has resided upon the old homestead in this town some portion of the time during the past few years. He was educated in the district schools until the age of fourteen, when he entered the Ithaca Academy, where he prepared for college. In the fall of 1866 he entered the Sophomore Class of Hamilton College. The succeeding year he taught in the Ithaca Academy and, upon the opening of Cornell University in 1868, he entered the Junior Class, graduating in 1870. Then followed two years of preparation for the bar, to which he was admitted in 1872. Although in politics a firm Democrat and hence in this county at a great disadvantage in the distribution of political honors, in the year 1873 he was elected and served as district attorney and, in 1876 and 1878, he represented Tompkins county in the Assembly at Albany, since which time, except that he was the candidate of his party for State Senator, he has taken no part in politics as a candidate for office, but has frequently been a delegate to state and national conventions.

In June, 1874, Mr. Halliday was chosen trustee of Cornell University by the alumni, a position which he held for ten years. He is now a trustee elected by the trustees themselves and, in more recent years, he has taken a prominent part in the management of the affairs of that great institution. Since the death of H. W. Sage he has been the chairman of the Managing Board, a position of great responsibility and trust, involving the leadership in the conduct of the business affairs of the University. For nearly twenty-five years Mr. Halliday has been acknowledged as the leading lawyer of the Tompkins County Bar, not in any particular branch of the profession alone, but as an "all around" lawyer. His connection with the Cornell University litigation, which, of itself, has been very prominent during the past few years, has formed only a small part of his extensive practice.

SAMUEL D. HALLIDAY.

GEORGE B. DAVIS was born in the town of Dryden in 1840. He attended the common schools and, from the village of McLean, went to the Homer Academy, and later to the New York Central College at McGrawville. He graduated from the Columbian College Law School,

GEORGE B. DAVIS.

Washington, D. C., taking the degree of L. L. B., in 1869. Like most of the self-made men in this part of the country, he taught school at intervals during his college days, and by this means, was able to pay his own expenses. He was engaged in teaching in the city of Syracuse, during the war, and, in the last year of the great conflict, served in the United States Military Telegraph Department under General Eckert. At the close of the war, he was appointed to a clerkship in the Department of the Interior at Washington. It was during this time that he pursued his legal studies, and his location at Washington gave him an opportunity of becoming familiar with public affairs, as well as legal proceedings in the higher courts.

GEORGE B. DAVIS.

He commenced practice in Ithaca, in 1876, and, for four years, was associated with Mr. S. D. Halliday. He has built up for himself a large and lucrative practice, and now stands as one of the prominent members of the Ithaca Bar.

Perhaps the most important victory, and the one which has extended his reputation as a lawyer of ability beyond the confines of this state, was in the celebrated Barber case. Great ability was shown by Mr. Davis in the conduct of this noted case, involving an immense amount of research and study, in which he was successful in establishing the theory upon which the defense was conducted.

Mr. Davis has never held office, although his party has honored him at different times, by naming him for county judge, supervisor, etc. He was offered by Gov. Hill the appointment of county clerk, upon the death of Phillip Partenheimer, which office Mr. Davis declined, since he felt that he could not sacrifice his large practice for the position. Mr. Davis is a graceful and fluent speaker, and has been in great demand in political campaigns and on other occasions.

He is a prominent member of the Masonic fraternity and for several years was a member of the Grand Lodge of the state, wherein he performed good service toward paying off the Masonic debt and establishing the Masonic Home at Utica. He is also a very active member of the Unitarian church of Ithaca, and has delivered several lectures in the popular course which that church has established.

Since 1872, Mr. Davis has affiliated with the Democratic party, and has given considerable time and attention to its success. He has been prominent in the county and state conventions, and very active in the anti-Hill campaign in 1892, and is a non-resident member of the Reform Club and of the Sound Money Club of New York City.

Mr. Davis has a wife and two grown-up daughters, and lives in a pleasant home on East State Street in Ithaca. Socially, he is friendly and agreeable and, though a member of several social clubs, he takes the greatest pleasure in the delights of his home circle.

JOHN D. BENTON.

JOHN D. BENTON was born in our neighboring town of Virgil, April 2, 1842, and was, at one time, in partnership with Peter Mineah, proprietor of the old hotel in Dryden village. He lived on the farm in Virgil, receiving a common school education, until the death of his father in 1856, after which he attended the Cortlandville school for one year and then engaged in the hotel-keeping business at Virgil, Dryden, and Cortland, until 1868. Like many boys who are early left without a father's care and guidance, he, in early life, neglected his opportunities, but, unlike the most of them, he had sense enough to see his mistake before it was too late and strength of character enough to profit by his experience. When twenty-six years of age he commenced the study of law with Duell & Foster, at Cortland, and, from

DR. FRANCIS J. CHENEY. 241

1871 to 1874, he held the office of sheriff of Cortland county, his manly figure, and gentlemanly bearing, as well as his good common sense, well adapting him to perform the duties of that office.

He afterwards attended the Albany Law School, graduating in 1876 and, going west, commenced the practice of law at Fargo, Dakota Territory, in 1878. He was sheriff of Cass county, Dakota, in 1887 and 1888; state treasurer under Gov. Church; nominee for Congress in 1890; and, in 1892, he lacked but one vote of being elected to the United States Senate, from North Dakota. Since going to Dakota, Mr. Benton has been actively engaged in the practice of law, together with large farming and banking interests in that section.

In politics he is a Democrat and has always represented the best element of his party, everywhere opposing dishonesty and corruption in political, as well as in business affairs.

We have already taken the liberty, in a previous chapter, to refer to his ability to remember and to relate the humorous anecdotes of Dryden village, in which capacity he has no superior.

DR. FRANCIS J. CHENEY, now principal of the Cortland Normal School, resided in Dryden village for seven years, during which time he was principal of the Dryden Union School, and, at the same time, studied law and was admitted as an attorney and counselor of the Supreme Court of this state. He was born in Warren, Pa., June 5, 1848. At six years of age, he removed with his parents to Cattaraugus county, N. Y. His father was a farmer, and the son lived on the farm until twenty-one years of age, working at farm work during the summer and going to school in winter. By dint of perseverance he thus prepared for college, teaching several terms in the district school, in the meantime.

In 1868 he entered Genesee college and graduated at the head of his class, taking the degree of A. B. in 1872, with the first class sent out after the above-named institution was merged into Syracuse University. In the spring of 1872, before graduation, he was elected to the chair of mathematics in the Northern New York Conference Seminary, at Antwerp. He remained in this position for two terms, when he was called to the principalship of Dryden Union School, where he remained for seven years.

Just as he was making arrangements to go west to engage in the practice of law he received a letter from the Kingston Board of Education, in which he was invited to become the principal of the Kingston Free Academy. The inducements held out by the Kingston board were such that he abandoned the project of going west and accepted

16

the invitation. He remained in this position until he had completed a term of service ten years in length for the Kingston people.

In 1885 he reaped the benefit, in culture, of an extended tour of Europe, visiting England, Scotland, Germany and Switzerland. In 1889 he took the degree of A. M. and Ph. D., upon examination in the School of History at Syracuse University. He has twice been elected to the presidency of the Associated Academic Principals of the state. After serving the Board of Regents as State Inspector of Academies, Dr. Cheney was appointed principal of the State Normal and Training School at Cortland, N. Y., Aug. 5th, 1891, which position he still holds. During his administration of this school the old building has been completely renovated and a large and substantial addition made, doubling the capacity of the building; the attendance of the Normal department has increased from 384 to more than 600; and it is now the second largest Normal school in the state, ranking among the first in thoroughness and efficiency. Its graduates are in constant demand because of the careful and thorough training which they get in preparation for their work.

DR. FRANCIS J. CHENEY.

In March, 1896, Dr. Cheney suffered the most terrible bereavement that can befall a man, in the death of his estimable wife, Lydia H.

WARREN W. TYLER.

Cheney, whom a large circle of friends in Dryden had learned to highly regard.

WARREN W. TYLER was born about three miles east of Dryden village, on a farm which is now owned by Eugene Northrup, and lived there until about eighteen years old, having worked on the farm the greater part of the time up to this date, when, with his father's family, he moved into the village of Dryden. His father, Moses Tyler, was born in Virgil in 1809, on the farm now owned by Ernest Lewis, which is bounded on one side by the east line of the town of Dryden. His grandfather, Oliver, was an early pioneer of Virgil and a brother of another Moses Tyler, who was a pioneer in the north-east section of Dryden. His mother was Mary Vandenburgh, his grandmother being the second wife of Selden Marvin, whom the latter married in Truxton, Cortland county, and who formerly came from Saratoga county, in this state.

WARREN W. TYLER.

The first day's work he ever did away from home was for a neighbor, gathering turnips and beets to be used in feeding stock during the winter. Although only a lad about ten years old, he worked from daylight till dark, for which he received twelve and one-half cents per day, and in payment, the good lady of the house where he worked made his first suit of clothes from new cloth. Before this he had been wearing the cast-off clothing of his older brothers, and he was very proud of this, his first new suit.

After moving to Dryden village, his time was occupied for two or three years in various occupations, including in summer farming and cattle-driving, attendance at school for a short time when possible, and teaching school in the winter. In 1864 he entered the employment of Sears & Spear, in the general merchandise business, and remained with them for three years, receiving as a salary for the first year four dollars per week, boarding himself. In 1867 he entered the employment of Dodge & Hebard, of Williamsport, Pa., in the lumber business, and remained in the employment of the Dodge interest for eleven years. In 1878 he started in the wholesale lumber business in Buffalo, and, from that time to 1891, was engaged in the lumber and shipping business. At that time he sold out his lumber business to his brothers, and retired from active business for six years, living in California during that period. Returning to Buffalo in 1897, he joined his brothers again, conducting business on a large scale, and they are now handling about forty million feet of lumber per year.

In his father's family were nine children, six boys and three girls; six of these are now living, three boys and three girls. One brother, James V. Tyler, died in the service of his country, after having been through the terrible battles of Spottsylvania and the Wilderness, through to Cold Harbor, where he contracted a disease from which he died in a hospital in New York soon after.

CHAPTER LIII.

THE DRYDEN CENTENNIAL CELEBRATION, HELD JULY 10, 1897.

In connection with the plan of the preparation of a local history of the first century of the town's inhabitation by civilized people, the prospect of a celebration during the one hundredth year of such inhabitation was undertaken. The preliminary steps for both projects were instituted at a public meeting, held on February 22, 1897, at Lyceum Hall, in Freeville, at which the Executive and Century Committees were named with authority to complete and carry out the plans thus far evolved. At a subsequent meeting in Dryden village, the subject of the construction of a new log-cabin, modelled substantially after the first known human habitation erected in the township in the summer of 1797, was considered, and a special committee was appointed to carry out that feature of the preparations by building such a cabin of the best available material upon the grounds of the Agricultural Society, where the celebration was to be held, and within eighty rods of the site of the original cabin of one hundred years ago. The farmers contributed the logs; Harrison Tyler, a former resident, now engaged in the lumber business in Tonawanda, provided the shingles for the permanent roof, which was temporarily covered with bark in imitation of the manner of the olden time; Andrew Albright, of Newark, N. J., sent his check for thirteen dollars to provide a log for each of the former members of his father's family in Dryden; and thus, with other contributions of labor, money and material, the new log-cabin was so substantially constructed that it is hoped it may, with some care, survive until Dryden's second centennial. For the cut of this cabin see page 12.

In perfecting the arrangements for the celebration, others were called upon by the Executive Committee and gave their aid in the carrying out of the enterprise, the full list of which committees and individuals officially connected with it is here given, as follows:

CENTENNIAL COMMITTEES.

EXECUTIVE.

Geo. E. Goodrich,	Mott J. Robertson,	Daniel M. White,
Almanzo W. George,	Willard Shaver,	Artemas L. Tyler,
Chester D. Burch.	Philip Snyder,	Joseph A. Genung,
	Jesse Bartholomew.	

Musical Director, - - - - Dr. F. S. Howe·
Leader of Morning Meeting, - - - Geo. E. Monroe, Esq·

LOG-CABIN CONSTRUCTION.

Daniel Bartholomew,	Martin E. Tripp,	Jackson Jameson,
Theron Johnson,	Archibald Chatfield,	Chester D. Burch,
	Jesse B. Wilson.	

LOG-CABIN INTERIOR.

Mrs. Wm. Hungerford, Mrs. John Lormor, Mrs. Abram Hutchings.

LADIES' AUXILIARY COMMITTEE.

| Jennie S. Wheeler, | Eva Goodrich, | Jennie Kennedy, |
| Rose Hubbard, | Anna Johnson, | Lilian Purvis, |

246   HISTORY OF DRYDEN.

Mrs. J. D. Ross,   Millie McKee,   Laura Jennings,
Mrs. Edd Mosso,   Anna L. Steele,   Lilian Mirick.

CENTURY COMMITTEE.

Albright, Aaron,   Hile, Sylvester,   Richardson, W. H.,
Allen, Dr. E. D.,   Hiller, Rev. F. L.,   Schutt, Robert,
Brown, Henry C.,   Houtz, Geo. H.,   Seager, Russel L.,
Bartholomew, Caleb,   Houpt, Henry H.,   Snyder, Harry A.,
Banfield, H. P.,   Hiles, John W.,   Smith, Wm. J.,
Baker, Wm. H.,   Hiles, Harrison,   Suttin, James,
Beach, Dr. J.,   Hanford, Geo. E.,   Suttin, W. J.,*
Bartholomew, D.,   Jameson, Jackson,   Skillings, Samuel,
Burch, Thos. J.,   Johnson, Theron,   Shaver, J. W.,
Brown, Frank E.,   Knapp, Cyrus,   Shaver, Ira C.,
Cook, Bradford,*   Lamont, John D.,   Shaver, W. J.,
Chatfield, Arch,   Lormor, Henry A.,   Spence, Rev. Fred,*
Collins, Arthur,   Luther, Orson,   Smith, E. C.,
Duryea, Richard,   Lawrence, Azel,   Sweet, G. C.,
DeCondres, Wm. F.,   Lumbard, James,   Sperry, Charles J.,
Deuel, Thaddeus S.,   Lupton, Seward G.,   Snyder, Bradford,
Darling, Edward,   Miller, Stanley,   Snyder, Alviras,
Davidson, Robert,   McArthur, John,   Seager, E. M.,
Ewers, Alvah,   McArthur, Benjamin,   Stone, A. C.,
English, Jesse U.,   Messenger, Levi,   Simons, Andrew,
Fox, James,   Mosso, C. A.,   Stickle, Theodore,
Ford, J. Giles,   Mineah, John H.,   Sheldon, Benj.,*
Fisher, William R.,   Mineah, N. H.,   Smiley, Artemas,
Fulkerson, S. C.,   McKee, Samuel,   Tripp, Martin E.,
Fitts, Leonard,   Montgomery, Dr. J. J.,   Terry, Rev. J. W.,*
Griswold, Benjamin,   Montgomery, Dan'l R.,   Tripp, Geo. W.,
Griswold, Charles D.,   McElheny, J. E.,   Wheeler, Enos D.,
George, Joel B.,   Pratt, John H.,   Watson, George E.,
Genung, Dr. H.,   Primrose, George,   Wilson, J. B.,
Grover, John S.,   Rowland, Moses,   Wheeler, D. T.,
Givens, Edward,   Rhodes, Truman,   Wheeler, Fred R.,
George, James H.,   Rockwell, G. M.,   Wade, Rev. E. R.*
Howe, Dr. F. S.,   Reed, Truman B.,
Hollister, Frank,   Rhodes, Omar K.,

*Since deceased.

A printed program of the exercises was prepared and distributed, containing the songs to be sung during the public exercises, including, in addition to some such familiar and popular pieces as "America" and "Auld Lang Syne," three original compositions written expressly for the occasion, which were as follows:

CENTENNIAL MUSIC. 247

Hail Heroic Fathers!

Words by NED NETTIRC. Welsh Melody.

1. Lift our voic-es in the cho-rus; Raise the praise of them that bore us; Hail the Fa-thers gone be-fore us Give them glad re-nown. Proud are we to own such breed-ing; Proud to send it on-ward speed-ing, Pure from pu-ri-ty suc-ceed-ing Gen-er-a-tions down. Hail, he-ro-ic Fa-thers! Hail, an-gel-ic Moth-ers! Give hon-or's meed to no-ble deed, And Vir-tue's o'er all oth-ers! Wor-thy is the way ye wrought us; Gra-cious is the land ye bought us;

2. Look ye on the land ye found-ed; See the palm of plen-ty round-ed— See the wa-vy mead-ows, bound-ed By the plum-ed wood. Hear the hum of thriv-ing mill-age; See the fields of fer-tile til-lage; Hap-py home-stead, farm and vil-lage— Know and name it good. Hail, he-ro-ic Fa-thers! Hail, an-gel-ic Moth-ers! Praise the har-vest grant-ed! No nig-gard stint of love's pure mint We give, from full hearts chant-ed! May no bas-er mood dis-traught us; May we heed the les-son taught us—

3. Dry-den is a name of learn-ing, Po-e-sy and loft-y yearn-ing; Let us keep the good way earn-ing Right to claim him kin. Dry-den was a mas-ter schol-ar— Min-strel Cour-tier in King's col-lar— Bet-ter so, than greed-y Dol-lar Goad the Mus-es in! Hail, he-ro-ic Fa-thers! Hail, an-gel-ic Moth-ers! Break-ing ty-rant fet-ters— Her plum-y flight—a-glow with light, Brings dawning o'er the wa-ters. Hail we glad-ly sound John Dry-den! May his fam-ed cy-cles wid-en!

Fair the her it-age thrift bro't us Our be-lov-ed Town!
Thrift and Faith and Hope the Mot-toes Of our lov-ed Town!
May its on-ward way be guid-en By our lov-ed Town!

THE OLD LOG-CABIN.

Tune—*Marching Through Georgia.*

1. Build the old log-cabin, boys, we'll honor it in song;
Build it with the spirit of a hundred years agone;
Build it as our fathers built, with noble hearts and strong;
    For we are celebrating Dryden.

CHORUS—Hurrah! Hurrah! we'll join the jubilee!
    Hurrah! Hurrah! then joyful let us be!
    Let us all unite in song and rule the hour with glee,
      While we are celebrating Dryden.

2. How our mothers trained us there in lessons true and sound,
How the children loved it, too, who played its doors around;
Now their children's children in the ranks of men are found,
    And they are celebrating Dryden.—CHO.

3. As we see it standing here the thoughts come crowding fast,
And our hearts are filled again with mem'ries of the past;
Scenes we see of long ago each fairer than the last,
    While we are celebrating Dryden.—CHO.

4. So to-day we'll honor it with songs and smiles and tears,
As it shows itself to us from out the mist of years;
And we'll bless its builders with three hearty, rousing cheers,
    As we are celebrating Dryden.—CHO.

THE DAY WE CELEBRATE.

Tune—*Glory, Glory, Hallelujah.*

1. We celebrate our hundredth anniversary to-day,
To greet old friends and neighbors from near and far away,
To commemorate with honor the past and present day,
    As we go marching on.

CHORUS—Glory, glory, hallelujah! Glory, glory, hallelujah!
    Glory, glory, hallelujah! As we go marching on.

2. Our new log-cabin as it is shall represent the old,
   The first one built in Dryden, as in history we're told,
   The latch-string now is hanging out to welcome young and old,
      As we go marching on.—Cho.

3. Then let our voices glorify the century that's gone,
   Giving praise to our ancestors with our music and our song,
   And may the mem'ries of this day our happiness prolong,
      As we go marching on.—Cho.

We here copy from the columns of The Dryden Herald an account of the celebration, as follows :

Dryden's great Centennial Anniversary has come and gone and the inhabitants of this village have resumed their usual occupations. The celebration began at midnight and from that time until sunrise the reverberation of cannon disturbed the slumbers of the villagers, who slept only to dream of mighty conflicts and the wars of by-gone years.

The day of the Centennial dawned cloudless and the sun was evidently on a triumphal march, shedding his beams on all with a glowing impartiality. A stray cloud or two might have been welcome, but every one was glad it did not rain and even accepted the intense heat with joyful resignation.

The streets of the village were indeed a pretty sight and Main street especially had never before been so profusely decorated as on the morning of Dryden's hundredth anniversary. The store fronts were one mass of red, white and blue, and the flags and bunting lent their folds to what little breeze there was. On other streets the decorations were also generous, as they should have been on such a day.

By ten o'clock in the morning the fair ground was a busy scene. The committee of ladies was diligently employed in arranging the ancient articles that were being brought in, and Mr. Goodrich was patiently trying to answer calls from all directions and be in several places at once. On entering Floral Hall one involuntarily expected to see masses of flowers in their usual place, but instead of that the Dryden Band occupied the "posy stand" and there breathed their sweetest notes. In compliment to the rural ancestors who were the sturdy pioneers in Dryden a hundred years ago, the Band attired themselves in farmer costumes, most fearfully and wonderfully made, but which could not disguise the military precision of the wearers or take away the classical expression of our true and tried musicians.

Shortly before eleven o'clock, the Band leading the way, the crowd proceeded to the grand-stand and to the platform erected over the opposite side of the track. On account of some delay the morning exercises were necessarily brief. The large chorus, led by Dr. Howe, sang "America" and "Glory Hallelujah" and then Mr. Monroe gave a few humorous sentences of welcome, finishing by saying that he preferred that the old men present, who knew so much of Dryden's history, should occupy the greater part of the time. He then read some letters of regret from those who would have liked to have been in Dryden but found it impossible. Among these were Hon. Andrew Albright, of Newark, N. J., who has shown his interest in Dryden by his beautiful gift of the fountain; Herbert Lovell, of Elmira, a former principal of our school; and Hon. Wm. Marvin, an old-time resident and honored citizen of this village. Mr. Monroe then introduced Mr. Smith Robertson, of Eau Claire, Wis., paying him an earnest tribute of respect by referring to his clear record as an official of Tompkins county, and his moral courage in saving the county from disgrace by putting down lynch law.

Mr. Robertson then came forward, saying that if he should try to make a regular speech he might feel like L. H. Culver, of Ithaca, who, called upon to make a patriotic oration, began thus: "The American Eagle soars aloft—ahem—the American Eagle soars aloft—By thunder, I've got her up, you'll have to get her down again." So Mr. Robertson, not wishing to be in Mr. Culver's predicament, declined speechmaking but said that he would talk a little of old times in Dryden, and this he proceeded to do in a very pleasast and modest manner. He said that his paternal ancestor, in company with two young relatives, found his way from the East through tangled forests, after weeks of traveling, to Lot 53, upon which his son, Mott J. Robertson, now lives, March 2nd, 1798. Here they camped for the night, and in the morning their beds were covered with two inches of snow. They made a clearing, built a log-house and kept bachelor's hall for awhile until the place was fit for womankind. He referred to the sturdy pioneers who founded Dryden, as a remarkable class, faithful and enduring, and also gifted with rare courage to surmount the difficulties that they did. He referred to the early history of the Agricultural Society, of which he was the second president, and spoke of his interest in its progress. He was president of the society forty years ago, at the time when the permanent site was bought and the large building was erected. He had not been in Dryden or about Tompkins county in thirty-four years and he was delighted at the evidence of growth and thrift which he had seen. He spoke of the grandeur of the scenery in different parts of the county and of the impressions it made on strangers.

Mr. Robertson's remarks were somewhat interrupted by the enthusiasm of the ball-players and on-lookers not far away and by the passing of the fusileer bicyclers, but all this he took good-naturedly, realizing that young America was trying to help along the celebration.

The fusileer bicyclers in strange array having passed the stand and the laughter died away, Mr. Monroe then introduced Mr. Hugo Dolge, the owner of the Dryden Woolen Mills, as a representative business man interested in the welfare of the village. Mr. Dolge spoke of the circumstances under which he came to Dryden and of his pleasant first impressions. He considered this a pearl among the villages of Central New York, offering better advantages, in most respects, than the average place of its size, and especially he commended our excellent school, churches, etc. Mr. Dolge said he had found good friends here whom he never could forget and his heartfelt wish was for the prosperity and progress of Dryden. He called for three cheers for Dryden, which were given with vim.

Mr. Daniel Bartholomew followed Mr. Dolge in a few wide-awake remarks with regard to the work accomplished by Mr. Robertson in the early days of the Agricultural Society. He considered him too modest in his estimate of his connection with the society, for he had been the projector of so much that had made for its welfare and, had it not been for his pioneer efforts, the society could not have made the progress it did. Just forty years ago that day Mr. Bartholomew and Mr. Givens were working on the Fair Building and could testify to the efforts Mr. Robertson made. He then proposed three cheers for Mr. Robertson, which were given heartily.

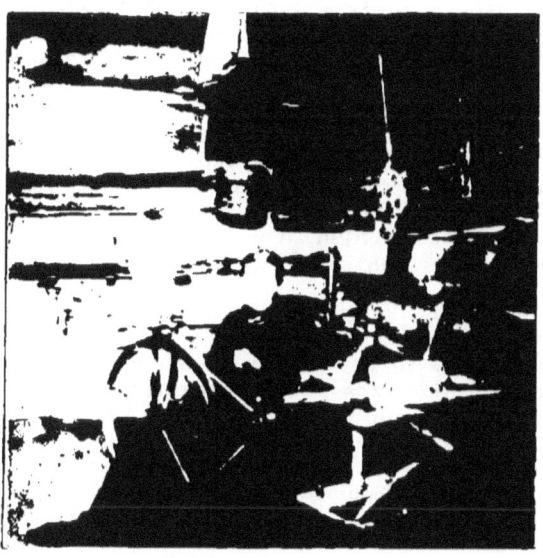

INSIDE THE LOG-CABIN.
Photo by Mrs. G. E. Monroe.

The exercises of the morning were brought to a close by a selection by the Band, and the people dispersed to find a supply for the wants of the inner man before listening to another "feast of reason and flow of soul" in the afternoon.

All during the day there were crowds about the log-cabin, which was presided over by Mrs. Abram Hutchings, Mrs. William Hungerford and Mrs. John Lormor. The ancient furnishings made it into a complete model of the old-fashioned log-house. Mrs. Lormor spun flax and little bits of this wound on cards were sold as souvenirs, the proceeds going as a fund for the laying of a floor in the cabin.

By noon it was fully apparent that Dryden was to keep its reputation for getting together crowds, for there were people coming to the fair grounds from every direction, and by the time the afternoon exercises were begun it was estimated that about five thousand were on the grounds. The noon hour made the celebration seem like one grand picnic. Many brought their lunches or procured them at the eating house and there was a general visiting time. The interesting relics were looked over and commented upon, and reminiscences of other days told by the older people. At times there was such a crowd in front of the door and window of the log-cabin that it was impossible to get a chance to look in before standing in line for some time. Evidently the young people who looked curiously at the ancient furnishings preferred to go to housekeeping with modern utensils. Just outside the window of the cabin was placed a piece of the boulder from which the first mill-stone was cut in 1800 by Daniel White and used for thirty years in the grist-mill at Freeville, the first in the town.

Among the portraits of the former Dryden people to be seen in the Fair Building were those of Judge Ellis, who in his day was known as "King John of Dryden" and in a certain sense merited the title from the fact that he served as supervisor of the town twenty-seven years and was elected member of Assembly for the county in 1832 and 1833, during which time the portrait in question was painted at Albany, besides serving as judge of the Court of Common Pleas in Auburn while Dryden was still a part of Cayuga county, and after the formation of Tompkins county in 1817 serving in the same capacity in Ithaca; an enlarged photograph of Major Peleg Ellis, who commanded the Dryden company of militia at the battle of Queenston in 1812, and was the pioneer of Ellis Hollow; Dr. J. W. Montgomery and Elias W. Cady, both of whom served as early members of the Assembly from Tompkins county; David J. Baker, Thomas Jameson, Sr., Abram Griswold, John Hiles, Ebenezer McArthur, Wm. Hanford, Geo. Hanford, Col. Chas. Givens, Wm. Nelson, Asa Fox, Leonard and Luther Griswold, and many others.

Among the relics were many different kinds of spinning wheels, swifts and reels; an ancient clock eight feet high and over a century old still keeping good time; a rocker over two hundred years old, originally from England, but which was brought here early in the century by an aunt of Jane McCrea, who was murdered by the Indians in the Revolution, and to whose family the chair belonged; an ancient desk brought by the Ellis family from their former home in Rhode Island as early as 1800; a griddle, hammered out by hand, the property of Joseph A. Genung; an old perforated tin lantern such as was used seventy-five years ago, this one having been presented by John McGraw to John R. Lacy about that time; a copy of Rumsey's Companion, published in Dryden in 1857; a printed call for Dryden volunteers of the War of the Rebellion in 1864; an almanac of the year 1797; several old Bibles of from one hundred to two hundred years of age, as well as numerous other old publications; swords and flint-lock guns dating back to the Revolution, as well as home-made linen, flax and thread, and hetchels and cards with which they were prepared; an old Dryden deed of 1790; and a letter directed to Lewis Fortner, of Dryden, in 1808, in care of the postmaster at Milton, then the nearest postoffice; as well as old canes, dishes, candlesticks, bottles and implements too numerous to mention here.

At one o'clock occurred the annual parade of the fire department with its four hose carriages, accompanied by the Band and a company of small boys with the small hand engine of years ago, as well as the larger hand engine, now superseded by the water-works.

THE CENTENNIAL CELEBRATION. 253

At two o'clock the fire company, headed by the Band, marched to the fair grounds and past the grand stand. This was the signal which brought the people together for the exercises of the afternoon. All the seats were soon filled and, though the thermometer registered ninety-six degrees in the shade, people managed to keep good natured and attentive. There was a liberal use of fans and once in a while members of the audience would turn their eyes longingly toward the cool-looking grove near the grounds.

The program began with the announcements by Mr. Goodrich, followed by two inspiring selections by the band and orchestra and a grand chorus led by Dr. Howe. Rev. F. L. Hiller made the opening prayer and then Mr. Goodrich introduced Prof. George Williams, who read in an able manner and with resonant voice "Alexander's Feast," a selection from one of John Dryden's poems. This was followed by the singing of Auld Lang Syne to orchestra accompaniment. Miss Victoria C. Moore then recited in a charming manner "The First Settler's Story" by Will Carleton. Miss Moore's voice was excellent for the trying occasion, and stood the test that was made upon it grandly. We venture to say there are few ladies that could have recited to a vast crowd in the open air on an intensely hot day and kept the attention of her audience as did Miss Moore. She was heartily applauded for her successful effort.

The music throughout the exercises was splendid and the people sang as though they heartily enjoyed it. Some of the songs had been written for the occasion and these were given with a peculiar zest. Dr. Howe well deserved the praise he received for the work he had done in preparation for the afternoon. He gratefully expressed his appreciation to all the musicians for their coöperation.

Mr. Goodrich pleasantly introduced Hon. J. E. Eggleston, of Cortland, the speaker of the day, who gave a very fine address, the true and noble sentiment of which will long remain in the minds of those who heard him and could not fail to inspire them with the wish to lead higher and better lives, and to make the best use of the many God-given opportunities of these remarkable modern days. After the benediction and three rousing cheers for Judge Eggleston, Mr. Goodrich, and Dr. Howe, the audience dispersed.

The selection from the works of John Dryden, read by Prof. Williams, was one of the most celebrated of that writer's shorter poems. It was included in the program of the day's celebration as a proper mode of showing respect for the great English Poet Laureate, after whom our township was named, and is inserted here for the same reason and as an interesting specimen of the learned and studied style of diction which flourished in Dryden's time, two hundred years ago. The title is "Alexander's Feast," and it was written in honor of St. Cecilia's Day, she being the patron saint of music in England, where her anniversary is annually celebrated with songs and music. The poem represents Alexander the Great seated with his conquering followers at a feast while his musician, Timotheus, with his performance on his lyre, exhibits the "Power of Music" upon his master. The story is related in the poem as follows:

ALEXANDER'S FEAST.

'Twas at the royal feast for Persia won
  By Philip's warlike son:
Aloft in awful state,
The godlike hero sate
  On his imperial throne;
His valiant peers were placed around,
Their brows with roses and with myrtles bound
(So should desert in arms be crowned);
The lovely Thais by his side
Sate, like a blooming eastern bride,
In flower of youth and beauty's pride.
  Happy, happy, happy pair!
    None but the brave,
    None but the brave,
  None but the brave deserves the fair.
  Timotheus, placed on high
    Amid the tuneful quire,
    With flying fingers touched the lyre;
  The trembling notes ascend the sky,
    And heavenly joys inspire.
  The song began from Jove,
  Who left his blissful seats above
  (Such is the power of mighty Love).
  A dragon's fiery form belied the god;
  Sublime on radiant spires he rode,
    When he to fair Olympia pressed,
    And while he sought her snowy breast,
Then round her slender waist he curled,
And stamped an image of himself, a sovereign of the world.
The listening crowd admire the lofty sound—
A present deity! they shout around;
A present deity! the vaulted roofs rebound.
    With ravished ears
    The monarch hears,
      Assumes the god,
    And seems to shake the spheres.

The praise of Bacchus, then, the sweet musician sung—
  Of Bacchus, ever fair and ever young;
  The jolly god in triumph comes;
  Sound the trumpets; beat the drums!

ALEXANDER'S FEAST.

      Flushed with a purple grace,
      He shows his honest face;
Now give the hautboys breath—he comes, he comes!
      Bacchus, ever fair and young,
        Drinking joys did first ordain;
      Bacchus' blessings are a treasure:
      Drinking is the soldier's pleasure:
          Rich the treasure,
          Sweet the pleasure;
      Sweet is pleasure after pain.

Soothed with the sound, the king grew vain;
Fought all his battles o'er again;
And thrice he routed all his foes, and thrice he slew the slain.
    The master saw the madness rise—
    His glowing cheeks, his ardent eyes;
    And, while he Heaven and Earth defied,
    Changed his hand, and checked his pride.
      He chose a mournful Muse,
        Soft pity to infuse;
    He sung Darius great and good,
      By too severe a fate
Fallen, fallen, fallen, fallen—
Fallen from his high estate,
      And weltering in his blood;
Deserted, at his utmost need,
By those his former bounty fed;
On the bare earth exposed he lies,
With not a friend to close his eyes.
With downcast looks the joyless victor sate,
    Revolving in his altered soul
      The various turns of chance below;
    And, now and then, a sigh he stole;
      And tears began to flow.

The mighty master smiled, to see
That Love was in the next degree;
'Twas but a kindred sound to move,
For pity melts the mind to love.
    Softly sweet, in Lydian measures,
    Soon he soothed his soul to pleasures.
War, he sung, is toil and trouble;
Honor but an empty bubble—
    Never ending, still beginning—
Fighting still, and still destroying;
    If the world be worth thy winning,
Think, O think it worth enjoying!
    Lovely Thais sits beside thee—
    Take the goods the gods provide thee.

The many rend the sky with loud applause;
So Love was crowned, but Music won the cause.
  The prince, unable to conceal his pain,
    Gazed on the fair
    Who caused his care,
 And sighed and looked, sighed and looked,
  Sighed and looked, and sighed again.
At length, with love and wine at once oppressed,
The vanquished victor sunk upon her breast.

Now strike the golden lyre again—
A louder yet, and yet a louder strain!
Break his bands of sleep asunder,
And rouse him, like a rattling peal of thunder.
  Hark, hark! the horrid sound
   Has raised up his head!
   As awaked from the dead,
  And amazed, he stares around.
Revenge! revenge! Timotheus cries;
  See the Furies arise!
  See the snakes that they rear,
  How they hiss in their hair,
And the sparkles that flash from their eyes!
   Behold a ghastly band,
   Each a torch in his hand!
Those are Grecian ghosts, that in battle were slain,
   And unburied remain,
   Inglorious, on the plain!
   Give the vengeance due
   To the valiant crew.
Behold how they toss their torches on high,
 How they point to the Persian abodes,
And glittering temples of their hostile gods!
The princes applaud with a furious joy,
And the king seized a flambeau with zeal to destroy;
   Thais led the way
   To light him to his prey,
And, like another Helen, fired another Troy.

    Thus, long ago—
  Ere heaving bellows learned to blow,
   While organs yet were mute—
  Timotheus, to his breathing flute,
   And sounding lyre,
Could swell the soul to rage, or kindle soft desire.
  At last divine Cecilia came,
  Inventress of the vocal frame;
The sweet enthusiast, from her sacred store,
  Enlarged the former narrow bounds,

And added length to solemn sounds,
With nature's mother-wit, and arts unknown before.
Let old Timotheus yield the prize,
   Or both divide the crown ;
He raised a mortal to the skies—
   She drew an angel down.

The verses from Will Carleton's poem, "The First Settler's Story," beautifully recited by Miss Moore, were the following:

THE FIRST SETTLER'S STORY.

Well, when I first infested this retreat,
Things to my view looked frightful incomplete ;
But I had come with heart-thrift in my song,
And brought my wife and plunder right along ;
I hadn't a round-trip ticket to go back,
And if I had, there wasn't no railroad track ;
And drivin' east was what I couldn't endure :
I hadn't started on a circular tour.

My girl-wife was as brave as she was good,
And helped me every blessed way she could ;
She seemed to take to every rough old tree,
As sing'lar as when first she took to me.
She kep' our little log-house neat as wax,
And once I caught her fooling with my axe.
She hadn't the muscle (though she had the heart)
In out-door work to take an active part ;
She *was* delicious, both to hear and see—
That pretty girl-wife that kep' house for me.

One night when I came home unusual late,
Too hungry and too tired to feel first-rate,
Her supper struck me wrong, (though I'll allow
She hadn't much to strike with, anyhow) ;
And when I went to milk the cows, and found
They'd wandered from their usual feeding ground
And maybe'd left a few long miles behind 'em,
Which I must copy, if I meant to find 'em,
Flash-quick the stay-chains of my temper broke,
And in a trice these hot words I had spoke :
"You ought to've kept the animals in view,
And drove 'em in ; you'd nothing else to do.
The heft of all our life on me must fall ;
You just lie 'round, and let me do it all."

That speech—it hadn't been gone half a minute
Before I saw the cold, black poison in it ;

And I'd have given all I had, and more,
To've only safely got it back in-door.
I'm now what most folks " well-to-do " would call :
I feel to-day as if I'd give it all,
Provided I through fifty years might reach
And kill and bury that half-minute speech.

She handed back no words, as I could hear ;
She didn't frown ; she didn't shed a tear ;
Half-proud, half-crushed, she stood and looked me o'er,
Like some one she had never seen before !
But such a sudden, anguish-lit surprise
I never viewed before in human eyes.
(I've seen it oft enough since in a dream ;
It sometimes wakes me like a midnight scream.)

Next morning, when, stone-faced, but heavy-hearted,
With dinner-pail and sharpened axe I started
Away for my day's work—she watched the door,
And followed me half way to it or more ;
And I was just a-turning 'round at this,
And asking for my usual good-by kiss ;
But on her lip I saw a proudish curve,
And in her eye a shadow of reserve ;
And she had shown—perhaps half unawares—
Some little independent breakfast airs—
And so the usual parting didn't occur,
Although her eyes invited me to her ;
Or rather half invited me, for she
Didn't advertise to furnish kisses free ;
You always had—that is, I had—to pay
Full market-price, and go more'n half the way.
So, with a short " Good-bye," I shut the door,
And left her as I never had before.

But, when at noon my lunch I came to eat,
Put up by her so delicately neat—
Choicer, somewhat, than yesterday's had been,
And some fresh, sweet-eyed pansies she'd put in—
" Tender and pleasant thoughts," I knew they meant—
It seemed as if her kiss with me she'd sent ;
Then I became once more her humble lover,
And said, " To-night I'll ask forgiveness of her."

I went home over-early on that eve,
Having contrived to make myself believe,
By various signs I kind o' knew and guessed,
A thunder-storm was coming from the west.
('Tis strange, when one sly reason fills the heart,

THE FIRST SETTLER'S STORY.

How many honest ones will take its part:
A dozen first-class reasons said 'twas right
That I should strike home early on that night.)

Half out of breath, the cabin door I swung,
With tender heart-words trembling on my tongue;
But all within looked desolate and bare:
My house had lost its soul—she was not there!

A penciled note was on the table spread,
And these are something like the words it said:
"The cows have strayed away again, I fear;
I watched them pretty close; don't scold me, dear.
And where they are, I think I *nearly* know:
I heard the bell not very long ago. . . .
I've hunted for them all the afternoon;
I'll try once more—I think I'll find them soon.
Dear, if a burden I have been to you,
And haven't helped you as I ought to do,
Let old-time memories my forgiveness plead:
I've tried to do my best—I have, indeed.
Darling, piece out with love the strength I lack,
And have kind words for me when I get back."

Scarce did I give this letter sight and tongue—
Some swift-blown rain-drops to the window clung,
And from the clouds a rough, deep growl proceeded:
My thunder-storm had come, now 'twasn't needed.
I rushed out-door. The air was stained with black:
Night had come early, on the storm-cloud's back:
And everything kept dimming to the sight,
Save when the clouds threw their electric light:
When, for a flash, so clean-cut was the view,
I'd think I saw her—knowing 'twas not true.
Through my small clearing dashed wide sheets of spray,
As if the ocean waves had lost their way;
Scarcely a pause the thunder-battle made,
In the bold clamor of its cannonade.
And she, while I was sheltered, dry, and warm,
Was somewhere in the clutches of this storm!
She who, when storm-frights found her at her best,
Had always hid her white face on my breast!

My dog, who'd skirmished round me all the day,
Now crouched and whimpering, in a corner lay;
I dragged him by the collar to the wall,
I pressed his quivering muzzle to a shawl—
"Track her, old boy!" I shouted; and he whined,
Matched eyes with me, as if to read my mind,

Then with a yell went tearing through the wood.
I followed him, as faithful as I could.
No pleasure-trip was that, through flood and flame ;
We raced with death ; we hunted noble game.
All night we dragged the woods without avail ;
The ground got drenched—we could not keep the trail.
Three times again my cabin home I found,
Half hoping she might be there, safe and sound ;
But each time 'twas an unavailing care :
My house had lost its soul ; she was not there!

When, climbing the wet trees, next morning-sun
Laughed at the ruin that the night had done,
Bleeding and drenched, by toil and sorrow bent,
Back to what used to be my home I went.
But as I neared our little clearing-ground—
Listen!—I heard the cow-bell's tinkling sound.
The cabin door was just a bit ajar ;
It gleamed upon my glad eyes like a star.
"Brave heart," I said, "for such a fragile form!
She made them guide her homeward through the storm!"
Such pangs of joy I never felt before.
"You've come!" I shouted, and rushed through the door.

Yes, she had come—and gone again. She lay
With all her young life crushed and wrenched away—
Lay, the heart-ruins of our home among,
Not far from where I killed her with my tongue.
The rain-drops glittered 'mid her hair's long strands,
The forest thorns had torn her feet and hands,
And 'midst the tears—brave tears—that one could trace
Upon the pale but sweetly resolute face,
I once again the mournful words could read,
"I've tried to do my best—I have, indeed."

And now I'm mostly done ; my story's o'er ;
Part of it never breathed the air before.
'Tisn't over-usual, it must be allowed,
To volunteer heart-history to a crowd,
And scatter 'mongst them confidential tears,
But you'll protect an old man with his years ;
And wheresoe'er this story's voice can reach,
This is the sermon I would have it preach :

Boys flying kites haul in their white-winged birds :
You can't do that way when you're flying words.
"Careful with fire," is good advice, we know :
"Careful with words," is ten times doubly so.

Thoughts unexpressed may sometimes fall back dead,
But God himself can't kill them when they're said!

JOSEPH E. EGGLESTON.

You have my life-grief: do not think a minute
'Twas told to take up time. There's business in it.
It sheds advice: whoe'er will take and live it,
Is welcome to the pain it costs to give it.

The final public exercise of the Celebration was the address of Hon. Joseph E. Eggleston, county judge of Cortland county, with which we conclude this chapter and our "History." As Judge Eggleston commenced to speak, an incident occurred which would have disconcerted most men, but, by his happy treatment of the matter, it was made to contribute to, rather than to detract from, the interest manifested in his address. The day was intensely hot; the crowd was large and somewhat weary; the boys were having a game of baseball on the grounds; and the gun-club was having some target practice in the neighboring grove, all of which contributed to the confusion and noise. To cap the climax, just as the Judge commenced to speak, an anxious mother, who was deaf and did not appreciate the situation, but who wanted to hear the speaking, as well as to escape the sun's fierce rays by getting under the shade of the awning which covered the speaker's stand, mounted the platform with her crying baby, of an unusually dark complexion, just in front of the speaker, where she commenced promenading in her efforts to quiet her child. Instead of being put out by the akward situation, the Judge, in opening, remarked in his usual commanding but good-humored manner: "Everything goes here to-day; the older people have been talking and now it is time to give the babies a chance." Happily at that moment a kodak was pointed at the platform and, with a "snap-shot," preserved the interesting scene, which we are able here to reproduce.

The address was then delivered to an attentive and enthusiastic audience, as follows:

Mr. President, Ladies and Gentlemen:
I deem it a privilege indeed to be present with you upon this happy occasion, and I hardly know why the distinguished honor of being your speaker was given to me, except, perhaps, that it is due to the fact that I was born and reared to manhood where I could daily look upon the dear old hills of Dryden.

It may be said that we are at the present time living in an age of centennial celebrations, for throughout our land, counties, towns and villages are seeking to do homage to the hundredth year birthmark by joining in festivities such as we are engaged in to-day.

A long time ago the poet sang:

"Breathes there a man with soul so dead,
  Who never to himself hath said
    This is my own, my native land;
  Whose heart has ne'er within him burned
  As home his footsteps he hath turned
    From wandering on a foreign strand?"

CENTENNIAL ADDRESS.

and that same spirit of love for your native land fills the breast and quickens the blood in the veins of many of you here to-day.

One hundred years ago this morning, the sun, as it gilded yonder hillside and lighted up this valley, smilingly looked down upon a scene far different from what we now behold.

The primeval forest had scarcely been disturbed in its solitude, the little stream wound its way along the valley secure in all its fastnesses, nature was undisturbed in her repose, as a solitary adventurer,

"EVERYTHING GOES"—AT DRYDEN CENTENNIAL. *Photo by J. G. Ford.*

seeking to find a home in some new country, caught the beauty of the location and commenced in a primitive way to break the spell that had so long existed and bring the forces of nature in subjection to his will.

Little did he know how well he builded.

The ring of the axe disturbed only the birds of the air and the beasts of the forest; the log-cabin, so rudely constructed, produced only astonishment to animal life as it then existed. There were no herds of cattle upon the hillside, no sound of voices to break the silence, no one to dispute the rights of this adventurer, for he was monarch of all he surveyed, and this was the picture presented a century ago, as the calm, soft rays of summer then rested upon the land.

The entering wedge to future civilization had been driven, a step was taken in the advancement of future progress, looking to further development of the resources of the country. The soil that had known no master but the red man was waiting only to be tilled by the hand of the white man in order that it might bring forth a bountiful harvest in its season, and the work of this first settler, followed by that of others, was the foundation work for the town of Dryden as it exists to-day.

What an interesting study is the settlement of any new country! What hardships were endured! What self-denial practiced! What labor and energy put forth to furnish sustenance for life! What joy and sadness alternates in quick succession in the lives of those early pioneers. To them it was largely an experiment, but they entered upon their work with a determination to succeed, and in that way the victory was half won. It is related of Father Taylor, that, when a young man, preaching in Boston, becoming entangled in a long sentence, he aptly relieved himself as follows: "Brethren, I don't exactly know where I went in at the beginning of this sentence and I don't know where I am coming out, but one thing I do know, I am bound for the kingdom of Heaven." So did these men with an object in view bend every energy to accomplish the desired result.

Reading your Centennial History I have been impressed with the strong individuality of these men, and their plain, common sense, matter-of-fact way of doing business. In their seclusion they had time and room to think, and another one of their peculiar characteristics is their originality. Reflection and solitude are prime factors in forming a good business education. The average man of to-day is too artificial, is too much a creature of society and custom, (when a man gets to be a society leader you may generally look for him at the tail end of every other procession,) his education has been so conventional that it has fettered his originality, by training the irregular growth of his genius into set forms, like a vine to its trellis.

It is the legitimate result, doubtless, of this education in the past that a higher degree of alertness has been born of our "brisk social commerce," that man's sympathetic nature has been quickened, that the surface virtues in human character have attained to more of polish and perfection. The average man of to-day possesses less of the individuality, the profundity of thought, the strength of character and moral principle that distinguished the generation of our fathers.

We need the training of seclusion if we would be original. Reflection develops the inner man according to the tendencies of his being, and from such developments the radical forces in society are always recruited for the conflict with conservatism; the originality thus grown by reflection is the material from which civilization gathers the successive increments of its progress. This discipline of reflection you will also find a necessity to the formation of a well-rounded character. The solitary maple of the open field attains a symmetry of development, a strength in resistance, that it could never possess if grown in the crowded, inter-dependent life of the forest. This self-education begets individuality, and success is born of reflection.

This explains how a lonely shepherd boy in England became her great inventor, how a thinking rail splitter in Illinois became America's most successful statesman, and a secluded tanner at Galena her greatest general; it may explain to us also why the plow handle has come to be the schoolmaster of our statesmen, why the lonely brookside is the cradle of our poets.

Your town has been honored in being named after one of the world's greatest poets, a name beautiful indeed, and one that is dear to you all. There is much in a name and in the giving of names to towns in this section of our state, and in near proximity to us, one can but admire the classical, poetical and historical genius of those persons who so furtunately acted as sponsors in those early days.

Dryden, honored and loved the world over, has a monument thus erected to his memory. Within hailing distance poetry finds herself remembered in the names of Virgil, Homer and Scott. Classic literature finds itself distinguished by such names as Cicero, Marathon, Pompey, Tully, Brutus, Aurelius, Scipio and Genoa. The legal lore of other days receives recognition at the hands of Cincinnatus, while the Prince of Ithaca and the brave Trojan Ulysses, the one the father, the other the son, names renowned in Grecian story, are next door neighbors, and designate a city far famed for her halls of learning, and a town in rural simplicity filled with prosperous and happy homes.

What a galaxy of names to conjure with; what a list of honored names of the world's greatest men and most distinguished places, famed in ancient history, and here at this time we would invoke all of the genius of modern times, music, poetry, eloquence and art, to speak in their praise.

Another thought which occurs to me now is the enjoyment we find in meeting here upon this occasion. To-day the past rises up before us and we seem to live over again the scenes of other days. What pleasant memories are recalled, what hallowed associations revived, how familiar the trees and rocks and streams look to us. Some of you who are older can say:

> "With what a pride I used to walk these hills,
> Look up to Heaven and bless God
> That it was so.
> It was free,
> From end to end, from cliff to lake, 'twas free;
> Free as our torrents are, that leap our rocks
> And plow our valleys, without asking leave;
> How happy was I in it then!
> I loved its very storms."

Time makes rapid changes, we look forward a hundred years and it seems a long time, but when we look backward over a hundred years how short it seems. Amos Sweet, when he constructed his log cabin, which was his castle, and was the sole resident of the town, could not in any flight of his imagination, foreshadow the rapid progress civilization would make here. Your happy homes, your cultivated fields, your schools and public library, your churches with their spires pointing toward heaven, all tell of the spirit with which they have been erected and preserved. In that time you have kept pace with the progress of the country, and have helped to write that history of which every American citizen has the right to be proud.

In that time, as a nation, we have aged a hundred years and the work we have accomplished has been the wonder of the whole world. Who that is capable of patriotic emotions can read and study that history during the past century without feeling a just pride in the past, with gratitude for the present and with confidence in the future! O, land of Washington, of Jefferson, of Lincoln and Grant, land of statesmen wise and warriors brave, and above all, land of liberty where our fathers died, land of the pilgrim's pride, on this glad day our hearts go out in glad praise and thanksgiving to the God of nations for that history so resplendent with good deeds.

In what part of that glorious record which you have helped to make, and which you have all been factors in making, is there a page that will provoke a blush or a line that will inspire apprehension of the future. As the citizen of to-day looks across the extent of the country which he rules, and contrasts its condition with the condition of the colonies which had just won their independence a little more than a century ago, he sees a change so marvelous, a development so great, a progress so wonderful that he is almost inclined to doubt history itself. He beholds a country which numbered, when it formed its government, a population of three millions, now maintaining in all their rights over seventy millions of independent citizens. That tree of liberty planted by our forefathers has taken deep root in the soil; its branches have become wide-spreading; its fruit abundant for the sustenance of this and other nations, and all of the people may repose beneath its shade. In territory it extends from the confines of monarchy on the north to the warm summer clime of the Gulf of Mexico on the south: on the east it is washed by the silvery waves of the Atlantic, and reaches across hill and valley and plain and mountain until it reaches where the waves of the Pacific roll and beat upon the golden sands of California's shore.

By rivers whose sources were almost unknown, one now sees countless cities where the footsteps of millions beat upon magnificent highways; the waters which were undisturbed save where the dwellers of the forest slaked their thirst in them, to-day bear upon their bosoms the freighted steamers of a mighty inland commerce which surpasses in its extent the wildest anticipations of the founders of this republic. In solitudes where the footstep of the hunter had never penetrated, where the silence was unbroken except by the roar of the wild beast, is heard the shrill whistle of the locomotive as it bears to the seaboard the product of the farm, the shop and factory as the results of American industry.

The flag of our country, the emblem of the free, purchased by the best blood of the land; its red as bright as the blood in which it has been bathed, its white as pure as the driven snow, its blue as clear as the expanse of heaven, has added to the original thirteen stars, states in their sovereign power until at the present day we find it contains a grand constellation of forty-five stars. That flag which we carry in all its glory to-day is a symbol of power and national strength throughout the world. As has been said, "Beneath its folds the weakest may find protection and the strongest must obey." It floats alike over the log-cabin in the forest, and the loftiest mansion of the millionaire; over the little red school-house by the roadside, and the massive walls of the university, built by wealth and maintained in luxurious splendor, "and like the bow of heaven is the child of sun and storm."

> "Is this the land our fathers loved,
> The freedom which they toiled to win,
> Is this the soil on which they moved,
> Are these the graves they slumber in?"

Yes, this is the land our fathers loved and we are to-day enjoying the blessings vouchsafed to us by them, blessings and privileges bestowed upon us by reason of their energy, perseverence and economy. But we have a lesson to learn to-day. If you shall go from this place without entering into the spirit of the occasion, or without feeling a just pride in the past and a determination to improve in the future, then have you kept the day in vain.

In reading the history of the pioneer settlement of this country, and it is true of your own town, one can but be impressed of the fact that these people had implicit faith that they would succeed. In any business, in any undertaking, faith is a necessary ingredient to success and a lack of it will in nearly all cases lead to a disastrous failure. I don't want any man around me who does not have faith in his work. In our work, individual or national, we need the faith of our fathers. The learned Bishop Duane says the men to make a state are made by faith, and if that be so, the men to protect, to guard, to improve, to make substantial progress in national affairs are men stimulated to action by faith in their work and the justness of the same. Why, faith is a heritage of our people, it was one of the first lessons learned and one that should never, no never, be forgotten. A little band of pilgrims, taking their lives in their hands, brave the dangers of the ocean wave and seek a home in an unknown land, in order that they may be free and independent and enjoy their religion after the dictates of their own conscience. From the tears and trials of Delft Haven, from the deck of the Mayflower to Plymouth Rock, what a step in the advancement of American liberty.

How, on the wings of the morning, that first prayer ascends to Heaven and how beautiful its language: "Father in Heaven, we thank thee that thou hath permitted us to place our feet upon these shores. In thy hand we leave our destiny, trusting that He who hath brought us hither will glorify our work to his own good." What a cross to bear, what a beautiful example of faith in the divine providence. What a corner stone upon which to rear this, our temple of liberty— there upon the eternal rock, beneath the soil and shifting sand, upon the basis of equal and exact justice to all men, to lay the foundation of the government, broad and deep. Oh, I sometimes think that in our worldly ambitions we are drifting away from Plymouth Rock and that we lose sight of that implicit faith as shown by those early settlers. As I have stood upon that consecrated spot I have thanked God for Plymouth Rock. There it stands, washed by the silvery waves of the ocean, surrounded now by all of the evidence of wealth and prosperity. What a contrast—then it was a cross to bear, now it is a crown to wear.

My dear friends, we want to live more the simplicity of life of our fathers. As a nation we are living too fast. Whenever our expenditures exceed our earnings we certainly will find our names in the debtor column. Practice a little of the economy and self-denial of those early days and we will be the better for it. In our national advancement let us occasionally go back to Plymouth Rock. We need that strength, we need more of that simplicity of life and character, we need to pray to God that all of our work may be acceptable in his sight, for I have learned to believe that that nation whose God is the Lord will live long and prosper upon this earth.

The republic was born by the fireside of the American home. It was maintained by those heroic women, who, as they spun the flax, taught their children to fear God and to live within their income. I believe that the mother who reared a family of children to manhood and womanhood in the log-cabin, such as has been constructed upon your grounds for this occasion, and sent them out into the world well equipped to engage in life's battles, taught them the lesson of honesty, sobriety and economy, and above all taught them in youth at her knee to say, "Our Father which art in Heaven," is deserving of being classed with those persons who successfully rule a kingdom. While we are to-day thinking of our fathers let us not forget our mothers. The grand corner stone upon which the wonderful fabric of our form of government is builded is the kingdom ruled by woman, the home. Some one has said that we could not have put down the Rebellion without the aid of the loyal women of the land. In time of war while the men were at the front fighting, the women were at home praying, and I am not sure but they did as effective work as the men.

You can find enjoyment in the celebration here to-day for the reason that you all contributed something toward making the town of Dryden the prosperous, beautiful town that it now is. I don't mean that you have simply paid money to be used upon this occasion or that you have builded houses and blocks or accumulated wealth. No, I mean that you have given something far more precious and long to be remembered than that. Go with me to your two beautiful cemeteries, where the roses now bloom, and where the green grass covers the graves of your silent dead. There I find cut in granite and marble names that I read in your history, illustrious and honored names, the numbers are legion, names that are dear to you, and the same that many of you bear to-day. The same blood that once coursed in their veins, and gave them strength and activity to do their work, now courses in your veins, that you may have continued strength and activity to pursue and perpetuate, to perfection as near as it may be attained, the work laid out and planned by them. Year after year you have borne to that final resting place the father, mother, husband, wife, brother, sister, and child, giving back to earth the body, and the spirit to God, who gave it, retaining only sweet and blessed memories of those dear ones. This is the precious gift that you have made and how it must touch your hearts at this time.

There is an old story that always had a charm for me: In some strange land and time they were about to cast a bell for a mighty tower, a hollow, starless heaven of iron. It should toll for dead monarchs, the king is dead, and make glad clamor for the new prince, long live the king, it should proclaim so great a passion or so grand a pride that either should be worship, or wanting these, forever hold its peace. Now this bell was not to be digged out of the cold mountain, it was to be made with something that had been warmed by human touch, or loved with a human love, and so the people came, like pilgrims to a shrine, and cast their offerings into the furnace and went away. There were links of chains that bondsmen had worn bright, and fragments of swords that had broken in heroes' hands, they even brought things that were licked up in an instant by the red tongue of flame, good words they had written and flowers they had cherished, perishable things that could never be heard in the rich tone and volume of the bell. And the fires panted like a strong man when he runs a race, and the mingled gifts flowed down together and were lost in the sand. And the dome of iron was drawn out like Leviathan. And by and by the bell was alone in its chamber and its four windows looked forth to the four quarters of heaven. For many a day the bell hung silent in the tower and the wind came and went and only set it sighing. At last there came a time when men grew grand for right and truth and stood shoulder to shoulder o'er all the land, and went down like reapers to the harvest death, looked into the graves of them that slept and believed that there was something grander than living, something more bitter than dying, and so, standing between the quick and dead, they quitted themselves like men. Then the old bell awoke in the tower and the great waves of its music rolled gloriously out, and broke along the blue walls of the world like an anthem, and every tone in it was familiar as a household word to somebody, because they had placed their treasure in it.

So, my dear friends, it seems to me that at this time, as we join in these exercises and lift our voices in song and praise, as the music shall float upon the air, every tone in it will be familiar to you all, for you have brought your treasure here.

One thought more in conclusion. What of the future of our country? Thus far we have been thinking of the past. That is, however, an utter waste of time, unless it stimulates us to new activity in our work and inspires us with new hope for the future. "To-day the man who tells us what we have done, must stand aside for the man who will tell us what we ought to do." The opportunity for future advancement is as great to-day as it was a hundred years ago, the lessons to be learned as important now as then. There are great questions yet to be determined which invite your most earnest consideration.

Where are the men who will solve the problem of how to reconcile the conflict between capital and labor, and cause them to go hand in hand, to the mutual benefit of employer and employed. To what school shall we go, and at the knee of what teachers shall we kneel that we may learn the economic lesson of living within our income, of paying our debts as we go along? Who will be the statesmen, masters in the science of government, who, knowing what is right, will dare to stand up and with massive intellect and giant arm break into fragments every monopoly which seeks to fetter, oppress or rob the people?

Again, the voice of your government is such that it welcomes within its jurisdiction people from all climes and countries, guaranteeing to all who shall come protection to life and property. The flow of immigration to this country at this time is wonderful, and how are you to receive the thousands who are seeking refuge within your borders? You must furnish them homes, you must educate them, you must surround them with the influence of the Christian religion; aye, you must make them citizens, as they have the right to demand it.

Freedom at the ballot box, purity of elections, the election of honest men to places of trust, these are important matters and must ever be guarded with zealous care.

You will doubtless remember the letter of Lord Macauley to the Hon. Henry S. Randall, of Cortland, in which letter Macauley prophesied that the time would come when the people of this nation would fail to intelligently perform their duties and when they would ignorantly allow bad men to be elected to places of trust and thus bring our government into anarchy and confusion. But Macauley spoke as one having knowledge of a monarchial form of government and where the people are kept in ignorance. He knew not of the little school-houses which dot our landscape, of the institutions of learning which are found in nearly every square mile of our territory and which are the jewels that shine brightest in the crown of American liberty. In making that prophesy Macauley had in mind English society and not American. In England the society is like the crusts of the earth, one above the other, strata upon strata, the royalty, the nobility, the aristocracy, and down strata by strata until on the bottom are found the peasantry and common people. People in one strata never rise to the next, unless by some volcano-like eruption in society or by the overthrow of the government, the lower stratas break through the overlying crusts and come up. Such are the people of England and for such reasons were certain rights not given to the lower classes. Were the powers of the government submitted to them, anarchy and confusion would at first follow. But the sociey of America may be likened to the ocean, where the drop of water which to-day lies down in darkness on the rocky bottom, to-morrow may be glittering in the sunlight, riding on the crest of the topmost wave. The strength of our government is found in the fact that the power is vested in the common people. Were our country in danger to-day you would witness the same sublime response of the people to the rescue as you did in '76, when they said "Give us liberty or give us death;" when they said "The Union shall remain one and inseparable forever;" when they said there should be no flag but the old flag, the red, white and blue, and bathed it in the best blood of the land.

I have no fear for the future of my country and the picture of to-day encourages me to indulge in the brightest visions. We never sing the old song "America," without its making us better; there is more music in it to the square inch, than any opera that was ever written.

Then this sea of happy faces coming from so many pleasant homes, the click of the mowing machine heard in the meadow, the fields of waving golden grain almost ready for the reaper, God forbid that anything should ever occur to mar the beauty of such a scene.

I call upon you, old men whose brows have become furrowed by time, whose step is somewhat feeble, whose hair has become silvered by the snows of many winters, whose memories go back far beyond mine, to see to it that the fires kindled upon the hearths of our fathers be kept alive. I call upon you, young men, as you shall grow up in the strength of your manhood, heirs of a rich inheritance, to remember whose sons you are. Oh, let me appeal to you all, that in the great conflict of life, where right is at war against wrong, where truth and falsehood walk side by side through our streets and vice and virtue meet and pass every hour of the day, you enlist in the great army with those who, disheartened by no obstacle, discouraged by no defeat, appalled by no danger, neither paused nor swerved from their clear line of duty until the battlefields of the past have been strewn with the wrecks of what was false, and truth and justice and right have triumphed in the glory of victory. "Whatsoever things are true, whatsoever things are honest, whatsoever things are pure, whatsoever things are lovely," think on these things, let your voice be raised in their behalf, let your work be earnest, and when others shall speak to your praise and tell the story of your deeds, they will rise up and call you blessed.

> "Who'll press for gold this crowded street
>   A hundred years to come?
> Who'll tread yon church with willing feet
>   A hundred years to come?
> Pale, trembling age, and fiery youth,
> And childhood with its brow of truth,
> The rich, the poor, on land and sea,
> Where will the mighty millions be
>   A hundred years to come?

"We all within our graves shall sleep
 A hundred years to come.
No living soul for us shall weep
 A hundred years to come.
But other men our land will till,
And others then our streets will fill,
And other birds will sing as gay,
And bright the sunshine as to-day
 A hundred years to come."

www.ingramcontent.com/pod-product-compliance
Lightning Source LLC
Chambersburg PA
CBHW031330230426
43670CB00006B/300